Raising Stanley

Raising Stanley

*What It Takes to Claim
Hockey's Ultimate Prize*

Ross Bernstein

TRIUMPH
B O O K S

Library of Congress Cataloging-in-Publication Data

Bernstein, Ross
    Raising Stanley : what it takes to claim hockey's ultimate prize / Ross Bernstein.
        p. cm.
    ISBN: 978-1-60078-393-7
        1. Stanley Cup (Hockey)—History. I. Title.

GV847.7.B47 2010
796.962'648—dc22

2010027660

This book is available in quantity at special discounts for your group or organization. For further information, contact:

Triumph Books
542 South Dearborn Street
Suite 750
Chicago, Illinois 60605
(312) 939-3330
Fax (312) 663-3557

Printed in U.S.A.
ISBN: 978-1-60078-393-7
Design by Amy Carter

Photos courtesy of AP Images unless otherwise indicated

For Sara and Campbell

Contents

Foreword

Scotty Bowman

I have been fortunate to win 11 Stanley Cups over my career, and I cherish each and every one of them. I remember them all with fondness, as each one came at a different phase of my life. The first one and the last one were probably the most special, though. That first one, in 1973 with the Montreal Canadiens, was the culmination of a lifelong ambition. It was very meaningful. I grew up in Montreal, and this had always been a dream, to raise the Cup for my hometown team. I would have loved to have done so as a player, but due to an injury early in my career I got into coaching instead.

I started out with the Canadiens organization as a coach and scout with one of their junior teams in 1956. They were dominant in those days, and I was just thrilled to have an opportunity to grow with them from the ground up. So I got to be a part of their eight Stanley Cup victories in the '50s and '60s. I got to soak it all in and learn about how they did things from the inside out; it was so eye opening how they were able to achieve success year after year. I learned about their culture and about how they treated people. It was fascinating. I got to attend the victory parties after those Stanley Cup wins and be a part of all of that. I just soaked it all in.

I finally got my opportunity to become a head coach in the NHL in 1967 with St. Louis. I was able to lead the Blues to three straight Stanley Cup Finals from 1968 to 1970, but sadly we lost each time. I left St. Louis in 1971 when I was given the opportunity of a lifetime, the head coaching position with the Canadiens. We lost in the first round of the playoffs that first year but came back to win the Cup the next year when we defeated the Blackhawks four games to two. We were ahead in the series three games to one coming home to Montreal. We could win on our home ice and were really excited. Our goalie was Ken Dryden, and he was facing Tony Esposito; they were two of the premier goalies in the league at the time. Well, we wound up losing 8–7. It was the most bizarre game I have ever been involved with in my entire career. Here we were, about to clinch the Stanley Cup on our home ice, on national TV, and we let in eight goals. I couldn't believe it. Fortunately we rebounded to win Game 6 in Chicago 6–4 to clinch it, but that was one game I will never forget. It will go down in my book as the strangest ever.

I was pretty hungry that season. I had been there before and did not want to be denied again. No way. Once you win one, you have that confidence, which is so important. As a coach in the National Hockey League you really need that. Hockey coaches get dismissed about five times more than the general managers do, which means their shelf life is not very long. So when you win it, not only are you happy and satisfied, you are also relieved that you have now bought yourself a little job security.

After Philadelphia won a pair of Cups in '74 and '75, we came back to win it again in 1976. It would be the first of four straight Stanley Cups, which was really a thrill. The last one, when we beat the Rangers in 1979, was maybe the most enjoyable because it was the only one where we won it on our home ice. That was really neat to finally be able to do it at home and to reward our fans with that. To drink champagne out of the Cup in your own locker room is something else, let me tell you.

To coach your team to the Cup is really a grind, though. To go back-to-back is extremely difficult, so to win four in a row is almost impossible. Everybody is gunning for you, night in and night out, and it becomes a battle. The playoffs are almost an entirely different season, a second season that is much more intense than the first one, physically as well as emotionally. It's a marathon to win all four series, which can be anywhere from 20 to 28 games, and you have to be able to overcome a lot of adversity. Sure, you do your homework, and you try to put together a winning formula, but you have to stay healthy, and you have to get lucky sometimes too. That's all a part of it.

Preparation is so important, especially for the playoffs. You play 82 games during the regular season, but once the playoffs start you have to be completely focused and dialed in on the task at hand. Another important factor is to be able to get past your weaker opponents quickly in order to get some days off for rest. If you can sweep a team early on in the first or second round, that is huge, especially if your next opponent has to go seven games. You need your guys rested at that point of the season, you really do. The guys especially enjoy getting a day off at that point too, to heal up and come back reinvigorated. If you go seven games and have a lot of overtime games mixed in, that is so tough. You need to keep your guys focused and prepared, but they need that physical rest in order to recharge their batteries.

Your role players become increasingly important at this point of the season too. As a coach, if you can play four lines versus three and get your guys a little less ice time, then that is big. When you are playing an opponent seven times in 14 days, there is a lot of strategy involved at that point. You can really get guys into certain roles and take advantage of mismatches here and there. Good coaches can shine in the playoffs, they really can. Experience counts. You have to be willing to make some changes in order to find those mismatches. You need a plan, and sometimes you have to be confident enough to go to Plan B. If what you are doing isn't working, then you have to change or you are dead in the water.

I needed a change of scenery after the Canadiens, so I wound up spending the next seven seasons with the Buffalo Sabres before joining the Pittsburgh Penguins in 1991 as the team's director of player development. I needed a break from the grind of coaching and was excited about working with Bob Johnson. Badger Bob was a great guy, and what a ride he took us on that year with Mario Lemieux and company en route to winning the Cup. It was an emotional roller coaster from there, however, as Bob suffered a brain aneurysm in August of that year and sadly passed away just six months later. It was just devastating. That was so tough on the entire organization. I agreed to coach the team on an interim basis for the 1992 season, but it worked out that I stayed on for the whole season. We struggled early on that year, but fortunately we were able to keep it all together and then get hot in the playoffs—winning 11 straight to win our second straight Stanley Cup over the Blackhawks. It was really an incredible experience.

From there I went to Detroit, where we would win three more Cups in the next nine seasons. We went back-to-back in 1997 and 1998, which was really neat, and then added what would be my ninth and final Cup in 2002. That year we went into Carolina in the finals tied at one game apiece. They were very good at home that year, and their crowd was really into it. Well, this one was a classic. It went into triple overtime, and Igor Larionov wound up getting the game winner, the oldest player ever—at age 42—to score a goal in a Stanley Cup Final. It was amazing. I will never forget that game; it was unbelievable. It didn't end until about 1:30 in the morning. That really swung the momentum for us and propelled us to the championship. No question. It lifted us and took the wind out of our opponents' sails at the same time. Just an amazing game. We didn't lose another game in the series.

I knew when we won it that I wasn't going to coach anymore. So I put my skates on and headed back out onto the ice to raise Stanley one last time. It was wonderful. You know, that Cup weighs 34 pounds; it's pretty heavy. But when you win it and you are out on the ice and your adrenaline is flowing, that thing is like a feather. That's why you see the players skating around with it effortlessly after they have won it. But for me, I had to really be careful lifting that thing up over my head. The hardest part was trying to avoid all the confetti and streamers that they blasted out onto the ice after the game. I didn't want to fall on my face on national television so I had to really watch where I was going.

One of the greatest traditions in hockey is the time players get to spend with the Cup. Now, the tradition of having the Cup for a day didn't start until the '80s, but we used to get some time with it during my days up in Montreal in the '70s. We would have a big party after the season and get to take pictures with it, but that was about it. We did, however, have some great parades in those days. I mean, Montreal really did it up. My young children were able to be a part of that too, which made it extra special for me. They got to be in the parade with me, which they just loved. Years later, when I was with Pittsburgh and later Detroit, I was able to spend some time with the Cup and really had some nice times with it. I had a handicapped son, and we would bring it to where he lived, which was nice.

We would have backyard barbeques and parties, stuff like that. Nothing too crazy, maybe 30 or 40 people would show up. One year, however, we had a party at the house, and my wife put a sign up in the driveway made out of hockey sticks that read "The Cup is in the backyard." She figured our invited guests would just walk around back, and that way we didn't have to answer the door. Well, before long a couple hundred people showed up, and we didn't know who any of them were! I looked at her and she looked at me and then we realized it was that big sign out front, basically inviting the whole world over to see the Stanley Cup. People would drive by and just stop over; it was crazy. It is pretty neat to see the expression on people's faces when they see that big beautiful Cup. That's what makes it so special, I think, that aura about it. And the fact that it is so accessible. It's the people's Cup, it really is.

I think longevity will always be a part of my legacy because I was able to coach for so many years. I would like to think that I helped a lot of young men along the way and that I brought a lot of joy to a lot of lives. I just feel very blessed to have been able to make my career doing my passion and to be a part of the greatest game on earth. I am also proud of the nine Cups that I won as a head coach, as well as the two others I was fortunate enough to be a part of as management. Eleven Cups is pretty humbling, but whenever I start to get a little full of myself I just think about Jean Beliveau, who won 10 Cups as a player and another seven as a member of management for a total of 17. That is a number that I can promise you will never be beat. Ever.

—*Scotty Bowman*

Bowman won 11 Stanley Cups: nine as a head coach (five with Montreal, one with Pittsburgh, and three with Detroit) and two as a member of management (one with Pittsburgh as director of player personnel in 1991 and one with the Red Wings in 2008 as a consultant). Incidentally, Scotty's son Stanley (named after you know who...) is the GM of the Chicago Blackhawks and recently led his team to the Stanley Cup Finals in 2010.

Foreword
Phil Esposito

Winning the Cup? There's nothing better. Nothing. The three most important things that have ever happened to me in my career were 1) winning the Stanley Cup; 2) having my No. 7 retired by the Bruins; and 3) when it was announced that "the Tampa Bay Lightning franchise was awarded to Phil Esposito and the Tampa Bay Hockey Group." The Hall of Fame was great too, but winning the Cup will always be the most near and dear to me because of what it symbolizes. It was about a team of guys coming together to do something bigger than themselves. It was about being a champion.

Winning your first Cup is always the most memorable, and for me that came in 1970 when my Boston Bruins beat the Blues. After beating the Rangers in the opener, we won 10 games in a row during that playoff run, sweeping Chicago and then St. Louis in the finals. In Game 4 against the Blues, Bobby Orr scored the iconic game winner in overtime on goalie Glenn Hall, when he was flying through the air with his arms raised in victory. Winning at home in front of our fans was amazing. That was such an exciting time. It was the first Cup in nearly 30 years for the Bruins, so it was a pretty big deal. It absolutely sparked the growth of hockey in New England too, without a doubt. A lot of youth hockey programs were started as a result of the

Stanley Cup. I remember Bobby Carpenter once told me that the reason he started to play the game was because of that win. So hockey became hugely popular around there after that game, and that was great to see.

We won it again in 1972, this time beating Toronto and St. Louis to make it to the finals. Once there, we faced off against the rival Rangers and wound up beating them four games to two. We clinched it in Madison Square Garden that time, and it was a wonderful experience. We had a great rivalry with those guys back then. Gerry Cheevers got the 3–0 shutout in the finale, and it was a moment I will never forget. To beat New York in New York was something special, it really was.

No question, we were on a roll, and in my opinion it all started at the top. Harry Sinden was the best coach I ever had. I will never forget the day he told me, "I'm going to teach you how to play the slot and make you our goal scorer." That sounded great to me. He worked with me on my footwork and on my positioning, and it just clicked. I knew where to go and how to work with my line mates. It was amazing. Harry was a good teacher and the guys respected him. He was a big part of our success in those days.

Heck, part of winning the Cup back then was getting that bonus check at the end of the season. We didn't make anything like the guys make today, hell no. So if you could make a few extra bucks for winning it, then that was serious motivation for a lot of guys. Teams were tight too. I will never forget scoring 76 goals in 1971 and then 66 in 1972. I won the scoring title both years, yet the headline in the newspaper after the 1972 season read "Esposito Slumps." I couldn't believe it. I remember going in to renew my contract that off-season, expecting a big raise, and our GM held up that paper and said, "Phil, I don't think so... Look here, it says you slumped!" We both had a pretty good laugh about that one.

Money aside, we just wanted to play hockey and wanted to win for our fans, even if that meant playing hurt. That just went with the territory. You just did it. Whether it was an ankle sprain or a wrist sprain or a sore knee or a concussion—you just played. That was the way it was in those days. We had no clue about concussions causing long-term damage or anything like that. I had to get my ankle frozen, my shoulder frozen—the doc would just stick that big needle in there and freeze it up, and then off you went. Afterward was the worst, when the medicine wore off. That was bad. But hey, if you could lace 'em up and play, then you played. That was it. You didn't want to let your teammates down; that would have been worse than any pain.

We had such a great team in the early '70s, and looking back I think it is ridiculous that we only won two Cups; we should have won at least four or five. Gerry Cheevers was an unbelievable goaltender, just fantastic. People underestimated him. And Bobby Orr was a phenom on defense; he revolutionized the game. We had great talent, but truth be told, I don't think we were very disciplined. We drank too much and partied too much, and that's a fact. We just screwed around way too much. Those were great times, though, and I have no regrets.

Then when the Lightning won it in 2004, that was something else. I was no longer a part of the ownership group at that point and was doing radio broadcasting for the team. I can tell you without a doubt that it was as exciting to watch that happen as a broadcaster as it was being a player. It was absolutely electrifying. I loved it. I felt almost like I had given birth to that team, so for me it was so validating. I had worked so hard to help land that franchise in Tampa, and to see them win it was unbelievable. I couldn't hardly contain myself when they won it; it was just wonderful. I will never forget it. Never. For them to win it the way that they did, in seven games, and in Tampa—you just can't make that stuff up. What a storybook ending to an incredible season. Wow! The fans almost brought the house down. Special doesn't even cut it. I was speechless. After the game I met my wife and my partners, who had started that whole thing with me, and we went to our favorite watering hole. We closed the doors at 1:00 AM and then sat in there drinking and laughing until nearly six the next morning. What a blast!

They even let me take the Stanley Cup home for a day, which was something I was never able to do in Boston. That was reserved for our team captain, Johnny Bucyk, who got to carry it around the ice both times we won it. That was how it was in those days, nothing like today where they all pass it around and celebrate. I thought I might get a chance to raise it in New York that second time, but we had to get off the ice in a hurry after the fans started throwing eggs and tomatoes at us. So to be able to spend some time with the Cup all those years later—what a gesture. It felt wonderful. I had a helluva time with it too, so much fun. Shit, I bet I had more than 300 people come through my house to see it and take pictures with it. That to me was just amazing. Even to think about it now I get goose bumps. I was so elated, proud as a kid in a candy store.

I had always dreamed of winning the Stanley Cup, ever since I was a kid growing up in Sault Ste. Marie [Ontario], so to be able to do it on two occasions as a player was very special. It's the hardest trophy to win in all of sports, and that is what makes it so special in my eyes. It's amazing to think about how many great players played for so many years in this league and never got the opportunity to win one. I finished my career with the New York Rangers, and we came close in 1979 under Freddy Shero, losing to Montreal in the finals that year, but that was as close as I would get. It's elusive. So I am thankful that I was in the right place at the right time in my career and was able to get my name on Stanley a couple of times. I had some outstanding teammates along the way, that's for sure.

—Phil Esposito, two-time Stanley Cup
champion (Boston 1970 and 1972)

Foreword
Brett Hull

The Stanley Cup is just the coolest trophy in sports. What's not to love about it? It's so old, and it completely reeks of history. Everybody's name is engraved on it, which is unique, and you get to have it for a day when you win it. The lore and the mystique of it are what make it unlike any other trophy in sports. Nothing can compare, it's just phenomenal. Winning it meant the world to me, it really did. It's what you play for in hockey. I would have gladly given back every goal I scored to have won one, had I not had that opportunity. Sure, the personal accolades are great, but without the Cup they don't mean much. So winning the Cup? Yeah, it means everything.

Unlike most players, however, I didn't grow up dreaming about winning it—which might sound odd considering the fact that my dad won it in 1961 as a member of the Chicago Blackhawks. I loved hockey as a kid, but I wasn't consumed with it. My dad never really talked about that championship too much, either, instead he mostly talked about all the other ones that his teams *should've* won. Maybe I could see how busy he was and was sort of turned off by it all. Who knows? I was into a lot of stuff as a kid. My obsession with the Cup wouldn't come until years later, when I realized that I too was going to make my career as a player. Now that I am retired and I look back, it's neat to think that my dad and I both have our names on the Cup. That's pretty special. It's forever.

The first Cup team that I was fortunate to be a part of was in Dallas in '99. We had a great regular season and then got really hot in the playoffs, advancing past Edmonton, St. Louis, and Colorado before meeting up with Buffalo in the finals. I will never forget how nervous I was heading into the playoffs that year. I had been labeled as the "missing piece of the puzzle" to win the Cup, and I was definitely feeling the pressure at that point. Honestly, I was so nervous that I could barely play. And I never got nervous. This was so scary to me, though, I just didn't know how to deal with it. Luckily, each game we played it got easier and easier for me. Once we got past Colorado I knew that we had a great chance to win it. Eddie Belfour played great for us down that stretch, and we were confident heading into the finals. The Sabres stole Game 1 in our building in overtime, but we came back and took Games 2 and 3. They answered in Game 4, but we shut them out 2–0 in Game 5.

So it all came down to Game 6 in Buffalo, where we made history. We were tied at one apiece at the end of regulation, so we went into overtime and battled back and forth. What a grind that was. Finally, with about five minutes to go in the third over-time, I did what every kid who plays hockey dreams about—I got the game winner to win the Cup. It was unbelievable. The way it happened was what makes it so unique. I was camped out in front of their goaltender, Dominik Hasek, and the puck just came my way. He made a save, and I got the rebound and put it in. I remember being mobbed by Mike Modano and Shawn Chambers, and then the rest of the bench emptied and we just celebrated out on the ice. What an incredible feeling; I will never forget it. The officials reviewed the goal, and there was some controversy about my foot being in the crease. I knew that I was all right, however, because I knew that if you had posses-sion in the crease you could score. The rule had been changed earlier in the year, and I knew it. So they reviewed it and the call stood. I don't mind that there was all that controversy surrounding it because the goal sort of lives in infamy, which I guess makes me infamous too. I think it's great.

Afterward, Derian Hatcher, our captain, got the Cup from Commissioner Bettman and hoisted it first. He then handed it to Mike Modano, and when I saw the look in his eyes I almost lost it. I was so happy for him. He then handed it to me, and I got to hoist it, which felt amazing. I then gave it to Pat Verbeek, who had waited a long time to touch it as well.

Mike Modano was the focal point for me in wanting to win the Cup that year. He had been with the organization since day one, and everybody was rooting for him, everybody. He was a former No. 1 overall draft pick, and the pressure had always been on him to deliver. So to win the Cup and to see how that affected him both personally and professionally was amazing. He was the face of that franchise, and the community down there just fell in love with him. I was so happy for him it was unreal. What a great guy.

We won the Stanley Cup that year because we were the consummate team. From our goalie, Eddie Belfour, to our defensemen to our forwards, we were solid from top to bottom. Plus we were all very good friends who went out together and genuinely liked each other. From that, we all had a single goal—to win that Cup. We all put our egos aside and played for each other that season. We just did whatever it took to win, and that was a big reason why we won the championship. We had a great coach too, Ken Hitchcock. Kenny was a great Xs and Os guy. He could really put game plans together that were tactically superior to those of our opponents. He studied and prepared and left no stone unturned. Nobody was better at that stuff; he was just fantastic.

You know, nobody was sure how hockey was going to fit in down in Texas, when the North Stars moved there in the early

'90s, but they embraced it wholeheartedly. They loved us, and why not? Hockey has the speed and the grace of basketball and baseball and the violence of football, and then you can drop the gloves and fight—what says Texas more than all of those things? Watching the excitement build around the city as we got closer and closer to the finals that year was really neat to see. Our home, Reunion Arena, had so much atmosphere in there it was unbelievable. By the time the finals came around you could hardly contain our fans, they were crazy. What a fantastic time that was.

One of the great traditions of winning the Cup is to be able to have it for a day. I took it back to Duluth, where I played college hockey and have a summer home. It was so much fun, just a great day. I just wanted everyone to be able to share it and to enjoy the experience. I took it downtown to Grandma's Saloon out on Canal Park, over to Norman's on the west end, and to Northland Country Club—I took it everywhere. I later had a big party at my house out on Pike Lake. What a great day.

Well, I wound up signing with Detroit in 2002 and as luck would have it, I was blessed to win the Cup yet again. Winning it for a second time was amazing. The ironic thing about this one was that our goalie that year with the Red Wings was Dominik Hasek, the guy I had scored the game winner on just three years earlier. Needless to say we never once spoke of that goal in Buffalo, never. What a great teammate, though, just a first-class guy. That season was very different than '99. The first one was full of so many emotions, and it was all kind of a blur. This time I knew what was going on a little bit more. I had the experience under my belt, and that made a big difference. I was able to soak it all in and enjoy it much, much more.

What a team that was. Holy cow. We had double-digit Hall of Famers on that roster, not to mention our coach, Scotty Bowman—arguably the best ever. We had so many great veteran players. In addition to Hasek we had Steve Yzerman, Brendan

Shanahan, Sergei Fedorov, Igor Larionov, Chris Chelios, Nick Lidstrom, Luc Robitaille, Steve Duchesne, Kirk Maltby, Kris Draper, and Tomas Holmstrom. Wow. All Scotty had to do that season was open the doors and let us go. We knew what to do. We won 51 games that year in the regular season and then headed into the playoffs on a mission. We beat Vancouver four games to two, St. Louis four games to one, and then got past Colorado in a very tough seven-game series. Detroit and Colorado did not like each other in those days, and that was a really tough series.

From there we met up with the Carolina Hurricanes in the finals. I remember losing in Game 1 on Ron Francis's overtime goal. That was a huge wake-up call for us, and we responded big time by winning the next four games to clinch it. The biggie was Game 3, when Igor Larionov got the triple-overtime winner. That was huge. It really deflated those guys, you could just tell. We clinched it at home at Joe Louis Arena 3–1, and what a feeling that was. Winning it on our home ice was great too, because in '99 we won it on the road, and it was a totally different vibe. This was pretty incredible. Steve Yzerman, the longtime captain of that team, got to hoist the Cup first, and what a moment that was. Then he passed it around for all of us to take our turn. After the season that year I brought the Cup back to Dallas, where I live, for a big Fourth of July party at my house. It was pretty low-key this time around but a lot of fun nonetheless.

Patience and trust are two of the biggest life lessons that I took away from winning the Cup. I didn't win it until I was 33 years old, so I had to *really* be patient. There were times when I wasn't sure if it would ever happen for me, and that got to be very frustrating because I wanted it so badly. I just wanted a chance. I began to question whether I had the right makeup to be a Stanley Cup champion. Finally, in 1999, everything came together in Dallas and we were able to win it. What a moment that was. Once you win it you realize that the belief in yourself and the belief in your teammates can in fact correlate into real-life success. Then to have it happen again in 2002 with the Red Wings—that was just icing on the cake.

—Brett Hull, two-time Stanley Cup champion
(Dallas 1999 and Detroit 2002)

Foreword

Joe Sakic

What did it mean to win the Stanley Cup? It meant everything. It was a lifelong dream come true, without a doubt. As a kid growing up in Canada, every spring I would watch the playoffs on TV, and I couldn't wait to see who was going to get to raise the Stanley Cup. That was the ultimate goal, to hoist that big beautiful trophy. It means that you are the best of the best that year. So for me to finally accomplish that in 1996 with Colorado was just an amazing feeling. In fact, it's really hard to put into words. It's excitement, it's a relief that you finally did it, it's the culmination of years and years of hard work.

I had played seven seasons with the Quebec Nordiques prior to the team moving to Colorado in 1996, and to be honest it was somewhat bittersweet winning it that first season with the Avalanche. On one hand I was so excited for my teammates and for our new fans in Colorado, yet I knew that the team's fans back in Quebec were disappointed that we had left. That was tough. Winning it was such an unbelievable feeling, though. I will never forget the pure raw emotion I felt the night we won it. It was incredible.

Winning our first Cup was a journey I will never forget. It was the beginning of our epic rivalry with the Detroit Red Wings too, arguably the most intense in the NHL in those days. I mean, for about six years straight it was who-was-going-to-beat-who between the two teams. We knew that we were going to have to face each other sooner or later in the playoffs, and when it finally happened, it was war. I really looked forward to those matchups, though, because they brought out the best in me. If you could beat them then you could feel satisfied in knowing that you had beaten the best. In 1996 Detroit had just dominated the regular season and were heavily favored to win the Cup. So for us to beat them in the playoffs was pretty amazing. That was the beginning of that rivalry right there. It was the two best teams in hockey who did not like each other, yet had an immense amount of respect for one another. Those were extremely physically demanding games to play, too; you really had to be on guard for whatever was coming your way. It was intense.

To wear the "C" on that team was definitely an honor. Being elected captain meant that you represented your teammates out on the ice, and that was a responsibility that I never took lightly. The biggest perk, however, is without a doubt getting to raise Stanley first. When Commissioner Bettman handed me the Cup in '96 it was such an incredible feeling. I just felt like the weight of the world lifted off of my shoulders. I hoisted it proudly and then handed it off to Curtis Leschyshyn, who had been my teammate in Quebec. We had gone through some tough times together, and I wanted to acknowledge him and let him know how much I respected him by handing it to him first.

Then to do it again in 2001, what a feeling. We had come so close to getting back there but kept coming up short. Between our two Stanley Cups in 1996 and 2001 we made it to the conference finals four other times, losing each of them in either six or seven games. It was so frustrating. So when we finally made it back to the finals in '01 we made sure to seal the deal. That year was so special too in that it was Ray Bourque's last season. He had decided to join us the year before so he could take one last shot at the Cup, something that had eluded him in Boston for more than two decades. So that season was all about Ray. We wanted him to raise that Cup so badly, and when he finally did, I don't think there was a dry eye in the house. It was so emotional, a moment I will never forget. As soon as the commissioner handed me the Cup that year, I immediately gave it to Ray, to let him hoist it first. It was awesome, just a great memory.

We had some great teams in those days, and each was led by a different coach. Marc Crawford coached the '96 team, and Bob Hartley coached the '01 team. They had their own unique styles, but both were great coaches. They each took us on their own path to winning the Cup, which was pretty neat to see as a player. Bob was more of an Xs and Os guy who was really good at putting together strategic matchups. He was a real student of the game, and his preparation was second to none. Marc, meanwhile, had a great feel for the game and was really good at in-game tactics such as line combinations. He had a good sense for which guys were playing well and which guys weren't at certain times and could make adjustments accordingly.

One of the great traditions that comes with winning the Cup is that you get to have it for a day. The first time we won it I stayed in Denver due to the fact that my wife was pregnant at the time. So we had some friends come over for a pretty low-key party. Then in 2001, I brought it back to Vancouver to celebrate with my friends and family from back home. We rented a boat and went out to the inlet to watch some fireworks with Stanley. It was a really memorable day, for sure. We had a party and let a lot of people celebrate with it. That's what the Cup is all about, sharing it and letting everybody enjoy it.

Looking back, I just feel so fortunate to have not only won the two Cups but to have played this wonderful game at a top level for 20 years. It was a dream just to make it in the NHL, and I feel so fortunate to have been able to have played alongside so many great players. To be with one organization means a lot too, first Quebec and then Colorado when the team was moved. The fans were amazing to me, and I will forever be grateful for all the respect and class that they showed me over the years. There have been so many life lessons that I have learned from winning the Cup. The biggest thing, though, is to just never give up. If you work hard and pay your dues, then anything is possible. Hey, I am proof of that.

—Joe Sakic, two-time Stanley Cup champion
(Quebec 1996 and Colorado 2001)

Introduction

My first taste of Stanley Cup hockey came back in the spring of 1981, when my beloved North Stars made a Cinderella run through the playoffs and all the way to the finals. I remember watching those games with my brothers and all of our buddies down in the basement of our home in Fairmont, a small town in southern Minnesota near the Iowa border. Hockey was almost nonexistent in those days in rural southern Minnesota, as opposed to the small towns of northern Minnesota up along the Canadian border—such as Roseau, Warroad, and International Falls—where they pull the kids out of their wombs by their skate blades. I, however, had recently gotten into hockey in a big way after watching Herb Brooks lead the University of Minnesota to a national championship in 1979 and then guide Team USA to the Olympic "Miracle on Ice" gold medal the very next year with a roster made up of mostly Minnesotans. I was hooked. We would play shinny out behind our house on Hall Lake after school and then warm up with hot chocolate as we watched play-off hockey at night. Mom and Dad would even buy us cases of frozen White Castle hamburgers, and we would sit down there watching our Stars while eating greasy "sliders" and drinking Mountain Dew. It was awesome.

The Stars opened that postseason with a trip to Boston, a place where they had never won. Ever. It was 35 games of futility and counting…in what would otherwise become known as the "Curse of the Garden." You see, there was a lot of bad blood between the two teams, as Boston had completely dominated them and showed them no respect over the years. Making matters worse was the fact that the season before Bruins tough guy John Wensink came over in the midst of a big scrum out on the ice in Boston and challenged the entire North Star bench to a fight. Sadly, not one North Star hopped over the boards to accept the challenge. Minnesota's coach, Glen Sonmor, himself a tough guy with the New York Rangers back in the '50s who had his career cut short after losing an eye during a game, was so upset by this that he vowed right then and there that the curse was going to be broken that next season, no matter what.

When the two teams met again in Beantown on February 26, 1981, Glen instructed his boys to go to war the very first time Boston tried to intimidate them. Sure enough, when Bruins centerman Steve Kasper brought his stick up and cut Bobby Smith's chin on the opening faceoff, it was on. Bobby, a Lady Byng award winner for "sportsmanship and gentlemanly conduct," dropped the gloves and went after him just five seconds into the game. The benches emptied, and what ensued was nothing short of insanity: 84 penalties for a combined 406 penalty minutes, a record that stood for more than two decades. The first period alone took more than an hour and a half, and they could barely finish the game because so many players had gotten ejected. Minnesota got beat that night 5–1 but Glen's boys, bloodied and bruised, partied like rock stars after the game. Glen was proud of them for having taken a stand, and he assured them that their acts of courage were going to pay dividends come the playoffs.

As luck would have it, the hockey gods smiled down upon us that postseason as Minnesota opened the first round at Boston. This time the North Stars came in with a swagger and confidence that the Bruins had never seen before. They weren't intimidated in the least, and they wound up breaking the curse when Steve Payne scored at 3:34 of overtime to win Game 1. From there they tallied a combined 16 goals in Games 2 and 3 to sweep the series and give the team its biggest upset in franchise history. The drama was so intense and so passionate, my buddies and I were hooked...we were fans for life. The Stars rode that momentum all the way through the playoffs, upsetting the Buffalo Sabres and Calgary Flames en route to making it to their first-ever finals, where they faced off against the defending champion New York Islanders.

Mayhem and bedlam would ensue as Stanley Cup fever hit Minnesota hard. Rabid fans were even running around the Twin Cities with gigantic tinfoil Stanley Cups on their heads. It was nuts. Seemingly everybody had jumped on the bandwagon, myself included. Bobby Smith, Steve Payne, Al MacAdam, Brad Maxwell, Craig Hartsburg, Dino Ciccarelli, Brad Palmer, Don Beaupre, and Gilles Meloche had suddenly become household names. For my buddies and me, however, it was all about Neal Broten—the former Gopher and 1980 Olympian who had joined the team just prior to the Boston series. He was *our* guy. I think we all had serious man-crushes on him, bad mullet and all...but I digress.

Minnesota opened the series in New York, where they lost Games 1 and 2 by identical 6–3 scores. The Islanders had a bunch of future Hall of Famers in Denis Potvin, Bryan Trottier, Billy Smith, and Mike Bossy, and it showed. The Stars lost Game 3 back in Bloomington at a jam-packed Met Center 7–5 but rebounded to take Game 4 4–2 behind 19-year-old rookie sensation Don Beaupre. The Islanders came out strong in Game 5, though, and showed why they were the best team in hockey. Behind Butch Goring's two first-period goals they never looked back, winning 5–1 and clinching their second straight championship. My buddies and I were all completely destroyed, just absolutely depressed. We wanted the parade; we wanted to see our guys proudly hoisting the Stanley Cup.

I remember watching the players afterward, all bloody and battered, hugging and smiling as they skated around with the Cup. Their fans had even jumped out onto the ice and were celebrating alongside the players; it was quite the scene. I was fascinated to see how emotional it was for the players—on both sides. I could see the raw jubilation of the Islander players, elated and ecstatic, satisfied that they had accomplished their goal of winning a second straight Cup. It would be the second of four straight in all, establishing the franchise as a true dynasty. For the Minnesota players, meanwhile, it was a deflated look of sadness and depression. They were spent both physically and emotionally, and it showed. Their dreams of raising Stanley had been shattered, and you could just tell that they knew that nobody really remembers who finishes in second place.

As Stars fans, we just figured our squad would be going back to the finals every year, because as fans we're eternal optimists. Well, it would take us another 11 years to get back to the finals, where this time we got beat by Mario Lemieux and the Pittsburgh Penguins in 1991. Sadly, two years later the team got hijacked down to Dallas by a disgruntled owner who still remains enemy No. 1 up here in the great north woods all these years later. We would get the expansion Minnesota Wild in 2000, and they would make a fantastic Cup run in 2003, making it all the way to the conference finals after upsetting Patrick Roy and the Colorado Avalanche. But that is as far as that franchise has gotten in its first decade of existence. So, in short, we are still waiting patiently for our chance to call the Stanley Cup our own for a season. This is the "State of Hockey," after all, so I am optimistic that it will happen sooner or later…I hope.

As for the legacy of that magical Stanley Cup run back in 1981, it took me from enjoying hockey to becoming obsessed with hockey. I wound up playing through high school and eventually even took a leap of faith in the late '80s by walking on at the University of Minnesota, a perennial powerhouse in college hockey at the time. Sadly I got cut after a very brief but very thrilling cup of coffee (as a practice pylon…) with my beloved Gophers. I had always dreamed of wearing the Maroon and Gold, so I was really crushed when I got the news. It turned out, however, that there was another job opening on the team—one not quite as sexy as an All-American defenseman but pretty darn close. Team mascot: "Goldy the Gopher."

There were two basic criteria for the job: first, you had to be a decent skater, and second, you had to be a complete moron. I apparently fit on both counts and got the gig. I had two older brothers with Ivy League MBAs, and I aspired to become a giant rodent. Go figure. Needless to say, my folks were not too thrilled about my career aspirations. Anyway, after three glorious years of battling badgers, bulldogs, and wolverines, I decided to write a book about the history of Gopher hockey from Goldy's point of view. Now, I had barely read any books at that particular juncture in my life, especially college textbooks, but I figured I would take another leap of faith and just go for it. Either way, I figured this would certainly help divert my attention away from the scary specter of entering the real world for at least one more year before all of Dad's cash dried up.

With that, I jumped in headfirst and started interviewing anybody and everybody who had ties to hockey in Minnesota. What a blast to meet and interview so many great players and coaches I had admired, from Neal Broten to Herb Brooks and from Lou Nanne to Glen Sonmor—each told me about how he had grown up dreaming of one day hoisting the Stanley Cup. A year later my book, appropriately titled *Gopher Hockey by the Hockey Gopher*, hit the shelves and immediately became a regional best seller. Who knew?

From those humble beginnings, I am proud to say that I have now written nearly 50 sports books, including a whole bunch about my true passion—hockey. Among them are *The Code: Hockey's Unwritten Rules and its Ignore at Your Own Risk Code of Honor, Slap Shot Original: The Man, the Foil, the Legend, and America's Coach: A Biographical Journey of the Late Hockey Icon Herb Brooks.* The latter of the three probably means the most. I've written a couple of books about my friend, hero, and mentor, Herb Brooks, and am also very proud of the fact that I am the president of the board of directors of the Herb Brooks Foundation, a wonderful organization that aims to "grow the base of hockey for boys and girls; give kids a positive hockey experience; and afford them opportunities to learn life lessons along the way." A special thanks to my publisher, Triumph Books, for donating a portion of the proceeds from the sale of this book to the foundation. It's an extremely classy gesture.

In March of 2010 the Herb Brooks Foundation hosted a fundraiser at the Minnesota State High School Hockey Tournament, the largest prep event of its kind in the country, which draws upward of 125,000 fans annually to the Xcel Energy Center in St. Paul. The star attraction that day was Stanley himself, who was delivered in style by Mike Bolt, who works for the Hockey Hall of Fame as an official "Cup Keeper." What a day it was to see all the wide-eyed faces staring in amazement at the greatest trophy in all of sports. We raised nearly eight grand that day for a cause that's near and dear to the hearts of many in the Land of 10,000 Lakes.

Anyway, Mike and I started chatting. The guy is hilarious, and you will read more about him later in the book. Eventually I asked him if I could please take a picture of me hoisting the Cup for the "author shot" on the back cover of this book. He looked at me, smiled, and said no. I thought that was odd, so I asked why. He said simply, "You haven't earned it." Ohhh. I hadn't earned it. He was right. How stupid of me. Hockey players are both respectful as well as superstitious when it comes to the Cup. They will never touch it unless they have won it. Never. They don't want to jinx it. That's why when they actually do get to raise it above their heads for the first time, it's undoubtedly one of the proudest and most profound moments of their lives.

Now, as the "Cup Keeper," it's Mike's responsibility to make sure that the only people who can raise it are those select few who have earned that privilege. As luck would have it, a handful of players who have been on Stanley Cup–winning teams stopped by that day in St. Paul to say hi, including Derek Plante, Shjon Podein, and Tom Chorske—all of whom you will read about in this book. Mike told each of them that they were welcome to pick up the Cup and raise it to have their photos taken. How cool was that? As for all the other collegiate and pro players who came by? They knew better and kept their distance.

Okay, back to the picture that I needed to take that afternoon with the Stanley Cup. If you look on the inside back jacket of the book you will see the finished product. As you can see I have my arm around Stanley. Also, and this is important, I am not touching him. I'm giving him an "air hug." Why? Well, at 41 years young I can't help but to think about Gordie Howe, who played well into his fifties, and Chris Chelios, who played into his late forties. Hey, you never know. I could still get that call! Maybe a team might want to take a flyer on an over-the-hill rodent for the playoffs? Maybe that cup of coffee is still out there for me yet? Maybe there are some general managers reading this at this very moment, and if so, all I can say is I'm ready. I'll sign for cheap. Heck, I'll pay you to sign! So just in case, I didn't want to touch the Cup that day and jinx it. Hey, you just never know…

Welcome to *Raising Stanley*, my new book, which celebrates the honor, courage, and sacrifice it takes to reach the pinnacle of professional hockey. I spent over a year researching and interviewing more than 100 players and coaches for it, and I couldn't be prouder of the final product. I had one simple criteria for the subjects I interviewed: they had to have their name on the Stanley Cup. Through the entire process I was able to capture a great mix of superstars, role players, enforcers, and grinders—each with his own unique story to tell. I didn't just want to hear from the same old people who get quoted all the time, either, I wanted to go off the grid and get some unique perspectives. From Scotty Bowman, who has his name on the Cup 11 times, to Joe Motzko, who barely got on once after playing a few shifts in the finals with Anaheim back in 2007, it's an eclectic and wonderfully diverse assortment of individuals. Their stories, memories, and life lessons will not only make you laugh, they will hopefully inspire you to reach heights you never dreamed possible.

I have chosen to give you their stories and answers in the form of quotes direct from the players, not rewritten in *my* words and then regurgitated back to you. Hopefully you will enjoy the format and appreciate it in its simplest and purest form.

The cool part about this book in my eyes was the fact that I was able to meet with and interview so many players, more than 100 in all, and get them to talk openly—some for more than an hour—about what it meant for them to fulfill their childhood dreams. Another caveat is that many of the players are clustered from certain teams—such as the '95 Devils or '86 Canadiens. Why? Because one interview led to the next interview, and as a courtesy I asked everyone I interviewed if he had a friend or teammate that he felt would be a good fit for the book as well. Invariably that led to several players from the same teams sharing the same stories. Lastly, there are a handful of players in the book with ties to Minnesota. Why? Well, I'm from Minnesota, and I'm an unabashed and unapologetic homer. 'Nuff said.

Truth be told, it was extremely difficult to track down everyone and figure out which guys had won Cups. It was a puzzle. There were so many players who I spoke with for background information that I couldn't include in the book; guys like Neil

Sheehy, whose Calgary Flames lost in the finals to the Canadiens in 1986, or Robb Stauber, who played solid between the pipes for the L.A. Kings but lost in the finals to those same Canadiens in 1993. Players like Reed Larson, Mike Ramsey, Willie Mitchell, and Phil Housley—all of whom played between 10 and 20 seasons, yet never came home with the hardware. It just goes to show you that no matter how good you are and no matter how much of a team player you are, a little bit of luck plays a part in this game.

You will read about not only what it meant for them to raise the Cup, but also about the deeper significance of how that achievement has affected or changed their lives. Some of the players I spoke to laughed out loud, while others broke down and cried. They wanted to thank their parents for all of the sacrifices they made, for getting them to early morning practices, and for allowing them to pursue their passion. That raw emotion about this sacred journey is the essence of what I hoped to capture in this book. I wanted to honor their achievements and chronicle them in a unique and enjoyable format that has never been done before. One of the things I am most proud of is the fact that I was able to interview at least one player from each Stanley Cup team from the past 50 years. What an odyssey that was! But I was up for the challenge, and I absolutely had a ball in the process.

For me it is all about the stories—they're priceless. Some brought tears to my eyes, including the one where Phil Esposito talked about how tough it was for him to slip the Stanley Cup ring off his dad's finger at his funeral just before they had to close his casket for good; or the one where Brendan Shanahan talked about what it meant for him to take the Cup to his father's gravesite after he had just won it so he could thank him; or the one where Gordie Roberts talked about how emotional it was to be at Bob Johnson's funeral, where each of the players from the '91 championship team that he had just coached tapped their Stanley Cup rings on his wooden casket as they walked by in single file to salute their fallen leader.

Some stories gave me goose bumps, including the one Scotty Bowman told me about how emotional it was for him to put on his skates and do a final victory lap with Stanley after he had led his Detroit Red Wings to the championship in 2002. It was his record ninth Cup, and Scotty, then pushing 70, knew it was going to be his last as a head coach, so he wanted to remember that feeling forever. Or there was the one Shjon Podein told me about how he cried after watching Ray Bourque finally get to hoist Stanley for the first time in 2001 with Colorado after spending more than two decades with the Boston Bruins. When team captain Joe Sakic handed the Cup directly to Ray to let him hoist it first, there wasn't a dry eye in the house. As a testament to just how respected a player Ray Bourque was, when he took the Cup back to Boston, more than 15,000 Bruins fans showed up at a rally to support him. Shjon, meanwhile, was so excited about winning the Cup that he refused to take off his equipment for the next 24 hours. That's right. Wanting the moment to last forever, he kept his entire uniform on—skates and all—to party like a rock star with teammates, friends, and fans alike all over Denver. It was epic; people still talk about it a decade later.

Some stories made me cringe, including the one Shawn Chambers told me about how Mike Modano insisted upon getting his broken wrist shot up before every game so he could play because he didn't want to let his teammates down during Dallas's 1999 Stanley Cup run. What a true professional. I will never forget Mike's gesture of appreciation on April 10, 2010, in St. Paul when Mike's Stars played my Wild in the season finale. It had long been rumored that this was going to be his last game ever, and it was only fitting that it would happen at the place where his career had started nearly two decades earlier as the No. 1 overall pick of the Minnesota North Stars. Mike was chosen as the third star of the game that night, and when he came out to tip his hat to the crowd he was wearing his old No. 9 North Stars jersey. Mike wanted to say thanks to the fans and let them know he still felt badly about how close they had come to winning the Cup back in 1991. As a working member of the media for the Wild, I can tell you that there were more than a few tears shed in the press box that night. I will never forget seeing Mike hug his wife and cry with her in a dark hallway just outside the locker room after the game. It was a touching moment.

Some stories made me laugh, especially the ones that happened when the players got to celebrate with the Cup for a day—like the one Penguins defenseman Phil Bourque told me about the time he tossed the Cup into Mario Lemieux's swimming pool from high atop his rocky waterfall. After he and his teammates were able to rescue the water-logged challis out of the drink, he then did his best MacGyver impersonation to fix it. As he was taking it apart, however, he noticed some engravings on the inside of the Cup from some old players, so he decided to leave his own legacy by etching out a message of his own in there, courtesy of a Phillips screwdriver. Nice. Or there was the one Clark Gillies told me about the time he let his German shepherd "Hombre" eat dog food out of the Cup after his Islanders had won it back in the early '80s. Last, but certainly not least, is the one I heard about the time Red Kelly, an eight-time champion, put his three-month-old son, Conn, in the Cup to take a picture—at which point the baby promptly "filled it up with pee." You know, whenever I think of players drinking champagne or baptizing their newborn children in it—I just can't help but think of Hombre and Conn. Yeesh!

The playoff beards, the dramatic Game 7s, the closed-door captain's practices, the coaching wisdom, the bench-clearing brawls, the crazy superstitions, the "playoff makeup" (the cuts, stitches, and bruises on their faces), and of course their "day with the Cup"—it all comes to life in the ensuing pages.

Inspirational, poignant, and hilarious stories on the quest to claim hockey's ultimate prize, that's what this is all about. I am truly honored and humbled to be able to share this wealth of information with you in my new book. I hope you will have as much fun reading about and celebrating this amazing history as I did in bringing it all to life. Cheers!

Introducing Stanley...

Before we dive into what the players had to say, here is a little history about the Stanley Cup. Originally known as the Dominion Hockey Challenge Cup, the Stanley Cup was donated in 1892 by Canada's then–governor general, Lord Stanley of Preston, as a trophy to reward the country's top-ranking amateur hockey team. Lord Stanley's children loved hockey. His two sons, Algernon and Arthur, formed a team called the Rideau Rebels, while his daughter Isobel was one of the first female hockey players in Canada. In 1892 Stanley issued a letter to the Ottawa Athletic Association that read as follows: "I have for some time been thinking that it would be a good thing if there were a challenge cup, which would be held from year to year by the leading hockey club in the Dominion. Considering the general interest which hockey matches now elicit, and the importance of having the game played fairly and under rules generally recognized, I am willing to give a cup which shall be held from year to year by the winning club."

His offer was enthusiastically accepted, and with that he took on the task of finding an appropriate trophy. According to records, a decorative punch bowl was then purchased in England from the London silversmith G.R. Collis and Company for 10 guineas ($48.67 at the time). On it he had the words "Dominion Hockey Challenge Cup" engraved on one

Most appearances on the Stanley Cup
(as a player or head coach, not including management)

- 11: Henri Richard (Montreal Canadiens)
- 10: Jean Beliveau (Montreal Canadiens)
- 10: Yvan Cournoyer (Montreal Canadiens)
- 9: Scotty Bowman (coach, Montreal Canadiens, Detroit Red Wings, Pittsburgh Penguins)
- 9: Claude Provost (Montreal Canadiens)
- 8: Hector "Toe" Blake (coach, Montreal Canadiens)
- 8: Red Kelly (Detroit Red Wings and Toronto Maple Leafs)
- 8: Jacques Lemaire (Montreal Canadiens)
- 8: Maurice Richard (Montreal Canadiens)
- 8: Serge Savard (Montreal Canadiens)

side and "From Stanley of Preston" on the other. The first winner was the Montreal Amateur Athletic Association in 1893, and the first team to have its players' names engraved on it was the 1907 Montreal Wanderers, although it didn't become an annual tradition until the Montreal Canadiens won it 1924. Over the ensuing years several pro leagues would come and go, fold and merge. The National Hockey League was formed in 1917, and for the next decade the trophy was awarded to the winner of a playoff between the NHL and its rival, the Pacific Coast Hockey League. Then, when the PCHL dissolved in 1927, the Cup became the de facto championship trophy of the NHL. It has been presented exclusively to its annual play-off champion ever since. Other pro leagues and clubs would occasionally issue challenges to play for the Cup over the ensuing years, but the NHL rejected those offers and stood its ground. Among them was the World Hockey Association, which also sought to challenge for the Cup in the early 1970s but was denied. Interestingly, there have only been two times in the last century when the Stanley Cup hasn't been awarded. The first came in 1919 as a result of the Spanish flu pandemic, and the second came in 2005, when a labor dispute between the NHL's owners and the Players Association led to the cancelation of the 2004–05 season.

According to the Hockey Hall of Fame, there are actually three Stanley Cups: the "Original Bowl," the "Presentation Cup," and the "Replica Cup." The Original Bowl that was purchased and donated by Lord Stanley is currently displayed at the Hockey Hall of Fame in Toronto, Ontario. It was awarded to each champion for the first 71 years of competition until the authenticated version, or Presentation Cup, was created in 1963 by Montreal silversmith Carl Petersen. This is the Cup that is given to the players out on the ice each year at the conclusion of the playoffs and is also the Cup that is given to the players for a day as a reward for winning the championship. The Replica Cup, meanwhile, was created in 1993 at a cost of $75,000 by Montreal silversmith Louise St. Jacques and is on permanent display at the Hockey Hall of Fame. It is used primarily as a stand-in whenever the Presentation Cup is not available.

The Presentation Cup stands 35¼ inches tall and weighs 34½ pounds. Its history is fascinating. There are more than 2,500 names chiseled onto the Cup, although not all are on there at the same time. In 1924 the Montreal Canadiens added a new silver band to the Cup in order to be able to engrave all the names of its players on it. Since then, engraving the team's names has become an annual tradition. Originally, a new band was added each year, causing the trophy to grow in size vertically until it became known affectionately as the "Stovepipe Cup." As a result it was redesigned in 1948 as a two-piece cigar-shaped trophy with a removable bowl and collar, and in 1958 a one-piece Cup design was introduced. At that point the old barrel was replaced with a five-band barrel, with each band able to display a total of 13 winning teams. When all the bands finally filled up in 1991 the top one was removed and put on permanent display in the Hockey Hall of Fame. Every 13 years a new blank band is added to the bottom to keep the tradition going. So nowadays players can expect to have their names on the Cup for about 65 years before having their band retired for good.

The criteria for a player to have his name inscribed on the Cup include either playing in at least 40 regular-season games for the championship team during the regular season or playing in at least one game of the finals. Among those who have taken advantage of this ruling are Aut Erickson and Milan Marcetta,

Maurice Richard (left) and Jean Beliveau of the Montreal Canadiens are all smiles in the dressing room after defeating the Boston Bruins 5–3 to win the 1957–58 Stanley Cup.

Stanley Cup typos

One of the things players and fans alike enjoy doing when they have
time to study the Cup is to find the misspellings and mistakes that
are etched onto its sides, something that only adds to the allure and
curiosity of hockey's holy grail. According to the Hockey Hall of
Fame, here are a few of the more common ones:

- Pete Palangio of the 1938 Blackhawks had his name engraved
  twice; as did Turk Broda in 1942 with Toronto, once as "Walter"
  Broda (his given name) and once as "Turk" Broda, his nickname.

- Pat McReavy's name is misspelled "McCeavy" as a member of the
  1941 Boston Bruins.

- Gaye Stewart's name was misspelled "Gave" as a member of the
  1947 Maple Leafs.

- Ted Kennedy was misspelled "Kennedyy" in the 1940s.

- Dickie Moore won six cups in the '50s, and his name was spelled
  differently five times: "D. Moore," "Richard Moore," "R. Moore,"
  "Dickie Moore," and "Rich Moore."

- Glenn Hall's name was misspelled "Glin," and Tommy Ivan's
  name was misspelled "Nivan" after their Red Wings won it in
  the early '50s.

- Alex Delvecchio's name was engraved as "Belvecchio" following
  one of his three Red Wings titles in the early '50s.

- Jacques Plante won five consecutive Cups with the Canadiens
  between 1956 and 1960 and had his name spelled five different ways.

- Toronto Maple Leafs was misspelled "Leaes" in 1963.

- The Bruins' city of Boston was misspelled "Bqstqn" in 1972.

- Bob Gainey was misspelled "Gainy" when he was a player for
  Montreal in the 1970s.

- New York Islanders was misspelled "Ilanders" in 1981.

- In 1984, Edmonton Oilers' owner Peter Pocklington included his
  father's name on the list for the engraver. But Basil Pocklington had
  no affiliation with the team, so the NHL insisted on the name's
  removal. Sixteen Xs now cover Basil's name on the Cup.

- In 1996, Colorado Avalanche's Adam Deadmarsh's last name was spelled "Deadmarch." It was later corrected, marking the first name correction on the Cup. Similar corrections were made in 2002 and 2006 for the names of Detroit Red Wings goalie Manny Legace ("Lagace") and Carolina Hurricanes forward Eric Staal ("Staaal").

who each played in one game of the 1967 finals with the Toronto Maple Leafs. However, the NHL will also consider other "extraordinary" reasons to include players on a case-by-case basis, which can be petitioned. For instance, Detroit Red Wings defenseman Vladimir Konstantinov, whose career was tragically cut short following a limousine accident after the team won the Stanley Cup in 1997, was allowed to have his name engraved on the Cup after Detroit defended their title in 1998. And in 1972 the Boston Bruins included Ted Green on their list of engraved names. Green had gotten injured in a preseason game that year and wound up missing the entire campaign but was deemed an integral part of the franchise nevertheless.

In addition to players and coaches, other key front-office personnel as well as members of ownership also get their names on the Cup. Jean Beliveau's name appears on it more than any other in history, 10 as a player and seven as a member of management with the Montreal Canadiens, for a total of 17 times. Henri Richard, however, holds the record for playing on the most Stanley Cup teams with 11. Scotty Bowman, meanwhile, holds the record for most wins as a coach with nine, but he has 11 total when you add in the two he won as a member of management. Those numbers will never be surpassed in the modern era of free agency.

CHAPTER

1

The True Meaning
of Winning the Cup

Every player's journey to that magical moment when he finally
wins a championship is both profound and unique. Here are what
the players and coaches had to say about what it meant to them to
reach the pinnacle of hockey and to finally get to raise Stanley.

WHAT DID IT MEAN FOR YOU
TO RAISE STANLEY?

"Winning the Cup meant everything to me. Growing up in
Canada, it's a dream of every kid to raise the cup, but for
me it was even extra special because I got to win it up in
Montreal, which was my boyhood team. Winning the Cup,
it's not about the money, it's about the experience and
about the rings. They are rare and can't be bought. That's
why they are so special."

Brian Bellows
Montreal 1993

"Once you make it to the NHL your goal is to win the
Stanley Cup, and it is not easy by any stretch of the imagination. When it finally happens, though, and you get to
raise it proudly over your head, it's just a huge feeling of

satisfaction and relief. It was as if my love of hockey was reaffirmed after winning it. It was just extraordinary. I had been to the finals early in my career, back in 1993 with Los Angeles, and lost. Sure, I was upset over losing, but I just figured that those opportunities would come around every couple of years or so. Little did I know that those chances are far and few between. So when I got traded to Colorado from L.A. midway through that '01 season, I knew that I had been given a huge opportunity. When you look at that team and how it was put together, clearly it was a 'win now' approach. They had pieces to the puzzle in place prior to that year, but the guys they brought in really helped to put them over the top. Maybe the biggest thing was the outstanding play of our goalie, Patrick Roy, who just carried us that postseason. The thing I remember most about that season was when our team captain Joe Sakic handed the Cup straight over to Ray Bourque, who had been patiently waiting to hoist it for more than two decades. What a classy act by Joe. Ray was so excited, I think he bench-pressed that thing about a hundred times! It was pretty emotional for all of us."

Rob Blake
Colorado 2001

"My belief has always been that when you grow up as a kid playing hockey, your dreams are always of winning the Stanley Cup, so when it really does happen as an adult it's the pinnacle of your career. It is the realization that your dreams are actually coming true. What is so neat about that is the fact that in sports or in life, most people rarely will ever have that opportunity. Throughout the whole process of playing youth hockey, college, minors, and then into the NHL, the vision is always on you. It's about what

it's going to feel like and what it's going to mean to *me*.
That all changes when you get to take the Cup home and
share it with the people who matter most, your friends and
family. When I took the Cup back to my hometown of
Powell River, British Columbia, it changed my whole attitude. Once I saw the expressions on not only their faces
but the faces of all the fans who came out to see it, and I
could see what it meant to them, I realized that winning the
Stanley Cup wasn't necessarily about me. Watching grown
men who had grown up as die-hard Toronto Maple Leafs
fans or Montreal Canadiens fans touch the names of their
childhood heroes on the Cup and seeing them cry was just
profound to me. They had never seen the Cup before, and
it meant so much to them that I had brought it back home.
You don't realize the effect it has on people, because while
you are in pursuit of it you think it is all about you. Well, it
didn't take me very long once I got home to realize that it
wasn't about me anymore. It was way bigger than that. So
that to me really symbolized what winning it is all about."

Brad Bombardir
New Jersey 2000

"Winning the Cup was the culmination of basically my
whole life. I started playing the game when I was five
years old as a kid in Boston, and I knew from a very early
age that I wanted to be a professional hockey player. That
was my goal, my dream. I always imagined myself raising
the Cup one day, I really did. Then when it finally happened, it was just surreal. Winning the Cup was an affir-
mation of all the decisions I made, many of which others
doubted along the way—specifically when I chose
to go to Canada to play junior hockey rather than play
in college. All the hard work, the time, the energy, the

sacrifice, the money that my parents put in—it was all worth it once I was able to finally raise that beautiful trophy above my head. It was amazing."

Phil Bourque
Pittsburgh 1992 and 1993

"As a kid I dreamed about playing in the NHL, scoring my first goal, and then raising the Cup. So to do it was literally a dream come true."

Dan Boyle
Tampa 2004

"For me it was the highlight of my career. It represented a sort of validation for all the hard work I had put in for so many years prior. When we won it that year, it was my 17th season in the league, and I wasn't sure if it was ever going to happen or not. I had always believed that the hard work would pay off sooner or later, though, and I was thrilled when it finally did. What made it even neater was doing it alongside so many other veteran players, such as Bret Hedican and Glen Wesley, who had also never won it up until that point. To see the joy in their eyes was amazing, and I am sure they would say the same for me. It was just a wonderful experience all the way around, and it felt good to be a part of something that brought so much joy to so many deserving people."

Rod Brind'Amour
Carolina 2006

"I grew up in Roseau, Minnesota, which is right on the U.S.-Canadian border, and was lucky enough to be able to

Carolina's Rod Brind'amour celebrates after scoring the first goal in Game 2 of the 2001–02 Stanley Cup Finals against the Red Wings. The Hurricanes won the series in seven games.

Why I love the Cup

"The Cup is so unique, starting with the look of it. It is unlike any other trophy in sports. It's gorgeous. It's iconic. It's big. It's revered. It has a history. What more could you ask for? The Cup to a lot of people is a character; something that is alive—a living, breathing entity. It just has that aura about it, that's what makes it so special. I love everything about it, I really do."

Brendan Shanahan
Detroit 1997, 1998, and 2002

watch *Hockey Night in Canada* on Wednesday and Saturday nights on TV. I remember watching those great Montreal teams win all those Stanley Cups during the '70s and thinking to myself, 'One day. One day it would be so amazing to raise the Cup.' But I didn't really think it would even be a possibility, it was just too far fetched. I was more worried about making my high school team and playing in the state tournament. Slowly but surely, though, I kept moving up the ladder. From there I was able to win a national championship at the University of Minnesota, which was followed by a gold medal in the 1980 Olympics. What an unbelievable moment that was.

Then, in 1981, I signed with my hometown North Stars right out of college and basically joined the team for their magical playoff run all the way to the Stanley Cup Finals. We got beat by the Islanders that year, but I got a taste of what it was all about. We made it back in 1991, only to lose to Pittsburgh that time, which was really painful. We were up in that series too; I thought for sure we were going to do it. The North Stars wound up moving to Dallas a couple of years later, and I wasn't sure what was going to happen in my career, to be honest.

"Finally, midway through the '95 season I got traded to New Jersey. That was a lockout year, but I knew that they had a great team so I was excited about our chances. Sure enough, we got hot at the end and we did it. I even got a couple of game winners against Detroit in the finals, which was pretty exciting. My folks made it out there to see some of the games, which was nice too. I guess I had finally gotten the monkey off my back, and it felt great. I will never forget celebrating afterward in the locker room with all the guys; it was just an awesome moment. So to win it after 15 years in the league, at a time in my career when I figured it probably wasn't ever going to happen, yeah, it was special. It meant a lot to accomplish something that not too many players get to do. I know a lot of players who have played just as long—if not longer—who never won it, so I feel lucky in that regard. To be honest, and I don't want to take anything away from what happened in New Jersey, I really wish I could have won a Stanley Cup with the North Stars. That was my team growing up, and that was the team that I started out with. It just would have been nice to have been able to give that to the fans there because they were so good to me. They truly deserved it. Anyway, looking back the only negative thing that came out of the whole deal was that when I got traded to the Devils the player I got dealt for was Corey Millen, who was also a former Gopher [University of Minnesota] and fellow northern Minnesotan. I just felt bad knowing that I was going to get my name on the Cup and he wasn't, but I guess that's just the way the puck bounces sometimes in this crazy business."

Neal Broten
New Jersey 1995

"Winning the Stanley Cup was such a great experience. We did it our way that year too, with an element of toughness, and I was really proud of that. I will never forget those final few seconds in that last game against the Senators. The clock was ticking down, and our video guy, Joe Trotta, yells out, 'And the Chiefs have won the championship of the Federal League!' I just burst out laughing, it was absolutely hilarious. I could just picture Jim Carr, the toupee-wearing play-by-play announcer of the Chiefs in my mind, screaming it out. It was just the perfect thing to say at this amazing time in our lives, and we had all heard that line a million times over our careers. Even *Sports Illustrated* wrote about that moment in their big article about us winning the Cup. I still have to smile when I think about that."

Brian Burke
Anaheim 2007 (GM)

"As a kid growing up in Roseau [Minnesota], I had always dreamt about winning the Cup. I even wished for it, I really did. So to finally do it, to win it, it's almost indescribable. What a feeling. To raise it up above my head was an experience I will never forget. You get teary eyed and it gets pretty emotional. It was a huge accomplishment for sure. It didn't hit me right way either. I think it finally sunk in when we were driving in a bus down Michigan Avenue in Chicago at our victory parade and seeing over two million fans show up to cheer us on. That was so amazing. Those fans had waited nearly 50 years for that, and I was just so happy that I played a small role in giving that to them."

"We had such a great team that season with so many great players, and I was just really proud and honored to be a part of it. My role was to bring an element of toughness to the team, and I think I did all right. We didn't have a heavy-weight, but we all stuck together, and that really united us. We didn't let anything get us down either, we just battled and battled every night. It didn't matter how many goals we were down, we never gave up. If you screwed up out on the ice nobody would get on you either, instead they would make a joke and ease the tension that way. What a great

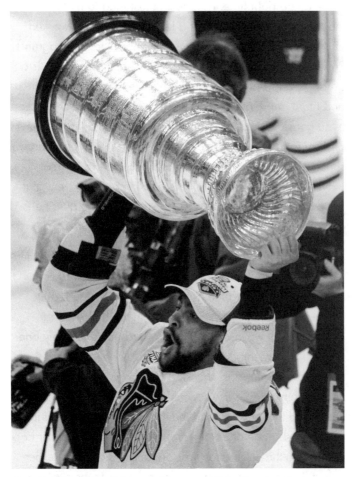

Dustin Byfuglien celebrates the return of the Stanley Cup to Chicago after nearly five-decades. The Blackhawks topped the Flyers 4–3 in overtime on June 9, 2010, to take the title.

group of guys. From Patrick Kane to Jonathan Toews to Duncan Keith, what a lineup. Duncan kind of epitomized our toughness I think. When he lost those seven teeth in the semifinals and still kept playing, that was epic. What a warrior.

"That entire playoff run was so emotional. I wound up getting five game-winners over that postseason, too, which was so crazy. What can you say? I think I was just in the right place at the right time, I suppose. I just tried to make the most of my opportunities, and luckily for me it all worked out. Looking back I will always remember the finals against Philly and the battles that I had with Chris Pronger. He is a great player, and it was tough to battle that guy night in and night out, that was for sure. There was so much media hype going on too, so I had to go out and play my game and try to tune everything else out. After the series when we shook hands I said, 'Thanks for battling, you're a great player, and you brought out the best in me.' We went at it out on the ice, but I have a lot of respect for the guy; he is one of the best in the business for sure.

"The biggest highlight for sure though came at the end when we won it in Game 6 out in Philadelphia. When Kaner [Patrick Kane] scored the game-winner, what a surreal moment. I think he was the only guy in the building that actually saw it go in, too. It was a weird goal, certainly one that will be remembered though. I was on the bench at the time and saw him start chucking his gloves and didn't know what to think. It was like super slow motion until we figured it out, and then it was just pandemonium after that, but for a few seconds none of us knew for sure if it was a goal or not. From there the celebration was on, and it didn't stop either. In fact, I didn't sleep for a couple of days—it was pretty nuts. I remember landing back in Chicago at about five in the morning. At first I thought it was raining, but then I figured out that the water was from the fire trucks that were hosing us down as we taxied in on the runway. They had their sirens going and everything—it was pretty cool. We got a police escort from there over to Harry Caray's, where we started the celebration with the Cup. From there everything is just a blur. The whole thing was pretty unbelievable."

Dustin Byfuglien
Chicago 2010

"For me it was a little surreal. I was fresh out of college at Minnesota State University, Mankato, and had been playing in the minors for most of the season. I then got a call up for the playoffs, and before I knew what was happening, I was raising the Stanley Cup. The whole thing was just a blur, but it was exciting, that was for sure. I was a black ace, or practice squad call-up guy—an insurance policy in case anybody got hurt. Well, one by one the organization started sending guys home, and none of us knew if we were going to be the next to go or not. It was pretty stressful, but luckily I stuck around just long enough to get some ice time—which got me on the Cup. I got into three games in the conference finals and then one game in the finals. I just stayed positive and worked hard, and eventually I was rewarded. I was really lucky and I know that.

"I think of all the guys who have played in the league for 10 or 20 years and never got their name on the Cup, and here I am playing four measly games. At first I would just wonder to myself, 'Did I really deserve it?' I guess it is what it is. We all have our own unique stories and journeys to get here, and mine was just different from everybody else's, I suppose. I had a role on that team, and they obviously saw something in me, so I have no regrets. It was an amazing experience.

To be out there afterward with all the guys on the ice, celebrating and hugging everyone, it was a moment I will never forget. I just hope that there are many more Stanley Cups in my future, that's why we all play this game."

Ryan Carter
Anaheim 2007

"Total dream come true. The '95 season was a wild one for me. I had gotten traded from Tampa to New Jersey right at the deadline that year. I remember getting the news; my wife was eight and a half months pregnant at the time. So I packed up and moved to New Jersey, where I wound up living at the same hotel as my old buddy Neal Broten, who had just gotten traded there from Dallas. Neal and I had gone to the finals together back in 1991 with the North Stars, and we were excited about our chances with the Devils. It was a lockout-shortened schedule that season too, which was great for a couple of old guys like us. What was so cool about that team was that we got hot late in the year and went on a roll that was just unbelievable. I had never seen anything like that before; I didn't think anybody could beat us. What fun that was, to have that kind of confidence in your teammates.

"We wound up sweeping Detroit in the finals, which was unbelievable. I scored a pair of goals in the last game too, which made it even more special. The second one came with about seven minutes left in the game to put us up 5–2. I will never forget John MacLean skating over and hugging me with his eyes all welled up with tears. He had been with the organization for so long and had suffered through so many tough seasons. We both knew that with Marty Brodeur back in the net, there was no way in hell that they were going to score three goals in seven minutes. So in that moment we both knew that we had finally won the Stanley Cup. What a feeling, that emotion was just incredible. Then when I came to the bench there was Mikey Peluso, our tough guy, just bawling uncontrollably. It was incredible, here is this huge guy who is so feared, yet he can't even bring himself to take another shift in the final six minutes of the game because he is so caught up in the moment. That's what the Cup is all about, though, just leaving it all out there, and when it's over, you're spent. That was Mikey, he was just spent. Wow, what a moment."

Shawn Chambers
New Jersey 1995 and Dallas 1999

"Winning the Stanley Cup as a pro hockey player is the ultimate accomplishment. When it finally happens, after you have won the game, it is completely surreal. You can't believe that you are actually doing it because you have watched so many great players before you over the years do it. And now here you are, raising the Stanley Cup. Honestly, it's like a delayed reaction; it just doesn't register right away. It's sort of an out-of-body experience, like you are up in the stands watching yourself as opposed to really doing it. There was a sense of satisfaction and contentment in that you had accomplished a huge goal that you had set for yourself. You realize that there is a beginning, a middle, and an end to that season, and once that final buzzer goes off you are officially a champion. It's extremely gratifying. When they played the Queen song "We Are the Champions," I lost it. Then about an hour later it hit me while I was in the locker room. This was something that I had dreamed about and thought about for my whole life, ever since I was a little kid. You think about all the long hours of practice and about the sacrifices your family made for you. You think about scoring your first goal and about your mom or dad congratulating you and reassuring you that all the hard work had finally paid off. Well, to raise Stanley means that all the hard work truly, finally paid off. When I realized that it was almost overwhelming, just really intense. I mean, it literally took the wind out of me. Then you look around and see all your teammates celebrating, and you are genuinely happy for them too because you know that you couldn't have done it without them. I got to New Jersey in 1991, and those were a rough couple of years. We weren't horrible, but we certainly weren't a contender either. So to see how far we had come in four years was pretty special. It just felt good to have contributed and to have been a part of the process. My teammates and I had paid our dues along the way, and this was our reward."

Tom Chorske
New Jersey 1995

"Raising Stanley didn't really have a concrete meaning at the time I won it because it was so surreal. I was only 23 when we won our first Cup, and it was almost like I was in a make-believe world at the time. As a kid it was something I had always dreamed of, though. Always. The strongest and most memorable emotion that I had when we won it was love. Immediately, it was love. The love I felt for my teammates at that moment was almost overpowering. I wanted to stay together with them forever and ever; I never wanted that moment to end. I can't explain it. It was amazing. Both Cups were special, but the second time was more meaningful in that I could wrap my head around it and really appreciate it. The first time I was almost in disbelief that it was actually happening. The second one was neat in that we won it on the road, up in Buffalo, and as a result we were able to enjoy the moment as teammates. We were all together without all the outside interference of the media and family and whatnot, which made it really emotional to a lot of us. It was just us, nobody else. We had won the first one at home, and the partying started immediately; it was just a blur. Whereas this one was more meaningful and ful-filling because we got to enjoy it a little bit more. We got to visit on the plane ride home and just talk about what we had just done. Winning that second one validated us too, it proved that we were no fluke. That meant a lot as well.

"I'm proud of what we accomplished in Philadelphia. We used fear and intimidation to change the game. Hell, we took it to another level. We figured out pretty quickly that when our opposition was scared on the ice they had little chance for success. As soon as we won a pair of Stanley Cups playing the way we played, all the other teams took notice. All of a sudden size mattered in the NHL. All of a sudden toughness mattered in the NHL. The wolf pack mentality that we were able to employ proved to be invalu-able, it really did. Based on Ed Snyder's [team owner] phi-losophy and Keith Allen's [GM] execution, we took toughness to a whole new level in professional hockey. Being an expansion team, Ed had gone through a lot over the franchise's first few years and taken a lot of abuse from those Original Six teams. Finally he said enough was enough. So he put together a lineup in which nobody was ever going to push one of his teams around again. We maybe had the most colorful team of all time in those days, and I just felt very proud to be a part of it.

"Some of my greatest memories from winning those two Cups came afterward, at the parades. After we won our first Cup we had a parade through Philly that drew something like two million spectators; it was utterly insane. They had us in cars driving down the street, and none of us could see a damn thing. It was actually pretty scary. People were hanging out of trees and off of buildings and on street lights; it was nuts. We were literally moving masses of humanity. Fans would just jump all over our cars. I had like 10 people on my car at one point, just hanging on for dear life. I was a smoker at the time, and I remember my wife and I taking my lit cigarettes and burning the fingers of the fans who were trying to come in through the sun roof. We thought we were going to die, we really did.

"Luckily they changed up the parade format for the second one. The next year they put us all on two huge floats that stood really high up so everyone could see us. They had the important people up on the first one, Bobby Clarke, Bernie Parent, and management. Then all of us grinders, we were in back. Well, we were driving down Broad Street in these things, waving to the fans and having a great time. We had been drinking quite a bit of beer for quite a few hours though, and eventually nature called in the worst way. I saw a gas station that was across the street and figured that was going to be my only chance. So I climbed down the side of our float as it was moving along and shoved my way, literally, into this gas station. I get there, and the gas station attendant at first wasn't going to let me use the bathroom unless I bought some gas, but luckily some fans reassured the guy that I was one of the players in the parade. He tossed me the key and I did my thing, and then when I got out I realized that the floats didn't wait for me. There was now a sea of tens of thousands of screaming fans between me and my teammates, and I didn't know what the hell I was going to do.

"Just then, these two cops came over to me. They had seen me jump off the float and knew that I was in trouble. So they instructed me to grab on to each of their belts and follow them, as they then proceeded to take their billy clubs and make a "V" shape with them to wedge through all of the people. It was crazy. There I was, like a plow horse, churning through all of these people. We were banging bodies out of our way as we went, and I was hanging on to these two guys for dear life. Finally, we got to the float, and they took one of their billy clubs, and each held on to one end of it, and they had me step on it like a ladder to hoist me up. Sure enough, I made it. I saluted them to thank them as we rode off; it was unreal. I was never so happy to finally sit down in my life.

"Then, maybe a minute later, both floats come to a screeching halt. We all wondered what was going on. We look up at the front float and quickly realized that they stopped so Bernie Parent could go to the bathroom. They pulled out these stairs from the side of the float, which I was of course oblivious to, and he gets off like some sort of king with everybody cheering for him. Meanwhile, our traveling secretary had gone over to this row house and arranged for Bernie to come inside to take a leak. So Bernie goes in, does his thing, and then comes out as we are all waiting for him. He kisses the homeowner, this little old lady who thought she had died and gone to heaven to have the world's greatest goalie pee in her toilet, and then he casually walks back up onto the float so we can start again. I am watching this, and it was at that very moment that I realized my level of importance in the grand scheme of things with the Flyers. I had to pee, and it was about a one-hour odyssey requiring two police officers and billy clubs. Bernie, meanwhile, has to pee and it's like the president getting off Air Force One or something. Unbelievable. You know, I still have a recurring nightmare where I am

begging the gas station attendant to let me use his filthy
bathroom and him not believing me that I am actually a
member of the Flyers. Then in this hazy dream sequence, I
see all these die-hard Flyer fans throwing coins into this
lady's toilet, which she had bronzed in Bernie's honor. How
crazy is that?"

Bill Clement
Philadelphia 1974 and 1975

"It's an amazing achievement and something I am so
proud of. I had worked so hard my whole life to get to that
level, where I might someday be in a position to have an
opportunity to raise the Cup. It was just incredible. I
remember after the game just sitting there with my teammates and my family and just having this feeling of calmness come over me. You realize at that moment that
whatever happens over the rest of your career, you can
now walk away from the game happily and peacefully
with no regrets. It's what every player plays for, and once
you have it you just feel complete. You feel satisfied in
knowing that nobody can ever take that away from you.
Winning it makes you think of your family too. Our parents
play such an instrumental role in our lives and make so
many sacrifices for us, and at that moment I just wanted to
thank them. It was pretty emotional."

Ben Clymer
Tampa 2004

"Winning the Cup was the fulfillment of everything I had
worked my whole life for. You never really expect to be
able to do it, but it's certainly one of those things you
always dreamed about. I tell you what, though, lifting that

thing up was unbelievable. It's crazy too in that while I was hoisting it I was literally flashing back to when I was a little kid playing on the outdoor rinks in northern Minnesota with my buddies. We had a rink in the backyard that my dad built. We hung lights from the gutters so we could play at night, and I can still remember the silver bucket that we used as our Stanley Cup. We'd play all day and well into the night until Mom called us in for hot chocolate. Some of my best hockey memories were made right on that rink. My dad was a longtime coach, and I certainly thought about him a lot at that moment too. As we were all cele-brating out on the ice I got caught up in the moment. I remember thinking about how happy I was for my team-mate Brett Hedican, who was someone I had always looked up to while I was at St. Cloud State University. Heddy was there a few years before me, but we had become great friends. I was *so* happy for Brett, maybe even more happy for him than I was for myself, believe it or not. For a guy who had gone through as much as he had, to now finally be able to raise the Cup, I just couldn't stop smiling for him. It actually brought me to tears. I was also extremely happy to see our team captain Rod Brind'Amour get to raise it for the first time as well. He was the first one to touch it, and to see the emotion on his face is something I will never forget. It still gives me goose bumps. What an inspiration he was for us that whole play-off run. He was such a great leader and scored so many big goals for us. Just some of the things he said and did when times were tough really stick with me. I had never respected a teammate as much as I respected him. What a great person."

Matt Cullen
Carolina 2006

"Ever since I was seven years old the only thing I dreamed of was to one day play in the National Hockey League. I said it to my mother every single day, probably 50 times a day. She used to pacify me by saying, 'Yeah, yeah. Sure, Kenny.' When I was 10 years old my buddies and I used to play shinny hockey, and the winners got to hoist a big garbage can above their heads, pretending it was the Stanley Cup. So when I finally was able to hoist the real one all those years later, it was beyond words. It was completely overwhelming. All of those memories came flashing back to me like an out-of-body experience. It was the greatest experience of my life.

"Now that I look back and realize that I have been fortunate to have won three of them, it's unbelievably humbling. The first one in 1995 was really special. When Jacques Lemaire came on the year before, we knew that things were going to fall into place for us. So we started adding pieces to the puzzle, starting with Marty Brodeur. You have to have great goaltending to win a championship, that's half the battle. Then we added Scott Stevens and Scott Niedermayer, two star quality-type players, which really helped to put us over the top. From that base we just started adding pieces, and eventually everything came together for us. It was amazing. What a feeling.

"I was blessed to have played in such a great organization, the Devils, and I am so proud to be associated with them. I spent my entire 19-year career with them and am very proud of that. I started out with them right after they moved there from Colorado, and we went through some tough times early on. We hung in there, though, and eventually we believed in ourselves. Eventually we became champions, and I feel very satisfied in knowing that I had a part in all three of the franchise's Stanley Cup victories. I was 32 when we won the first one and 40 when we won the third, so I definitely paid my dues."

Ken Daneyko
New Jersey 1995, 2000, and 2003

"I was a lowly rookie that season, and it's kind of a blur, to be honest. We had all these great veterans on that team, guys like Kevin Stevens, Neal Broten, Ken Daneyko, and John MacLean, and my whole focus was basically to not be the one who screwed it up for those guys. I felt so unworthy even being around some of those guys; I was just in awe of them. What a thrill, though, to win the Cup and to be a part of such an amazing group of guys. It was an unbelievable feeling, it really was."

Kevin Dean
New Jersey 1995

"For me to win the Cup with New Jersey in New Jersey, my home state, was indescribable. I grew up in Brick and dreamed of one day playing for the Devils, so to get drafted by them and then to be a part of winning the Stanley Cup with them was one of the greatest moments in my life. To win the Stanley Cup after winning a state high school championship and a national championship at Lake Superior State, it was as if my life was complete. Words can't explain it."

Jim Dowd
New Jersey 1995

"I came to New Jersey in 1984 and suffered through a half dozen pretty miserable seasons before we finally started to turn things around. We had a young group of guys on those teams, though, including myself, John MacLean, and Ken Daneyko, and we all sort of grew up together. Eventually it all came together for us, and after a couple of solid playoff runs in the early '90s we won the Cup in 1995. After going through that many years of futility, words almost can't even describe what it meant to me. It was a pretty amazing feeling, just really special."

Bruce Driver

New Jersey 1995

"The Stanley Cup is the ultimate punch line to the story, and the story is what makes the punch line work. The story is about that particular season and of all the hard work, preparation, and sacrifice that went into that season. The Stanley Cup is the culmination of your goals that you set out in quest of many months before. So, in the quest for anything that is worthwhile, you have to be willing to hope for it—which is so hard, because chances are it won't turn out—and that can be extremely painful. You also have to have your teammates hope for it just as hard. You have to go through moments where it doesn't seem remotely possible and nothing seems to be working and then fight your way back. So no matter how good your team is, you have all of those things going on over the course of a season. And if that weren't enough, you are also carrying everybody else's hopes as well, including the fans'. In our case it was the fans in not only Montreal, but also the entire province of Quebec. You hope big, and you hope hard, and you make yourself completely vulnerable in the process. You can't emotionally prepare yourself for the possibility of it not turning out the way you hope. I mean, if it doesn't go your way you've got nothing there to protect you from that disappointment. So you work and you work, and then it finally happens, and everything comes together, and you are the champions.

"I love the moment of the celebration right after winning. Then, about a half hour later, when you are in the locker room, you go into a sort of deep mellow where you know it's done. It's over. You set out on a path, and you had no way of knowing that you could get there, but you got there and you won. That is the moment that was the most gratifying for me. That was real satisfaction, to look around at your teammates and to realize that you were the champions that season. You sit and you reflect, and it feels very good. Very good. It's a quiet internal smile and it's wonderful. It's freedom. Then you get to enjoy it that next week with the parades and the parties. Best of all, though, you get to enjoy it that entire summer. You see that scoreboard in your mind with the final score on it, and you remember how good that felt. Then, when someone comes up to you and has something to say about a certain goal you blew back in December or a game you lost in February, it's as if you can just point to that scoreboard and all is forgotten. You just carry that around with you until September, when you have to work toward earning another scoreboard. It's that incredible freedom that you rarely feel about anything in life. It's amazing. I miss that.

"I was so fortunate to have won six Stanley Cups. They are obviously all very special to me, but my most memorable are the first, the third, and the sixth—all for very different reasons. The first was special because it was the first. It was special because it was new and exciting. I was a rookie that year and just being there was such a thrill. It was fun. I was trying to find my way and trying to fit in. I wanted to see what I could do, I wasn't sure. Probably the best part was that you don't yet know what you can't do either. My favorite one was probably the third, which came in 1976, when we beat the Flyers in four straight. We had won it in 1973, and then they had won the next two in '74 and '75, so this was a big rivalry for us. We were on a mission that season to win back *our* Cup. It started in training camp, and we were relentless that year. We were simply not going to be denied. To sweep them felt so good. They were the best at the time, and we beat them soundly, which said a lot. We discovered just how good we might be that year, and we carried that momentum en route to winning four straight Stanley Cups from 1976 to 1979. We didn't lose too many games over that time either; it was just a wonderful time to be a Montreal Canadien. Truly wonderful.

"Now the greatest part of that victory was the plane ride home, back to Montreal. It's a great story. You see, for the third game in Philadelphia the Flyers brought in Kate Smith, the famous singer, to sing 'God Bless America.' This was their secret weapon, so to speak, their superstition that had never before failed them. Whenever she performed live at the Spectrum, the Flyers had never lost. Ever. The fans there absolutely adored her. Well, before the last game I wrote out the words to the song and made 25 photocopies for my teammates for the plane ride home. I didn't tell anyone about it though because it was without a doubt the most presumptuous thing I had ever done in hockey. I didn't want to get too cocky or disrespectful or anything like that, I just figured that if we won then this would be a neat thing to do—to sort of neutralize their secret weapon. Sure enough, we beat them, Kate Smith and all, and on the flight home we sang like choir boys—a bunch of

Canadian kids heading back to Canada, singing 'God Bless America.' What a great moment.

"The last one, meanwhile, was memorable for the opposite reason. It was such a struggle that season. Knowing it was my last year was tough too. I had told the organization the year before that this was going to be my last year, which added even more pressure to go out with a bang. I wasn't playing well, and I was trying to pull it all together. All of the things that seemed to have come together for me in years past come playoff time weren't coming together this time, and it was so frustrating. I will never forget playing the Rangers in the finals. It was the opening game, and I got benched at the end of the second period by Scotty Bowman and replaced by Bunny Larocque. I was shocked. I had played every minute of every playoff game for the Canadiens prior to that since my rookie year. I never missed one minute. Here I was suddenly sitting on the bench, having gotten taken out. I completely deserved it, though, because I wasn't playing well, and it showed as we wound up losing the game 4–1. I figured that my time there was over, and I understood it, but it hurt. Ironically, Bunny got hurt in the warm-ups for the very next game, and I wound up going back in and stayed in for the rest of the finals. We wound up winning that game along with the next three straight to clinch our fourth straight Cup, four games to one. I had gotten the message, I suppose, and was able to pull it together for my teammates. Winning that last one was difficult, but very satisfying nevertheless."

Ken Dryden

Montreal 1971, 1973, 1976, 1977, 1978, and 1979

"It means you have completed the journey, the vision that you set out for at the beginning of the season. Twenty-nine other teams started out with that same vision, and here you are as the last man standing. What a feeling. To get there, though, what an unbelievable grind. Your team has to get through four grueling rounds over two months of nonstop battling. Then when you finally win it it's overwhelming. The sheer elation of winning—you are almost overcome by emotion. Later, when you have time to reflect on your accomplishment, you appreciate just how difficult, yet satisfying, it really is. You feel blessed and lucky at the same time because so few people have had the privilege to raise Stanley.

"You know, I grew up as the son of a hockey executive, so my experiences as a kid growing up and dreaming of raising the Cup were a little different than most other kids. My dad, Cliff, was the general manager of the Calgary Flames. I saw the disappointment in his eyes when his team lost in the finals in 1986, and then I saw his excitement and satisfaction when they finally won it in 1989. So I was able to experience some of those emotions and feelings at an early age, which was unique. It certainly created the desire for me to choose the same career path, which I have obviously now done. And it was a good thing too, because I realized pretty early on that I didn't have the talent necessary to make it as a player in this league! I remember my dad was able to bring the Cup home for a few days after they won it. It was just sitting on a coffee table in the living room like it was no big deal, which is kind of surreal to think about now. I have a lot of fond memories from that time, including having all my buddies over to eat ice cream out of it. I even remember my cat sleeping in it. How crazy is that? I remember my dad and I taking it to the hospital one day to visit a family friend who was dying of cancer, which was really tough. He was so happy to see it though. What a neat thing to see the joy on his face at that particular moment in his life. To be able to share it with people is what the spirit of the Cup is all about, I think. Just to be around it as a young person and to read all those names on it sitting there all alone at night by myself was pretty awe inspiring. Needless to say, it was pretty motivating in encouraging me to pursue my dream of winning it myself one day."

Chuck Fletcher
Pittsburgh 2009 (Assistant GM)

"Growing up in Sweden I didn't dream of winning the Stanley Cup, like so many of the players from Canada and the U.S. do, but as soon as I got here it quickly became my dream. I started my career in 1995 in Quebec with the Nordiques, and we moved to Colorado that next year and won it right away, which was pretty amazing. It was really neat to see how the people of Colorado reacted to us coming to town and just how they embraced us right away. We had a magical season that year, and it was certainly a moment I will never forget, when I got to raise the Stanley Cup. Then to do it again five years later, that was very special too. I was older and wiser at that point and maybe appreciated it a little bit more. It was tough, though, because I wound up getting emergency surgery to have my spleen removed after facing Los Angeles in the conference semifinals that year. I will never forget the look in Ray Bourque's eyes when he finally got to raise the Cup, though; that was pretty special. I was just very fortunate to have played alongside so many great teammates; those were both incredible teams. I have many wonderful memories from those days in Colorado, absolutely."

Peter Forsberg
Colorado 1996 and 2001

"The Stanley Cup is the holy grail. It's why we play this game. It's the ultimate accomplishment in hockey. For better or for worse, once you make it to the 'show' your career is ultimately judged by whether or not you were able to win it. There are plenty of great players out there, even Hall of Famers, that I am sure would give up a lot of the things that they achieved personally in order to have just one Stanley Cup ring. I was so fortunate to have won four of them alongside so many outstanding teammates. Then to think we would go on to win it three more times, no way. I still can't believe it. Each one of the Cups was special in its own unique way. Every one was a little bit different.

"The first one was special because it was the first one. It was an unbelievable feeling, just total joy and happiness. I went through a lot of battles that postseason and had a lot of blood on my jersey by the time it was all said and done. So when I finally got ahold of the Cup, when Dennis Potvin handed it to me, I took it and hoisted it above my head and then skated around the ice like a madman in total jubilation. I just took off with it; I don't think anybody could catch me! It was such a release of emotions. What a feeling. I was spent at that point. I felt as if I had paid the price and wasn't sure at that moment if I had anything more to give. There were some really tough battles along the way, especially with Boston in the second round. We did not like those guys and the feeling was mutual. I remember getting the overtime game winner in Game 1 of that series, and that was such a thrill. It put a big target on my back, though, which was no picnic. I had so many epic battles with their tough guy, Terry O'Reilly, that series. We fought a ton, it was brutal. Then to beat Philly in the finals, that was such a thrill. We won it in overtime in Game 6 on Bob Nystrom's game winner, and it was a moment I will never forget.

"The second didn't have as much drama as the first one did. We knew what to expect that time, and it wasn't a mystery to us. We beat Minnesota that time, and it felt very validating in that it proved that we were no fluke. By the time the third one rolled around we were so confident. We felt as though we were so much better than everybody else that year, and we knew that as long as we played up to our potential that we couldn't be denied. I remember nearly getting upset by Pittsburgh in the first round of the playoffs that year, though, what a wake-up call that was. We beat them 8–0 and 9–2 in the first two games and figured we were going to sweep them in three, but they won the next two and then had us on the ropes in Game 5 back on the Island. We were down 3–1 with five minutes to go in that one when we rallied to win behind John Tonelli's overtime game winner. From there we got hot, though, and we eventually swept Vancouver in the finals.

"The fourth and final Cup over Edmonton was unique in that we felt like we still had something to prove. People were predicting that Edmonton was going to upset us, and we didn't take too kindly to that and wound up sweeping them in four straight. It was pretty shocking to me, to be honest, because they were a damn good team. We could see the writing on the wall, though; these guys were the heir apparent. They had so much talent on that team it wasn't even funny. Sure enough, they got us in the finals that next year, 1984, and that was the end of our dynasty. They were hungry and determined to get revenge, so you had to tip your hat to them. The 'Drive for Five' sadly came to an end that year as the house of cards came tumbling down.

"I just love everything about the Stanley Cup. In fact, to this day I always make sure to watch the final game every season. I love seeing the Cup celebrated in the fashion that it deserves. I love seeing how the players react to winning the Cup, whether it is their first or their fifth, to see that raw emotion is amazing. To see grown men just lose it and go out of their minds, that is so awesome. Seeing how they break down and cry after going through several months of hell, with their bodies broken down and beaten—that's what hockey is all about. Nobody takes it for granted, that is for sure. It gives me goose bumps every time."

Clark Gillies

New York Islanders 1980, 1981, 1982, and 1983

"I was so fortunate to be a part of that team; what an amazing experience. Truly a dream come true. We went on such a magical run that postseason, and the way it ended against Detroit was incredible. What an unbelievable Game 7 that was. Max Talbot came through for us with two goals, and Marc-Andre Fleury came up huge in the net down the stretch. I will never forget him stopping Henrik Zetterberg's shot from the circle and then denying Nicklas Lidstrom's rebound attempt in the final couple of seconds—it was crazy. Just to be a part of that team was so exciting. I had spent most of the '08 season with the team's minor league affiliate in Wilkes Barre/Scranton but then got a call up late in the year. I then made the club in 2009 and was just really fortunate to have been able to play a small part in that team's success. To play alongside Sidney Crosby and Evgeni Malkin was really a thrill. It's pretty ridiculous how good they are. Just unbelievable. They are a lot of fun to watch and even more fun to play with. They see things that other players can't see, and that's what makes them so special. I had been playing sporadically that season and then got thrown into the lineup for the Eastern Conference Finals against the Capitals when Sergei Gonchar got hurt, which was definitely a little nerve wracking. I hung in there, though, and did all right. I wound up playing in 45 games that season, which was luckily just enough to get my name on the Cup. Hopefully it's the first of many, but to have it on there at this stage of my career is pretty humbling."

Alex Goligoski
Pittsburgh 2009

"You dream of raising the Cup from the moment you start playing this game, so to do it was really incredible. As a kid in Alaska I had certainly thought about it many, many times. I was a rookie in 2000 with New Jersey the year we won it, so it was pretty much a whirlwind for me as I look back. To win it that quickly in my career was neat and all of that, but I didn't really know what was going on. I thought, 'Gee, this is easy, I'm going to do this every season.' I was fortunate to win it again a few years later in 2003, but since then I have been chasing it. It's an elusive piece of hardware, no question about it. That's what makes it so special, though; it's so hard to win. Once you do, you just never want to give it up."

Scott Gomez
New Jersey 2000 and 2003

"As a kid growing up in Canada, this was it. This was what we all dreamed about as young boys. It was the light at the end of the tunnel, so to speak, in that all of that hard work finally paid off. To win it was just a wonderful feeling of accomplishment."

Butch Goring
New York Islanders 1980, 1981,
1982, and 1983

"To go 15 years between Cups is pretty surreal. I mean, the first one back in '95 was so exciting, just a dream come true. It was such an amazing accomplishment and something I had always hoped to achieve in my career. I was in my fourth year as a professional with the Devils, and it was neat to see that team's progression as we got better and better each year leading up to that. Then in 2009, to win it with Pittsburgh was such a thrill. I had gotten traded midway through the year from the Islanders and was really excited to be a part of that amazing Stanley Cup run. What made it so neat for me personally was that I now had my four kids to share it with. It was so emotional, just a wonderful moment I will never forget. I could really appreciate the journey this time around, the process of winning it."

Bill Guerin
New Jersey 1995 and Pittsburgh 2009

"Like everybody, I'm sure, it was a dream come true. To realize what you can achieve in hockey, it's pretty surreal. I was so fortunate to not only win it once, but twice, in back-to-back seasons—which is something I am so grateful for. It's just incredible, it really is. Winning it with the Ducks in 2007 was a pretty unique situation. I had gotten traded from Columbus to Anaheim late in the year and was just fortunate to be in the right place at the right time. I wound up getting into the very first game of the playoffs, that was it, but it was just enough to get my name on the Cup. I certainly wished I could have played in more games, but that's just the way it goes sometimes. I prepared myself as if I was going to play every night, but that obviously didn't happen. Just to be a part of that team was such an amazing honor though. It was really exciting.

"That off-season I wound up signing with Detroit, and as luck would have it, I was able to win it again that very next season. Winning it this time was a little more satisfying because I started the year with the Red Wings and was able to get to know a lot of the guys better. I felt like I was a little bigger piece of the puzzle this time around. I was up and down in Grand Rapids at the beginning of the season but then got called up for about the last 20 games in Detroit. It was pretty amazing. That was such a great team.

"In both instances I didn't get to dress for the last game, where we got to raise the Cup out on the ice, so I got dressed and waited in the chute until the final buzzer went off. From there I just ran out onto the ice and joined in the festivities. What an experience. In Detroit I will never forget standing there with Chris Chelios, who was also a scratch. We were both so nervous. I remember Marian Hossa scored a power play goal with about a minute and a half to go in the third period to cut the lead to 3–2, and from there it's just a blur. I just remember our goalie, Chris Osgood, denying Sidney Crosby and then Hossa again in the final seconds before time ran out. It was so nerve wracking. Then, afterward, being in that tiny locker room in Pittsburgh and celebrating with the guys. We were all passing Stanley around, drinking champagne and beer, just having a great time. We were all so spent, so it was like an amazing release. But to able to spend that special time with your teammates like that, celebrating so passionately, I will never forget it."

Mark Hartigan
Detroit 2008 and Anaheim 2007

"I grew up playing pickup hockey at Northwood Park in North St. Paul, and my buddies and I would always play for the Stanley Cup out there. So to have the honor of raising the real Cup in the real world, that was pretty surreal. Never in my wildest dreams did I ever think it would be possible. Winning it was just the culmination of so much hard work and sacrifice. I had previously been in two Stanley Cup Finals prior to winning it in 2006, so I had definitely paid my dues. You don't realize how hard it is to win it until after you have gone through it. Once you do, though, it just reaffirms what it means to be a true professional in this game. If you work hard enough and play the game the right way, with respect, then good things will eventually happen to you."

Bret Hedican
Carolina 2006

"I was a rookie when I won it back in 1993 so it didn't really hit home with me. I was so young and naïve back then, I figured I would be winning a whole bunch of them. Little did I know that that would be it for my 17-year career. Looking back, the whole thing is kind of surreal. I didn't really appreciate it, I don't think, but now I am so humbled to have my name on it. It just means a great deal. I firmly believe that it is the toughest trophy to win in sports, so it's pretty special to be in such an elite group of people."

Sean Hill
Montreal 1993

"To me it was a culmination of everything. Everything came together for me at that moment when I raised it, like 'Okay, so this is what it's all about.' The journey for every player is different. For me it started on a pond near my house in Minnesota when I was eight years old and my babysitter put skates on me and threw me out there. I was hooked and just fell in love with the game. From there I remember all the 5:00 AM practices, all the times I was told that I wasn't good enough, all the people who told me that I should focus more on getting a college education because I would never make it as a professional hockey player, then making it to the minors only to get cut in the minors—all of those events literally flashed before my eyes right then and there as I was holding up this big trophy. It was incredible. All of that hard work and sacrifice, all of that criticism, all of the garbage that I had to deal with—it all became worthwhile right then and there. And it wasn't just me I was thinking about, either. I thought a lot about my family and friends and coaches and teammates who had supported me along the way. I was holding up that Cup and in a sense honoring everybody who had had a hand in it. It was a culmination, and it was a vindication at the same time. It was wonderful."

Dan Hinote
Colorado 2001

"As a hockey player it is the single greatest thing you can do, to win the Cup, and I was fortunate to have won five of them over my career. When I was a kid, my father's favorite player was Rocket Richard, who starred for Montreal back in the '50s. So I grew up watching that team and dreaming of one day playing for them. I was the happiest guy in the world when I got to put on that beautiful sweater for the first time. To be French Canadian and to be able to play for Montreal, it is almost indescribable just what it means.

"The first time I had the privilege to win the Cup was in 1971. It was a tremendous honor. I was just thrilled to be on the same team as so many truly outstanding players: Jean Beliveau, Henri Richard, Yvan Cournoyer, Guy Lafleur, Larry Robinson, Serge Savard, Jacques Lemaire, Guy Lapointe, and Frank Mahovlich. Wow, what an honor to be on the ice with those guys, just amazing players. Winning five Stanley Cups was incredible, and each was unique in its own way. I was only 20 years old when I won the first one, so my perspective was much different when I won the fifth one 10 years later. I could see how I had grown as a player over that time, and it was very humbling. I appreciated each one differently; each had its own special story.

"There is just so much history with the Montreal organization and throughout Quebec, and I was very lucky to have been able to play in front of so many wonderful fans who truly appreciate and respect the game. We played for the crest, for the C.H., that was what it was all about."

Rejean Houle
Montreal 1971, 1973, 1977, 1978, and 1979

"What did it mean for me to win the Stanley Cup? Everything. It's a team trophy, though, and I don't think players should say 'I won the Stanley Cup.' Instead they should say 'We won the Stanley Cup.' There's a big difference in my mind. It's a respect thing. As far as raising the Cup? We never got to raise it in those days; they didn't want us to do that. The commissioner would present it to the team captain, and then he would just set it on a table out there on the ice for us to come up and touch it and have our pictures taken with it. It was nothing like it is today, when you see each player hoist it up out on the ice and skate around with it. We did get to drink champagne out of it afterward, which was pretty neat for me, being a 21-year-old back in 1950.

"We only had six teams in those days too, so you never really knew how well your team was going to do until you took one lap around the league. Once you played everybody at least once, then you could sort of gauge just how well you thought you were going to do against them. You could tell whether or not you liked your chances. It wasn't like we had all the scouting and the TV and all of that like we do nowadays; back then you had to play your competition to see how you good they were.

"We had some wonderful fans in Detroit, and I just appreciated so much all the support that they gave us. When we won, it wasn't for us, it was for them. I knew that those fans were paying top dollar to see their home team win, and I wanted to do everything that I could to make sure we gave them their money's worth. I will never forget the advice Sid Abel, our great captain, gave me when I was a young player. He told me that whenever you scored a goal, that you should bow your head to acknowledge and thank the fans. He reminded me that they were paying our salaries, and I never forgot that.

"You know, we had some great teams back in those days, and I was very proud to have been a part of such a great organization. I worked extremely hard and gave it everything I had every time I went out on the ice. I always figured that if you went out and gave a hundred percent then you could feel good about yourself at the end of the day, win or lose. I was proud of the fact that I always stood up for myself as well as for my teammates too, that was important. I never wanted anyone taking liberties with me or my teammates, and I was willing to stand up for them, no matter what, even if that meant dropping the gloves every now and then. The way I saw it, you were never going to win any Stanley Cups if other teams knew that they could push you around. Heck, I had eight siblings growing up as a kid in Saskatoon, so it seemed like I was always fighting!"

Gordie Howe
Detroit 1950, 1952, 1954, and 1955

"Growing up I scored many Game 7 overtime winners to win the Cup out on the driveway with my buddies. It's every kid's dream to hoist it, so when I finally got to do it for real it was almost indescribable. What a thrill and honor, far and away the biggest highlight of my career."

Tony Hrkac
Dallas 1999

"I came from a small town in southeastern Ontario, and we didn't have a TV or hardly a radio that worked, so I never grew up dreaming of winning the Stanley Cup. It was a different time, back in the 1940s. I didn't even really know anything about it until I was in junior hockey. When I got to the Blackhawks in 1957 I was just an 18-year-old wet-behind-the-ears kid; I wasn't dreaming of raising the Cup—I was dreaming of making the team and earning a paycheck. I was just trying to find my way, to be honest. Well, we had a pretty good team in those days, and we finally got it together and won it in 1961 after beating a very good Red Wings team four games to two. What a

Bobby Hull (left) and Jack Evans of the Chicago Blackhawks celebrate the Golden Jet's only Stanley Cup, won by topping Detroit in the 1960–61 championship series.

thrill. I wound up scoring the game winner in the first game, and then Stan Mikita got the game winner in Game 5. It was special, but at 21 years old, what the hell did I know? I didn't realize that it was going to be the toughest trophy ever to win in professional sports. Looking back, I feel so bad that I was too young to realize just how important it was going to be, winning the Cup, because I thought that was just going to be one of many over my career. Sadly

though, that was it. We came close after that, but thanks to
the Montreal Canadiens we were always the bridesmaids,
never the bride. You just never know in this game. I wish I
could tell you what it meant to raise Stanley, but I can't.
Back in my day when you won the championship, they
would wheel the Cup out onto the ice and place it on a
wooden table. We would then gather around it and listen to
the league president say a few words, at which point he
would present it to the team captain. He would then pick it
up, smile for the cameras, and very gingerly set it back
down on the table. A few of us then had our pictures taken
as we stood behind the cup, but that was it. We were never
allowed to hoist it above our heads and skate around the
ice like they do today, no way. Times have certainly
changed. In fact, the first time I even got to drink out of it
was at Chris Chelios' golf tournament back in 2002. My
son, Brett, and some of the guys knew that I had never been
able to enjoy a cold one out of it so they filled it up with
beer and held it for me as I got to take a big swig. My
shoulders were so bad that they had to hold it up for me,
but it was wonderful. Beer never tasted so good."

Bobby Hull
Chicago 1961

"I had never grown up dreaming of winning the Cup like
so many other players do. I just wanted to get a college
scholarship, and once Notre Dame said that they would
take me I thought I had hit the lottery. Once I made it to the
NHL, however, then raising Stanley quickly became my
No. 1 goal and priority. Winning that first one in 1984
was a pretty special time. When I got my turn to lift the
Cup I lifted it up as high as I possibly could. It was a big

moment in my life. We had just dethroned the New York Islanders, who had won four straight Stanley Cups and were on the 'Drive for Five.' They had beaten us the year before in the finals, and we used that as motivation all year long. So beating them in that highly anticipated rematch was pretty sweet. It was significant too in that it was the beginning of an Oilers dynasty that would dominate pro hockey for the better part of the next seven years. As for me, just to play alongside so many outstanding players was such a thrill, especially Wayne Gretzky, the greatest of all time. Whenever anybody would ask me about what it was like to play with him I would always answer this way: that he was a better person than he was a player. And I think that says a lot. I was fortunate to win another one that next season too, which officially made us a dynasty in my book. We had some great teams in those days, and I feel very honored to be associated with them."

Don Jackson
Edmonton 1984 and 1985

"Growing up in Russia I never really knew about the Stanley Cup. Once I started playing hockey, however, and got older, then I began to hear about it and about what it meant. As soon as I was fortunate enough to make it in the NHL, then my No. 1 goal became to win the Cup. That was it. It's the toughest trophy to win in sports, so when you win it you feel like you are on top of the world. You know that when you have won the Stanley Cup that you have accomplished something really incredible in your life. To win it in Tampa was special too because hockey obviously isn't huge down there, yet we were able to make a lot of new fans during our journey. They really came out to support us, and they really got behind us that season. I appreciated that so much; they made a big difference for us at home for sure. They were loud and they were fantastic."

Nikolai Khabibulin
Tampa Bay 2004

"I have been fortunate to have had the privilege of raising the Cup twice now, and obviously it was an unbelievable moment each time. Winning it for the first time in Anaheim was such a thrill. My parents got to come down on the ice and share the moment with me too, which was something I will never forget. It made me appreciate all the times as a kid that they had to get up and take me to the rink for practice before school. It was like that very moment paid off all of that somehow, like it validated it. Like it was worth it. I had dreamed about it for my whole life, I really did. Whether it was with the boys out on the pond or even in the street, that last goal was always for the Stanley Cup. Even shooting pucks in the backyard or playing mini-sticks in the basement, it was *always* for the Cup. Always. I had grown up watching those great Oilers teams hoist it so many times, and that was what I wanted to do. My dad played hockey, as did my two older brothers, so for me hockey was pretty much my whole life during the winters. When we weren't playing it we were watching it. Whether it was Don Cherry's *Rock-'em-Sock-'em* fight videos or the Stanley Cup Finals, we were just consumed with the game. We loved it. It bonded us together."

Chris Kunitz
Anaheim 2007 and
Pittsburgh 2009

"Winning the Stanley Cup is built into the DNA of all young hockey players, and I was fortunate to have won it as a member of *the* model organization in the NHL, the Montreal Canadiens. To be able to play alongside and learn the game from so many Hall of Fame guys like Jacques Lemaire, Serge Savard, Larry Robinson, Bob Gainey, and Guy Lafleur was just amazing. Just to be connected to and associated with that franchise means so much, and I will proudly carry that with me forever. I was a young player, just 23 at the time we won it in 1986, so I didn't realize all of that back then, but looking back I sometimes have to pinch myself to think about what I was actually a part of. We beat Calgary in the finals that year, and it was a big deal because they had just knocked off Edmonton, which had won two straight Cups and was on the verge of winning five in seven years with Gretzky and company. Patrick Roy was a rookie goalie for us, and we just went on an incredible run to win it. As for me personally, sadly, I never got to suit up for our playoff run because I got injured late in the season. We won it on the road in Calgary that year too, which meant I didn't get to hoist the Cup out on the ice with my team-mates. That was tough too, to not get to be a part of that. A few of us were left behind for that trip, and unfortunately I was one of them. I played 62 games that year which meant I still got my name on the Cup, but I will always regret not being out there on the ice. It's painful, it really is. That's hockey sometimes, though, you can't control injuries, and it affects everybody at some point of their career if they play long enough. I did get to party with the Cup afterward back in Montreal and have a few beverages out of it, which was great. We had an amazing parade, and the organization even sent the entire team to the Bahamas afterward to celebrate with the Cup as well. Typical Montreal class to do that too; I mean, how many other teams do stuff like that? Not many. They are the Yankees of hockey, there is just an aura about them. The way they do things and the way they treat their alumni, it's second to none. They just have a different level of reverence for the game, there are no two ways about it. Looking back, I am just grateful to have been able to have been a part of winning the Cup as a member of such a storied franchise."

Tom Kurvers
Montreal 1986

"I have been fortunate to win the Cup twice in my career, and it means a great deal to me. It's the only time in your career when you end the season feeling completely satisfied in that you have accomplished the goal that you had originally set out to do. It's indescribable, really. I grew up in International Falls, right on the Minnesota-Canada border, and used to watch *Hockey Night in Canada*. So I was a huge NHL fan early on, especially the North Stars. That was my team. My family later moved to Cloquet when I was about 11, a small town a few hours south, but I was always just a huge fan of the game, whether it was high school or college or whatever. So to win the Cup was just a dream come true, it really was."

Jamie Langenbrunner
Dallas 1999 and New Jersey 2003

"Winning the Stanley Cup makes everything that you have gone through in this sport worth it. All the injuries, the training, the time away from home, the sacrifices we've made through the years—winning the Cup makes it all worthwhile. I will never forget the first one, it was just brutal. In those days you played games back to back, and it got to be so exhausting both physically as well as mentally. I was drained. Every team was big and physical, and you just got worn out. It was such a grind, I think I lost 10 pounds during the playoffs due to fatigue. I will never forget that epic Game 6 against Philadelphia, where we won it in overtime 5–4 on Bob Nystrom's game winner to clinch it. What a relief. I honestly don't know what I was more happy about, winning the Cup or just knowing that I wasn't going to have to play anymore. I was totally spent.

"From there it was just total pandemonium on the ice, everything from that point on is just a blur. You know on TV how they show something dramatic happening, and they go to slow motion, and it gets all quiet and then turns noisy when they go to real time? Well, that was exactly what happened to me when I was out on the ice when we won it. To this day I have no memory of skating from the blue to behind the net; all I remember was sort of awakening from a dream with Stefan Persson on my back and then the deafening sounds of all of us out there celebrating. It was unbelievable. The bench emptied, fans were going nuts trying to get out onto the ice, just complete chaos. What an amazing memory.

"The second one is special because you want to make sure the first one wasn't a fluke. It validated it. Plus, nobody wants to be a one-time winner, you want to keep the streak going. It was extra special to me too in that we beat Minnesota, the team I grew up rooting for. So to be able to play there in front of my hometown friends and family, that was special. The third one, against Vancouver, was because we were the best team in the league that year, 1982, and we deserved to win it. We dominated from start to finish and really made a statement. We were so confident and so firm in our convictions. We just weren't going to be stopped that season. Then the fourth one, in 1983, was to confirm that we were a dynasty. Edmonton was the up-and-coming team that year, and you could see that with a young Wayne Gretzky and company they were poised to dethrone us. Well, not that year, but they did get us the next year in the '85 finals before going on to win a whole bunch of them in the late '80s. They were an unbelievable team, but I still think we should have beaten them that year. It still really bothers me, to tell you the truth."

Dave Langevin
New York Islanders 1980, 1981, 1982, and 1983

"I grew up in Montreal dreaming of hoisting the Cup. Guy Lafleur was my hero, and I used to love watching him on *Hockey Night in Canada*; that was my all-time favorite thing to do. When my parents used to make me go to bed before the games were over it was as if I were being severely punished, it was the worst. The first thing I would do when I woke up would be to run into my parents' room to wake them up so I could find out if my Canadiens had won or not. So winning the Stanley Cup means a great deal to me, and I just feel very fortunate to have won a pair of them with the Detroit Red Wings. What a fantastic organization. I remember losing to the Devils in the finals back in '95, and that was tough. It was a real learning experience for us, though, and I think it brought us closer as a team. I truly believe that in order to be able to win a Stanley Cup you have to lose first and then learn from your mistakes. We looked long and hard at that loss, and it prepared us well for our Stanley Cup wins in both 1997 and 1998. We were really mentally focused those years too, not too many highs and not too many lows. We were steady. It was an even-keeled mind-set, that was what kept us strong those two seasons. We were so mentally strong, it was all business for us. We swept both teams in the finals in those years, and I think that says a lot about just how determined we were to win the championship."

Martin Lapointe
Detroit 1997 and 1998

"I grew up in Russia, where winning Olympic gold medals and World Championships were always the goal. After winning a Stanley Cup, however, nothing compares. The Stanley Cup is the most coveted trophy in professional sports, no question. To go through an 82-game schedule and then have to win another 20-plus games in the play-offs is such a grind. To win it means everything, it is a very special moment. Everyone who plays this game, without a doubt, plays to win the Stanley Cup. So to have been able to win it and raise it was extremely gratifying."

Igor Larionov
Detroit 1997, 1998, and 2002

"To have grown up in Montreal and then to play for the Canadiens was a dream come true for me. Winning the Stanley Cup for Montreal was so special because everybody was a part of it; it was such a source of pride for the people there. The expectations in those days were to win, and any-thing but the Stanley Cup wasn't really acceptable. We lived and played by extremely high standards. We had some great teams in those days too, and I cherish those memories. I was fortunate to have played alongside so many great players, many of them who were heroes of my own when I was a kid growing up. Guys like Henri Richard, Jean

Beliveau, Yvan Cournoyer, and Claude Provost showed me the way, and then I did the same for the next guys. That was how it went, and that was why we had so much success."

Jacques Lemaire
Montreal 1968, 1969, 1971, 1973, 1976, 1977, 1978, and 1979

"Winning it the first time was unbelievable. We won it that year up in Minneapolis, after we beat the North Stars, and it was just a dream come true. To finally get to grab it and touch it, out on the ice, was something I can't even really describe. I think I was maybe the eighth guy to get a turn to raise it, and I will never forget waiting for what seemed like an eternity to finally get my turn. For me, it was probably more enjoyable the second time we won it because I could enjoy it a little bit more. I was able to sit back that time and enjoy watching everybody else as they experienced it too, which was pretty neat. We won that second one on the road too, which was great and all—but it would have been so amazing to have been able to have won it in front of our home fans."

Troy Loney
Pittsburgh 1992 and 1993

"It's hard to put into words just what it means. I remember back in 1993 when Jacques Lemaire took over as our new head coach with the Devils. We were all excited because we figured since he had won so many Cups as a player with Montreal back in the '70s that it was going to rub off on us somehow. We were asking him a bunch of questions about what it was like to win the Cup, and he was struggling to find the words to explain it. Finally, after thinking about it for a while, he said, 'I wish everybody could experience it just once.' He then talked about what it felt like to be on top of the world, celebrating alongside your teammates. We all just sat there listening to the guy, sort of in awe. So when I finally won it a couple of years later, I understood how hard it was to explain. You just have to feel it and experience it to appreciate just what it means. So much sacrifice goes into it, not only by you but by your family, that when you finally do win it it's almost indescribable. It's just a wonderful feeling."

John MacLean
New Jersey 1995 and 2003 (Assistant Coach)

"The first one is always the most meaningful, and for us to beat the Islanders in '84 was a huge deal. They were the four-time defending Stanley Cup champions, and we had officially dethroned them; it was pretty intense. I wound up getting the lone goal in the 1–0 opener of the finals too, which will always rank up there as one of the big highlights of my career. It really set the tone early on, as we wound up winning four games to one. We had so many great players on that team, from Gretzky to Messier to Coffey, just a who's who of the hockey world at the time. What a thrill just to be associated with those guys. I mean, Gretz scored 205 points that year, just unbelievable.

"You know, so much goes through your head as you are standing there, waiting for your turn to hoist it. I remember thinking about all the pond hockey games as a kid and about all the hard work it had taken to get to that very moment in my life. I thought about my childhood hero, Bobby Clarke, and that iconic picture of him without his two front teeth hoisting the Cup with the Flyers. Well, just the thought of my name going on that same Cup somewhere alongside of his was pretty fantastic. The thing that meant the most to me was the fact that my parents were in the crowd that night. I acknowledged them too when I lifted it, to say thanks for all their support and sacrifice over the years, which ultimately allowed me to live out my childhood dream. What a great feeling to be able to share that moment with them. Overall, to be able to look back and realize that I was a part of four Stanley Cup teams, that is just amazing to me. What an honor and privilege to be a part of such a classy organization, just first class."

Kevin McClelland
Edmonton 1984, 1985,
1987, and 1988

"Growing up in Canada it's something you dream about. You play peewee, you play bantam, you play junior, and eventually you hope to make it to the National Hockey League. Then, for those fortunate few, the goal becomes all about winning the Cup. So for me to do it was really the realization that I had achieved my dream."

Brian MacLellan
Calgary 1989

"I was lucky enough to win six Cups in my career, which is something I am very proud of. Ever since I was a four-year-old kid growing up in Timmins, Ontario, I dreamed of raising the Stanley Cup. So to finally win it meant the world to me. It was 1962, and I was a member of the Toronto Maple Leafs. We beat the defending champion

Chicago Blackhawks that year, and it was a moment I will never forget. I remember raising that Cup over my head down in the locker room after the game. Many people have since told me that I was the first to do so, or at least to be photographed doing so. Who knows? Back then the players usually just stood next to it, but I wanted to touch it. I remember thinking that it wasn't very heavy, so I hoisted it over my head to get a feel for it. What a feeling that was. So much hard work and sacrifice had gone into it, and when it finally happened it was just a huge relief. We went on and won three straight Cups from there, and those were some incredible times. Hockey was a lot different back in the '60s, and you really had to work for everything you got. Nobody gave you anything, you had to earn it. One of my favorite memories came in 1971, when I won it with Montreal for the first time. I got the game-tying goal in Game 6 against Chicago in the finals and then set up my kid brother, Peter, for the game winner, which was a very special moment. We have 10 Cups between us, only the Richards [Henry and Rocket] have more, with 19, and I'm very proud of that."

Frank Mahovlich
Toronto 1962, 1963, 1964, and 1967;
Montreal 1971 and 1973

"I had played for Pittsburgh for seven seasons back in the late '70s and early '80s, so to finally be able to raise the Cup was very meaningful for me. I have been a part of the organization for a long time, and this was certainly something I felt very proud to be a part of. It really hits you when you are able to spend some time alone with it, after all of the partying, where you just sit quietly and study all of the names on it. To see all of that amazing history and then to think that you are now a part of that, it's almost overwhelming. Then to see your own name on it alongside so many great players, that's pretty special."

Greg Malone
Pittsburgh 1992 and 1993 (Scout)

"Winning the Cup was the ultimate satisfaction in the sense that I had been training and working and dreaming about being in that situation my whole life. I had even started to question whether or not it was ever going to happen, so it was really gratifying in that regard. You spend years and years and years just trying to get to that position, and when it finally happens it's very difficult to even put into words. Your emotions just take over. I remember being in the locker room right after the game, and my dad was there with me. I said, 'Dad, we did it.' He said, 'No, you did it.' And I said it again, 'No, Dad, *we* did it.' It wasn't just me the player who did this, it was way bigger than that. I thought about my family: my mom, my dad, my brothers, my wife, my kids—and all the sacrifices that they have had to make for me over my career so I could do this. I thought about all my teammates who had helped me along the way. It was a pretty profound moment in my life, it really was. Winning the Cup also meant that no matter what, from there on out I was always going to be labeled as a champion. Nobody could ever say 'Todd Marchant had a great career, but he never won a championship.' Too many athletes get that label, and to be honest I was really glad that I never would. I worked hard to become a champion, and I was extremely proud of it."

Todd Marchant
Anaheim 2007

"For me it was unbelievable to be a part of that team. It was my first year in the league and my first year as a pro. I had just finished my senior year at the University of Minnesota and had played much of the season in Albany, the team's top minor league affiliate. That was the lockout season, so we only played 48 games that year. I got called up as soon as it ended and joined the team. We started out slow but got hot in the playoffs and then just took off from there, ultimately sweeping Detroit in the finals. I dressed for all the postseason games but unfortunately never got into any of them. It was tough not to be out there helping my teammates, but I understood my role as a lowly rookie. To play with so many great players, though, it was really a thrill.

"We had some great players on that team, guys like Scott Stevens, Scott Niedermayer, John MacLean, Stephane Richer, Martin Brodeur, Ken Daneyko, Bruce Driver, and Bill Guerin. In addition, we also brought in some guys midway through the season, including Neal Broten. I will never forget the first time I was out on the ice with Neal. I was standing there next to him thinking, 'Wow, I wonder if this guy knows that I have a poster of him on my bedroom wall at my parents' house as this very moment.' I was just dumbfounded being out there with him; he was my child-hood hero growing up in Minnesota. Well, Neal played a big role on that team, and it was great to see him finally win a Cup too, because he was at the end of his career and really deserved it. Beyond all of those superstars, we also had probably the best fourth line in the game that year: the 'Crash Line,' with Mikey Peluso, Bobby Holik, and Randy McKay. Those guys were just phenomenal. The way they played with such reckless abandon, every single game, was inspiring. They were really, really effective. We had a lot of selfless players on that team and were just really balanced from top to bottom. From there, everybody bought into Jacques' [Lemaire] system. The stars aligned for us that year, it was amazing.

"I will never forget when Scotty Stevens handed me the Cup, it was just unbelievable. I get chills just thinking about it. He was our captain and had it first, and he had passed it around to all the veteran players. Then, toward the end, he saw that I hadn't had my turn yet so he grabbed it and handed it to me. I was standing there with Brian Rolston, who was also a rookie at the time, and we both just freaked out. What a moment, I will never forget it. Well, that was it for me. I went on and played for 11 seasons, and that was my only Cup. As a rookie I just figured, 'Hey, this is great, this is easy, this is going to happen every year!' Then reality sets in and you realize, especially when you are on some struggling teams, just how difficult it is to get through that 82-game grind and then win four playoff series. I mean, that very next year, 1996, the Devils didn't even make the playoffs. So you just never know. One thing is for sure, though, it's gotta be the toughest trophy to win in sports, no question."

Chris McAlpine
New Jersey 1995

"To win the Stanley Cup is the ultimate achievement in hockey and maybe in all of sports. It's something that every Canadian kid grows up dreaming about. I was very fortunate to have been on four winning teams. Winning that first one, though, it was very exciting and very fulfilling. It happened in Montreal in 1958 when we beat the Boston Bruins, four games to two. I was a rookie and had just gotten called up from our American League team in Rochester for the playoffs. I didn't get a whole lot of ice time, but it sure was a thrill to play alongside guys like Henri and Rocket Richard, Jean Beliveau, Claude Provost, Dickie Moore, and Boom-Boom Geoffrion. I was a big part of the next two, however, in 1959 and 1960, when we beat Toronto back to back. We had some great teams in those days, just outstanding. We were a very disciplined team. You had to go both ways if you played for the Canadiens, otherwise you were out of there. Our coach, Toe Blake, wouldn't tolerate guys loafing out there. No way. If you bought into that philosophy, then you were all right. If not, then you were shown the door. It was a total team effort in Montreal, and that's why that organization has won so many Stanley Cups over the years. They're just top notch in everything they do. I remember my last year there, in 1960, they gave each player a mini replica Stanley Cup that we could take home. It was the first time any team had ever done it, and it was such a popular idea that the next year Chicago did it as well. Luckily I was there to get that one too, which means I have the first two in history—which is kind of a special deal. Playing with Chicago was a neat experience too. To play there with guys like Stan Mikita, Bobby Hull, and Glenn Hall was a real treat. One of the highlights of my career came that first season with the Hawks when I got the game-winning goal to clinch the Cup against Detroit in Game 6. I will never forget it. I just feel very blessed to have been a part of four great championship teams, those are some great memories. It's hard to believe that it's been more than half a century since I first raised the Cup, a lifetime ago, yet it seems like only yesterday."

Ab McDonald

Montreal 1958, 1959, and 1960;
Chicago 1961

Phil Housley on his record for the most NHL games played without winning a Cup

"Not having won the Stanley Cup will never define me as a player or as a person. I don't know if my life would be any different today had I won one, but I do know that it would have been very fulfilling to have won one. It's a big disappointment for sure, because that's why you play this game. It's the ultimate accomplishment in hockey. I played for 21 seasons and nearly 1,500 games, but it just wasn't in the cards for me. It's a team sport, and you have to get lucky along the way, I suppose. When I look back at my career and think about all of my teammates and all of the games, sure, it would have been a great feather in my cap. But I still go about my life the way I always have, so in that respect it hasn't changed me as a person whatsoever. I think my numbers speak for themselves, and overall I think I had a very good career. I am very proud of it. I was a part of a lot of great teams and have so many wonderful memories, so not winning the Stanley Cup is in no way, shape, or form the end of the world for me. No way. It would have been nice, absolutely, but it's not going to be a footnote on an otherwise solid career. Look in the Hall of Fame, there are a lot of players who had outstanding careers who never won one. It's the toughest trophy to win in sports, and it takes the efforts of an entire team—not just one individual. Timing, luck, the team you play on, a bounce here or there—those all factor in at the end of the day.

"I came close in 1998 when I was with Washington. We lost to Detroit in the finals that year and that was tough. They had won it the year before, and they had an awesome team. We had our chances, though. I remember in Game 2 we had a 4–2 lead in the third period, and it looked like we were going to steal one in Detroit. We could have iced it too, but Esa Tikkanen missed an open netter late in the game, and they rallied back to tie it and send it into overtime. Kris Draper then scored with about four minutes left in OT to give the Red Wings a 5–4 victory and a 2–0 lead in the series. We lost Game 3 by one goal back in Washington, and then they beat us pretty good in Game 4 to complete the sweep.

Who knows, though? Had we won Game 2, maybe the momentum would have shifted for us heading back to Washington tied at 1–1 versus down 2–0? Coulda-woulda-shoulda…you just never know.

"I watch the Stanley Cup Finals nowadays, and I think about what these kids must be thinking. They have no idea just how close they are to winning it. They are playing in the moment, and that is where their focus is. One team will be remembered forever and the other will not, it's sad but true. That's sports nowadays. The younger players all figure that they will get back there too, but the reality is that they probably won't. It's so elusive, it really is. You only get so many kicks at the can in this business, and you have to take advantage of your opportunities when they present themselves. Otherwise it may never happen again. I was fortunate to have a chance, but it didn't work out for me for whatever the reason. No regrets, though, just great memories.

"As for touching the Cup, I still won't come near it. I haven't earned that right. I've been close to it, but I won't get too close. It's that respect factor, and you never want to jinx yourself. Hey, who knows? I am coaching a high school team in Minnesota right now, in Stillwater, and my main goal is to win a state championship. I find it very fulfilling to teach kids the right way to play this game, and I am having fun spending time with my family. Down the road, though, I would love to be in a position to get my name on Stanley as a head coach someday. That burning desire to compete at a high level is still there for me. I look at Randy Carlyle, who was my defensive partner when I was playing with Winnipeg. He too played a long career and never got his name on the Cup. Then he got into coaching and wound up winning one with Anaheim in 2007. It must have been so sweet, what a wonderful moment that was. I called him up right away to congratulate him. I remember when Dave Andreychuk finally won one down in Tampa Bay in 2004 too. He had been the all-time leader in games played without a Cup until then, but I guess that dubious distinction now belongs to me. Oh well, that's life. As long as the coaching avenue is still an option for me, then my dream is still alive. Hey, I still have a chance to raise Stanley!"

"I will never forget those last 30 seconds of Game 7 of the '87 Stanley Cup Finals against Philadelphia. I just started thinking about the long journey that had gotten me to that point in my career. You see, I grew up on a farm in a small town in Canada in a household that lived for hockey. We watched it on TV, and my brothers and I played it every chance we could. And when we did, whether it was on the pond or in the chicken barn with a tennis ball, it was always for the Stanley Cup. The winner got to hoist it and then rub it in. That was the deal. Now here I was all these years later about to hoist it again, only this time it was for real. Wow. After the game got over and I got to actually touch it and hoist it, it was almost as if it wasn't really happening. It was like a dream that I had played out in my head a thousand times before. I just wondered to myself, could this really be happening? My dad even got to come out onto the ice with me after the game, which made the moment even more special. I later gave him my Stanley Cup ring, and he wore it until the day he died. I remember my first year in Edmonton, 1986, we lost to Montreal in the finals. So to stay focused and to come back and win it the very next year was very gratifying.

"Another odd thing about winning it was that because it had been such a lifelong goal of mine to win it, I now needed a new goal. Luckily for me I figured out pretty quickly that winning it again would be a great goal—and thankfully that was exactly what we did the very next season when we beat Boston in the finals in 1988. Even though we had won back-to-back Cups, we never took it for granted. I will always remember Gretz [Wayne Gretzky] talking about how there was no guarantee that we would ever be back to the finals. And then Mess [Mark

Mark Messier (left) and Wayne Gretzky lift Stanley together after the Edmonton Oilers defeated the Boston Bruins 6–3 to win the Cup in May 1988.

Messier] would talk about how hard it was to win it and about how so many things had to go right. In his opinion it was almost a miracle to win it. He talked about how easy it was for things to go wrong and how hard it was for things to go right. I never forgot that.

"We all had roles on those teams too. As a heavyweight my role was to be aggressive and to come down hard on any opposing players who wanted to take liberties with our top guys. They would look over their shoulders to see when my line would come out. I didn't come out to beat people up per se, but that threat of repercussion was always there. If they were instigating then I would react accordingly. That was my job. It was what I called the 'policeman mentality' of keeping the peace. Gretz and Mess used to say, 'Let's not change the tempo,' meaning they didn't want the game to get out of hand with a bunch of scraps all over, slowing things down. We were a speed and finesse team, and we wanted to use that to our advantage. So when I went out there I would run into guys and wear them down in the corners. I tried to be especially hard on the guys who were trying to slow down Gretz and Mess so that they would be deterred from going near them. It was psychological warfare, it really was. We wanted our star players to score goals, that was their job. My job was to make sure that they could do their job, no matter what. Don't get me wrong, I loved a good fight every now and then, absolutely. To win that fight and swing the momentum in our favor? What a great feeling, sometimes even better than scoring a goal. The appreciation that you are shown from your teammates is like a drug. I always felt like the ultimate compliment you could get as a fighter in this league was when you got to play in the playoffs. Most heavyweights are a healthy scratch come the postseason because they are typically one-dimensional players. Well, our coach Glen Sather believed in me and valued my role on the team, so I got to suit up and take a regular shift. That meant a great deal to me."

Marty McSorley
Edmonton 1987 and 1988

"More than anything it was a huge sense of relief that you had finally done it. I had come close early in my career with the North Stars when we lost to Pittsburgh in 1991, so to get back and win it was very satisfying. I grew up like most guys, fantasizing about what it would feel like to win it. I simulated scoring a few Game 7 over-time winners out on the pond as a kid, for sure. I know it's cliché, but yes, it was a childhood dream. So to do it means everything. To reach that echelon that so many players try but never get to is really gratifying. Even though I was 29 when it happened, I think it pretty much completed my career. I mean, I always felt after winning it that if I ever had suffered a career-ending injury or something, that my career would still be complete. It is very meaningful, though, and it makes you appreciate how lucky you are to have done it. I know a lot of players who have never gotten the opportunity to do so, and it makes you count your blessings for sure. Winning one was such an accomplishment, I can't even fathom how some of those dynasty teams were able to win four or five in a row. After you have been through it once, it just doesn't even seem possible."

Mike Modano
Dallas 1999

"When you win the Cup you are flooded with a variety of emotions. The first thing I thought of were all of the people who helped me along the way, because you certainly don't get there by yourself. You are out on the ice holding up the Cup, but you are thinking of all these other people: coaches, parents, friends, and teammates—the ones who made it possible. Beyond that, winning it was just a huge relief. The playoffs are really a survival of the fittest. I would certainly say that winning the Stanley Cup is the hardest championship to win in any sport. Just to get there is such a grind. Not only are you relieved when you finally win it, you are also relieved that you don't have any more games to play. By the end you are so completely spent. Afterward the guys just crash, physically as well as emotionally. It just feels a whole heck of a lot better to have won it than to have lost it, though, trust me. After winning four straight from 1980, 1981, 1982, and 1983 and then losing to Edmonton in the finals in 1984, that was really tough. It definitely makes you appreciate all the hard work it takes to win it, that is for sure."

Ken Morrow
New York Islanders 1980, 1981,
1982, and 1983

"In 2007 I was playing with Columbus and got traded to Anaheim late in the season. I wound up finishing the year with their minor league team in Portland and then got called up to play with the Ducks for the playoffs. I was what they call a 'black ace,' or an extra player who was on hand in case somebody got hurt. So I wasn't planning on playing. We beat Minnesota in the first round and then got past Vancouver in the second round, which set us up to play Detroit in the conference finals. Chris Kunitz got

hurt during Game 3 of that series, so I wound up getting
into two of the games. We beat Detroit and then wound
up facing Ottawa in the finals, where I was sort of 'on
call' as to whether or not I was going to get any playing
time. I would warm up with the team before the game and
prepare myself mentally to play, but I usually just sat on
the bench—which was tough. I knew that in order to get
your name on the Cup, you had to get into a game during
the finals. Then, as luck would have it, I wound up getting
into Game 4 up in Ottawa. It wasn't much, just a few minutes, but it was enough to make history, I suppose. We
wound up winning it the next game, so I got it in just
under the wire. I took warm-ups for Game 5 back in
Anaheim but watched the game in our weight room with
the other guys who were scratched from the lineup. We
were up a few goals with a few minutes to go in the game,
and one of the PR guys told us to put our gear on. From
there we all waited down in the gate for the final buzzer
to go off. Once we heard it we bolted over the boards
and joined in the festivities. It was pretty amazing.
Looking back, it is crazy to think about all of the players
who have played for 15–20 seasons and never got their
name on it, and here I was getting my name engraved
with just a few shifts. Hey, it's every hockey player's dream
to win the Cup, and I was just happy that I was in the
right place at the right time. You know, I wound up
moving on to play with Washington that next season, so
that moment on the ice with everyone was my last with the
team. Just to be around guys like Scott Niedermayer and
Chris Pronger, what an amazing experience. I learned so
much from those guys, about what it takes day in and day
out to be successful at this level. Those guys really prepare
themselves, and that's why they are winners. The entire

organization had bought into that same work ethic, from top to bottom, and I think that was why we were able to win it all that year."

Joe Motzko
Anaheim 2007

"No question about it, it was a lifetime dream that finally came true. It took me nine years as a professional to finally win it, but when it happened it was just incredible. To raise the Cup means you are a champion. It means for that season that you are the best of the best. It's for sure the toughest trophy to win in sports, no question. To play 100-plus physical games, where you could get injured in any given day—it's a grind. The sacrifice and the commitment is extraordinary. As a kid growing up in Canada there was nothing that I wanted to do more than to one day raise it. That was it for me. I will never forget getting to grab on to it for the first time back in 1993; it was as if my whole childhood flashed before me. It was like an out-of-body experience, like I was living this fantasy. I thought I was going to pass out. Then, to raise it up, it was just like *wow*! I was so fortunate to have scored the game winner to clinch it too, in Game 5 against the Kings, just like I had envisioned myself doing so many times before as a little kid out in the driveway. To win it with Montreal, in Montreal, that means so much. Their fans are so passionate about the game. It's the most storied franchise in hockey, so that was a pretty big deal too. What makes the Cup so special in my mind is that it brings you that much closer to your childhood idols. Growing up I was in awe of Bobby Clarke. He was my guy. So to now have my name engraved on the same Cup as him? Are you kidding me? Amazing. Just amazing. Afterward I was completely physically and mentally drained, just spent. I remember going into the locker room and getting drenched in champagne. It was wonderful. To drink out of Stanley was so sweet. I even went up with Mike Keane and had a cigar up in the seats at the Forum. We just sat back and reflected upon what we had just done. That was a moment I will never forget, just me and Keaner smokin' a stogie, smiling together all alone in those hallowed grounds. Pretty cool stuff."

Kirk Muller
Montreal 1993

"I never had any vivid dreams of raising the Cup as a kid, but it was certainly a goal of mine to make it into the National Hockey League. So just to make it was more the dream come true for me. Once you make it, though, then your focus immediately shifts toward doing whatever you can to help your team win the Cup. You work so hard and put your body through so much that when you finally do win it, there is just no better feeling in hockey. I mean, that is what everyone who plays this game strives for. I was pretty fortunate to have been able to have raised it on three separate occasions. It was such a thrill to do it each time too, that never got old—believe me."

Joe Nieuwendyk
Calgary 1989, Dallas 1999, and New Jersey 2003

"Winning the Cup was something that I dreamed about as a kid. In grade six I remember my family getting a TV, and all I wanted to do was watch *Hockey Night in Canada*.

Seeing those guys play for the Cup made such an impression on me. I just knew that was what I wanted to do. So to finally win it was beyond words. Then to go on and win four in a row, what can you say? We had so many great players on those teams, and I just feel very blessed to have been a part of it."

Bob Nystrom
New York Islanders 1980, 1981, 1982, and 1983

"To beat Montreal in Montreal was pretty special. They had beaten us back in the finals a few years earlier in 1986 behind a rookie goalie by the name of Patrick Roy, and we were not going to be denied this time around. One of the things I remember most about winning the Cup in '89 was the class those Montreal fans showed us the night we clinched it at the Forum. It was really neat. They stuck around and cheered for us, which was a very classy thing to do. The commissioner presented the Cup to our captain, Lanny McDonald, and from there we just started passing it around. I got it from Brad McCrimmon, and then I gave it to Haken Loob. What a feeling. Then to know that my friends and family were all watching on TV back home in Minnesota, that was just icing on the cake. Although we never got to have the Cup for a day like they do now, we did have a big party at Lanny McDonald's house afterward where we all got to celebrate with it. Lanny was a huge fan favorite up in Calgary, they loved him. He scored a huge goal in Game 6 of the finals and also notched his 500th career goal that year as well. He then went out on top, retiring after we won the Cup that year."

Joel Otto
Calgary 1989

"Winning the Cup was pretty incredible, but the way it all went down for me was pretty topsy-turvy. I was a member of the L.A. Kings that season but got released during the preseason. They had brought in a whole new coaching staff and wanted to go in a different direction. So I didn't know where my future was going to be at that point. From there I luckily got picked up by Colorado off waivers. I spent about a month and a half there until I found out that Anaheim had traded for me. Their enforcer, Todd Fedoruk, got hurt so they worked out a deal to acquire me for a second-round pick. I just fit right in with their aggressive style, and I couldn't have been happier with how things worked out. To finally win the Cup though was amazing, truly a lifelong dream come true."

George Parros
Anaheim 2007

"It's really something. To do it, to win it…it's a dream. It's beyond belief. It's almost as if you have to pinch yourself while it's happening to make sure it's real. We had a three-goal lead with a few minutes to go in that last game against Detroit to win it. That's when it really hit me. Even though we would ultimately sweep the series and were up by a comfortable margin at the time, I just never allowed myself to think we had it in the bag. I had been to the finals before, in 1992 with Chicago, and remembered how horrible it felt to lose. I never wanted to feel that way again. Then when the realization hit that we were in fact going to win it, I just lost it. I was a mess on the bench. My emotions came pouring out of me, and I just started bawling. It was surreal. I thought about growing up on the Iron Range in northern Minnesota and about going to college in Alaska; nobody ever thought I would make it in the

National Hockey League. Nobody. So for me to not only get there but to win the Stanley Cup was so vindicating and so satisfying. I can't even explain it. There were so many battles with so much blood and tears that lead up to it. Even when I think about it right now I get extremely emotional, goose bumps, you name it. It's the ultimate exclamation point you can put on your career. Very rarely do they talk about players who finish second, so it means you're a champion."

Mike Peluso
New Jersey 1995

"Obviously winning the Cup was the thrill of a lifetime and certainly something that I think every young Canadian aspires to do. I can tell you that I had hoisted it many, many times out on the street or at the park with my buddies growing up. I had it all planned out as to what I was going to do with it when I won it, or so I thought. Then when it finally became a reality, it was as if I had forgotten everything and didn't know what the hell to do with it. None of us knew what to do with it; we all just sort of stood there in awe, staring at it. Then I remember Bryan Trottier just grabbed the Cup and took off to do a victory lap with it. We figured that since he had already won four Cups with the Islanders that he knew what was going on, so we all just followed him. It was such a surreal moment.

"It was the greatest accomplishment of my career for sure. I will never forget it. We had gone through some tough years in Pittsburgh prior to that too, so when it finally happened it was very satisfying. To win it against the North Stars in '91 was extra special for me, given the fact that I had graduated from the University of Minnesota just prior to that. We clinched it at the Met Center in Bloomington too, so I had a lot of friends there that I was able to share that moment with.

"I was very fortunate to have won four games during the playoffs, and that was something I take great pride in. It doesn't happen very often where the backup goaltender gets that much ice time during the playoffs, so that was neat. Our coach, Bob Johnson, had prepared each one of us to be ready at all times, regardless of our positions or our roles on the team. He continually preached to us that our time would eventually come. So I practiced as if I was going to start each and every game. Bob was the eternal optimist, so it was easy to blow him off when he said stuff like that. But then, sure enough, my time did come and because he had prepared me, I was ready to go. When Tom Barrasso got hurt I was ready and able and per- formed at a very high level. I even won the pivotal Game 5 of the finals against Minnesota in Pittsburgh, which was really a thrill. My teammates appreciated that, and it was certainly very gratifying for me as well."

Frank Pietrangelo
Pittsburgh 1991

"I can't even really put it in words. It was something I had fantasized about since I was a kid. When it finally hap- pened it was actually quite an odd experience. You see, I was a scratch for that final Game 6 up in Buffalo, so I was watching nervously in the locker room with a few other guys. It went into overtime, then another overtime, and then another overtime—I thought I was going to pass out I was so nervous. Then when Brett [Hull] scored the game winner we ran and put our skates on so we could join our teammates out on the ice. What a moment that was. It was especially odd for me, however, because I had just gotten traded to Dallas at the trade deadline from Buffalo, where I had spent the last six years of my career. So to be back out on the ice was weird, especially for the Stars versus the Sabres. I was happy for my team, yet I felt bummed out for the fans there too because they so wanted to win a Stanley Cup. That city is just so in need of a championship, and they really thought that was their year. I mean, they are still reeling from the Bills' four Super Bowl losses all these years later. Shaking hands afterward was certainly interesting too. I felt badly for a lot of my good friends and former teammates who had worked so hard. They were hurting, but hey, that's hockey."

Derek Plante
Dallas 1999

"I was a young kid with wide eyes back in 1971, just trying to take it all in. I had actually gotten injured that year and missed much of the regular season. I came back for the playoffs and dressed for a handful of games but sadly didn't get any ice time in the finals. As a result, I never got my name on the Cup, which was unfortunate. To be there and to celebrate with my teammates was very special though. And even though my name isn't on the Cup, I still take great pride in knowing that I was a member of that team. We clinched in Chicago in Game 7, and it was quite a thrill. I remember Jacques Lemaire scoring from center ice past Tony Esposito, and Henri Richard scored a pair of goals, including the game winner late in the third.

"Our goalie that year was Kenny Dryden, who won the Connie Smyth trophy as the MVP of the playoffs as a rookie. What's even more amazing about Kenny was that he then won the Rookie of the Year award the following season, as a result of him not playing enough regular-season games in '71 to become eligible. That was a first. So it was great to be a part of that championship team, and it was even better to sip champagne out of the Cup afterward. Just to have the opportunity to be associated with the Montreal Canadiens organization was a huge honor and something I was very grateful for.

"You know, it's kind of funny looking back, but not only did I not get my name on the Cup that year, I also didn't get a ring that year either. Believe it or not, there were so many players who had won so many Cups on that team that they wanted other stuff that was more practical—like TVs and stereos and stuff like that. How crazy is that? I mean, some of those guys had more rings than fingers to wear them on, including Henri Richard and Jean Beliveau, who had 11 and 10, respectively. Amazing. The alumni association later decided to do the right thing, though, and about 25 years later those of us who wanted one were able to buy a ring. So I finally got my ring.

"Later in my career I was finally able to get my name on the Cup as well, this time as the assistant general manager and director of player personnel of the New York Rangers. What a wonderful experience that was being a part of such a tremendous hockey team. Who can forget Mark Messier, the captain, practically carrying that team on his back during the playoffs that year? He had guaranteed the win against New Jersey in Game 6 of the conference finals, and then he backed it up with a hat trick. We then won it the following game on Stephane Matteau's double-overtime game winner, which was just an amazing moment and one I will never forget. Then in the finals, to be up three games to one on Vancouver only to watch them force a final Game 7—which we won dramatically at home in the Garden. It was amazing, it really was. I will never forget looking into the crowd as that iconic Game 7 was winding down and seeing all of the fans holding up newspapers that had already been printed with the headline: "The Rangers Win the Cup!" What a run that was. The city of New York had waited so long to win the Stanley Cup, 54 years to be exact, so to be a small part of making that happen was pretty neat."

Larry Pleau

Montreal 1971 and New York Rangers
1994 (Assistant GM)

"When we finally won it in 2001 I thought I was going to be super happy and elated, but it turned out to be more of a moment of reflection. When that final buzzer went off I just immediately started thinking about all of the people who gave up so much of themselves so that I could pursue my passion. All of the time, money, energy, and the sacrifices that they made, I just felt so fortunate at that moment, and really it became less about me and much more about them. There were just so many people along the way who helped me and encouraged me, and I just can't thank them enough. Without them, I never would have been in that position. I tried to reward all of those people and to thank them when I had the Cup for a day, which was just an amazing experience. You know, I had come very close a few years earlier in Philadelphia when we made it all the way to the finals, and in Colorado we had lost twice in a couple of conference finals that had each gone all the way to Game 7. So I had certainly paid my dues, so to speak, as far as getting there and understanding just what it took to get past that last barrier. When it finally happened, though, words really can't describe how I felt. Aside from family, it was one of the greatest moments in my life."

Shjon Podein
Colorado 2001

"I remember being on vacation during the summer of 2000 and I got the call telling me that I had gotten traded from Carolina to Colorado. My family immediately reacted by being a little bit upset about having to move, but I instantly said to myself, 'Wow, I'm going to win the Stanley Cup.' I just knew that team was poised to win it all that year, and I was so excited knowing that I was going to be a part of that. I wound up not getting to play as much as I would have liked to, but to be a part of that amazing team was something I will always remember. Then, three years later, to be a part of an upstart Tampa Bay team that won it was very special too. I played a bigger role that season defensively, which was very gratifying. Being a part of two Stanley Cup–winning teams means the world to me. I dreamed of it as a kid up in Canada, and it had always been a lifelong goal of mine. I had paid my dues in the minor leagues for several years and worked very hard to get to the NHL, so I am very proud of the accomplishment. Just to be able to make your career playing a sport that you absolutely love and that you have such a passion for is hugely rewarding. To be able to share that with not only my family growing up but my current family now—it doesn't get much better than that."

Nolan Pratt
Colorado 2001 and
Tampa Bay 2004

"Growing up in Canada I spent my childhood chasing pucks around on my backyard rink dreaming of one day getting to hoist that thing. That scenario played out millions of times in my head in those days, so to finally get to do it was beyond anything I can even think of. It wasn't even reality at that point, it was just a dream. Winning the first one with Calgary was extra special because we got to win it up in that hallowed shrine of hockey in Montreal, the Forum, where their fans showed us so much respect after beating the Canadiens in Game 6. Being the classy fans that they are, they hung around and cheered for us after the game; it was a gesture that I had never seen before or since. They had never lost a Stanley Cup at home up until that point, and they wanted to show their appreciation, so it was pretty memorable. The memory that will always be etched in my mind was being out on the ice standing next to Brad McCrimmon when the final buzzer went off. I was standing in the left faceoff circle in the Montreal zone. I can still picture it like it was yesterday. I even get goose bumps just thinking about it. I will always just cherish that moment in my mind until the day I die.

"Then to win it again in Montreal, this time as a member of the Canadiens in 1993, was unbelievable. Those fans up there, what can you say? Hockey is religion for them, they're the best. What a season we had that year too, and then to beat the Kings in the finals…amazing. It was kind of ironic how I wound up there too. I had been with Tampa Bay that season, and midway through the year our GM, Phil Esposito, called me into his office and said that Los Angeles wanted to trade for me. Phil, being the classy guy that he was, said that I was a veteran and that it was my call as to whether or not I wanted to go. Well, at the time I was battling a horrible flu and the only place I wanted to go was to bed, so I respectfully said no. It was a hard call, though, because it would have been pretty neat to have played with Wayne Gretzky. So I went back to work. Then, just before the trade deadline, Espo called me back into his office again and said that three teams— Chicago, Detroit, and Montreal—were all interested in acquiring me. I was a veteran at this stage of the game and was flattered that anybody would want me. Espo then said that the catch this time, however, was that I couldn't choose which team. He said that he would have to go with the one that made the best offer—probably a couple dozen sticks and a few water bottles, I suppose! Anyway, I talked it over with my wife and she said sure, go for it. We were out of the playoffs, and I figured this might be my last chance to raise the Cup again. As luck would have it, Montreal was the one that came through, and lo and behold, who did we wind up facing in the finals? Old No. 99 and the Kings. How cool is that? Kinda hard to put into words."

Rob Ramage
Calgary 1989 and Montreal 1993

"It was a goal that I had set for myself ever since I was a young boy growing up in Moose Jaw, Saskatchewan, watching *Hockey Night in Canada* on TV. When you finally win it, it's kind of surreal. I will never forget when Bobby Nystrom scored the Cup-clinching overtime game winner against Philadelphia in the finals, it was unbeliev- able. It was an emotional explosion for all of us. We had been up two goals in that game, and they had come back to tie us, so we were so nervous right up until the final second. I remember celebrating out on the ice afterward and all the fans running out there, it was just wild. What a scene. It's a cherished moment. I think that's why guys don't want to go to bed the night they've won it; they stay up all night because they want that moment to last forever. That emotion right after you win the Stanley Cup, it's priceless. You hear everyone saying the same clichés: 'I just love these guys! It's the greatest team ever!' It's just pure, raw, uncontrollable emotion. You feel a wonderful sense of having been a part of something bigger than yourself. It's very satisfying. When we won that first Cup in 1980, it had taken us years to get to that point. Years. I had been with the club since the early '70s, and we had been on a mission ever since I had gotten there. That was when the core of that team got there too, guys like Denis Potvin, Bob Nystrom, Clark Gillies, Bryan Trottier, and Billy Smith. We struggled for years before we were finally able to put it all together, so when it finally happened it was extremely gratifying. I only wish I could have been around for all four Cups, but I got traded to Colorado in 1981 at the trading deadline. I was excited about getting a new opportunity but sad at the same time to be leaving all of those teammates I had been to war with for so many years. Just knowing that I was a part of arguably the best hockey team in the world, that's pretty special."

Chico Resch
New York Islanders 1980

"It meant everything. I had imagined what it would be like as a little kid, and when it finally happened, it was even better than I had imagined. The minute it happened; that was the new standard by which you measured yourself. It was almost like anything but 'that' would never feel right again. As an individual playing on a team sport, this is it. This is the pinnacle. This is what you have grown up dreaming about doing. It is what you have been working for your entire life. Beyond that, it is what you have been entrusted to do by the organization that signs your pay-check, and it is the expectation of the fans who pay to watch you day in and day out. It's a big deal. It makes you appreciate everything so much more too. I thought about all of the great players who had played this game for so long that had never gotten the opportunity to raise the Cup. You just feel so fortunate that you were able to get through the grind of it all and get your name on it. To drink out of that Cup is so, so sweet. Winning it in New York, for those fans who had waited 54 years for the Cup, was indescribable. It was insane and wonderful all at the same time."

Mike Richter
New York Rangers 1994

"Winning the first one is always the most special. I was just a 21-year-old kid at the time so it was pretty amazing—especially sweeping the 'Broad Street Bullies' on Philly's home ice. I remember just before that last game got under-way the Flyers brought in Kate Smith to sing 'God Bless America.' Now, they had never lost a playoff game when Kate sang that song, and their fans were jacked. It was so loud in there you couldn't hear yourself think. It was already the most hostile environment to play in, and now they added this. We knew that [we] were going to have our work cut out for us that night, no doubt about it. Well, we wound up surviving and clinching the Cup, but the best part came on the flight home when our goalie, Kenny Dryden, handed out sheet music to 'God Bless America' for all of us to sing. So here we were, the Montreal Canadiens singing 'God Bless America' as we flew back to Canada. It was just classic, we had officially stolen their song!

Whenever I see anybody from that team we always have a good laugh over that; it was a moment none of us will ever forget.

"Then, when the partying stops, you have time to reflect. The initial reaction is obviously that of happiness for your team's success. Never mind the historical perspective of being a kid and growing up hoisting Stanley every day out on the pond. Then when it finally happens for real, the accomplishment is almost overwhelming. The thing I took away the most is that it was a real unifying team accomplishment. You just feel so happy for all of those guys who were along for the ride on that same voyage. It's the ultimate team trophy in my opinion because you have to overcome so much adversity every step of the way. It's such a test on so many different levels. Then when you win it, you pause and you reflect, and that's when you think a lot about your family, who sacrificed and helped you to get to that point in your life.

"While the first Cup was the most sentimental, it was the fourth one that was the most satisfying. It was the only Cup we won at home, which was special too in that we got to share it with our fans right then and there, versus the next day. Plus, we weren't the best team that year. The other years we were always the best team in the league, but not in '79. Case in point, in 1977 we lost a total of eight regular-season games and then won the Cup in just 13 games—which is probably the record for fewest losses ever. Anyway, we got hot in the playoffs and wound up beating the Rangers to make it four straight Cups, securing our right to be called a dynasty. I will never forget the night we clinched it; it was without a doubt the best game that team had played in all four of those seasons. We were just not going to be denied. We wanted to win it right then and there in front of our fans. To hear the final horn go off and to celebrate with my teammates that night, what a moment. I will always remember that night.

"The expectations for winning the Stanley Cup in Montreal are unlike any other organization in professional sports, with the exception of probably the New York Yankees. We were expected to win. Period. The history and the ghosts up there weigh on the players. In fact, the playoffs in those days really only represented the Stanley Cup. I remember walking down the street one day during the summer of 1975, shortly after my rookie season. We had lost to Buffalo in the conference finals that year in seven games. A group of fans came up to me and said, 'Gee, it's too bad you guys didn't make the playoffs.' I said, 'No, we made the playoffs, we made it all the way to the conference finals, just one goal away from the finals.' They just sort of smiled and said, 'No, no, no…that's not the playoffs. The playoffs; are the Stanley Cup.' That was how they saw it up there, anything less than winning the Cup didn't even matter. They had set the bar higher than anybody else. Those were their expectations. They expected and demanded excellence, and as players we did not want to disappoint them.

"Conversely, I later played for Calgary, and we lost to Montreal in the finals in 1986. What a contrast in organizations. In Montreal the Stanley Cup was the norm. It was expected. In Calgary it was a goal, something that we were all hoping to achieve. Three years later I then won the Stanley Cup as an assistant coach with Calgary, again against Montreal. So to see the growth of that organization as they gained confidence, that was pretty neat. One was a bar that was set, where the other one was a goal that was set from ground zero, so to speak. So after winning four straight Cups with the Canadiens, to winning the first Cup in franchise history with the Flames, it was meaningful. Very meaningful. It wasn't just about the team, either, it was about the fans and the city too. Everybody was so into it, it was such a big deal. Just huge. For them to beat Montreal, to dethrone those guys who had beaten them so many times previously, was an enormous achievement to so many people. What a thrill to be a part of that, just amazing. I mean, in Montreal when we won a Cup, sure the fans were excited, and we had parades. But it was expected. We had done our jobs. We were a dynasty in those days. In Calgary, meanwhile, where they had never won a Cup before, it was like an explosion of emotions. The city erupted. What a contrast.

"Montreal, though, that organization is just totally unique in all of sports. The fans, the city, they take so much pride in their team. In 2010 I attended the 100th anniversary of the Montreal Canadiens. It was a really neat black-tie affair, very classy. That night they invited all the players who had won Stanley Cups onto a stage. Everybody cheered and applauded. Then, one by one, they said all the one-time winners, please sit down. Then the two-time winners, three-time winners, and on and on. It was incredible. They eventually got to double-digit winners. It was crazy. Just to be up on stage as they read off all those iconic names: Henri Richard, Rocket Richard, Jean Beliveau, Yvan Cournoyer, Claude Provost, Scotty Bowman, and Jacques Lemaire—it was so humbling. I was in awe."

Doug Risebrough
Montreal 1976, 1977, 1978, and 1979;
Calgary 1989 (Assistant Coach)

"What a great moment, to finally win it. I was lucky enough to win a couple of them toward the end of my career, but that first one was the one I will always remember the most. I didn't know if it was ever going to happen for me. I was with St. Louis the year before and thought I was going to be put out to pasture on the veteran castaway line, so to speak. Luckily, Scotty Bowman saw me play one weekend and felt like I still had the passion, so he traded for me, and it was as if I had hit the lottery going to Pittsburgh. Winning that first one against the North Stars was really neat for me because I had played for that organization for eight seasons earlier in my career and had come close to winning it with them back in 1981 when we lost to the Islanders in the finals.

"I remember seeing my dad right at the end of the final game against Minnesota the night we clinched. He was sitting near the glass, and we made eye contact. I could see his eyes well up and how proud he was. I grew up the youngest of four boys, and my dad had done so much for me over the years and made so many sacrifices. So to see him right then, and to get to share that moment together when my dream finally came true was just extra special. I later thanked him by giving him my Stanley Cup ring, which was a moment I will never forget.

"I will never forget the parades and the genuine emotion that the fans felt. Seeing those 25,000 fans waiting for us at the airport when we got home from Minnesota, all wearing their jerseys—what a feeling. They felt so connected to those teams, and the atmosphere at our rink night in and night out that they created for us was amazing. We couldn't have done it without them. That's something that you really take away from the whole thing when it's all said and done, just how important those memories are to the fans who all felt as though they were a part of those teams. When you win a Cup, the whole city wins the Cup."

Gordie Roberts
Pittsburgh 1991 and 1992

"Winning the Stanley Cup is the end-all be-all for any kid who plays hockey. For me to get that opportunity in my first year in the league was pretty amazing. I was just so lucky to have been a part of that. Here I am 16 seasons later, still chasing my second Cup. You just never know in this league."

Brian Rolston
New Jersey 1995

"Like every kid, it was a lifelong dream come true to raise Stanley. I had always been aware of the tradition that you were never allowed to touch it unless you won it, so when I finally got to touch it I really grabbed on for dear life. It was incredible. Even now, whenever I see it at various charity functions, I am so proud to be able to put my arms around it anytime I want. I earned that and I am very proud of that. I grew up watching Bobby Orr lead the Boston Bruins to two Stanley Cups in the early '70s, so to be on the same shrine as Bobby is such a thrill."

Steve Rooney
Montreal 1986

"As a kid out on the street I played many, many times for a fake Stanley Cup, so when I finally got to win the real thing it was an incredible feeling. I had always dreamt about it but never really believed it would ever happen to me. I was

Avalanche goaltender Patrick Roy raises the Stanley Cup for the third time in his career, this time after Colorado defeated the Florida Panthers in 1996.

a rookie back in '86 when we won that first one, and I will never forget it. We had a big party after we won it at my house, and at one point everybody, including Stanley, was in my pool. It was pretty crazy. We won another one in '93, which was very special, too. We had a really close team that year. We had lost in the finals in '89 to Calgary, so we were very hungry to win it again. I had so many great teammates in Montreal and just feel so fortunate to have been able to have been a part of that organization. Then, to win it in '96 in Colorado, that was really special. I had just gotten traded, and a lot of people thought that my best years were behind me. So for me that time it was personal. Real personal. There was a lot of pride on the table for that one, absolutely. Then, the fourth one in 2001, that was all about Ray Bourque. I will never forget when we won it, there was not one guy on our team who wasn't thinking about Ray at that moment. We wanted it for him so badly, and when we did it, it was a very special moment—one I will certainly never forget. Overall, just to be remembered as a champion, that is what it's all about to me…to be a champion."

Patrick Roy
Montreal 1986 and 1993,
Colorado 1996 and 2001

"Raising the Cup was not only a thrill, it was a huge relief. I'd been playing pro hockey for 15 seasons at that point and just figured it was probably never going to happen. I had started out the 2004 season as one of the six starting defensemen in training camp, but that all came to a screeching halt when I hurt my back. Later on, when I got healthy, I didn't want to make a big issue out of getting my job back. The team had moved on, and other guys were

filling in nicely, and I really didn't want to become a dis-
traction for Torts [Head Coach John Tortorella] in the locker
room. I didn't want to rock the boat. I remember telling
Torts that I would do whatever he asked me to do and that
I just wanted to contribute any way I could. As a guy who
had spent many years in the minors, I didn't care if he
wanted me to fill water bottles; I just wanted to be a part of
the team. I think he really appreciated me doing that, as to
not upset the chemistry we had going at the time.

"I figured I would hang in there and eventually get back
when somebody got hurt or something. Well, incredibly,
we set a record that season for the least amount of man-
hours lost due to injury. We were just super healthy as a
team, which was great—because that meant we were winning. As a result, however, I never got a shot at cracking
the lineup and wound up playing in only five games all
season. I was a healthy scratch for most of the season. I
practiced with the team, traveled with the team, and essen-
tially became a cheerleader rooting my teammates on. It
was probably the most challenging thing I have ever had
to do in my entire career. It was a situation that was
beyond my control. I could never really feel good about
myself because I rarely saw any ice time. It wasn't like I
was going to root for guys to get injured, though. I just
accepted it and made the best of it.

"We wound up going on a magical playoff run, starting
with a win over the Islanders, followed by a sweep over
Montreal. From there we beat the Flyers in a tough seven-
game conference finals series to get to the finals, where we
met up with Calgary. The Flames were a great team, and
that one also turned out to be an epic seven-game battle.
Game 7 was in Tampa and it was a classic, just back and
forth all night. Then, with just a few minutes to go in the

game, myself and the other scratches for the game got suited up so we could run out there as soon as the final buzzer went off. It was a one-goal game, though, so we weren't sure if we were going to get out there or not. I was green I was so nervous. Thanks to Nikolai Khabibulin, who played huge in net and just slammed the door in the last few minutes, we won the game 2–1. With that, we all raced out there like chickens with our heads cut off. The fans were going crazy, and it was amazing. After shaking hands I got to hoist the Cup, which was such an incredible experience. So memorable. Even though I was one of the older guys on the roster I went last, just out of respect. The neat thing about that was that I got to hand it to Torts, which was a pretty cool moment for me as well. Then we drank champagne out of it in the locker room and even had a couple of cigars for good measure. We did it up right.

"While I was thrilled that I got to be a part of all the postgame festivities, I was still bummed out, knowing that because I didn't play enough games that season, nor did I get to play in the finals, I wouldn't get my name on the Cup. You think about your legacy at that point and about how cool it would be for your great-grandkids to read your name on there one day. Well, to my surprise I later found out that the players all went to bat for me and lobbied to get my name on it. It was sort of unprecedented, which made it even more special. I was so blown away by their gesture, it just meant so much to me. I never really knew for sure, either, until I saw it on my day with the Cup. As soon as the Cup Keeper got there I immediately grabbed it and started searching. Sure enough, there I was alongside all of my teammates. I just smiled and cried. Pretty cool."

Darren Rumble
Tampa Bay 2004

"Growing up in Waldheim, Saskatchewan, we didn't have a TV so I used to have to walk down to the hardware store just to watch *Hockey Night in Canada*. I used to stand there and imagine what it must have felt like to play in the National Hockey League. I would go home and lie in bed, dreaming about winning the Stanley Cup. So what did it mean for me to raise the Stanley Cup? The fulfillment of a lifelong dream. And I didn't dream about being an enforcer either, hell no. I dreamed about scoring the game winner in Game 7 in overtime, like all kids.

"In fact, I never fought, ever, until I was drafted by the Flyers and went to their minor league team. I wasn't afraid of it, certainly, and as soon as I realized that I was pretty good at it I just embraced it. I figured out that I was willing to do whatever it took to make the team, and if that meant protecting my teammates, then so be it. I wanted to be the best at what I did, and I think that eventually I became one of the best in the business in my role. I was proud of that because I knew that without me doing my job, then a bunch of my teammates couldn't do theirs.

"So when we finally won our first Cup in 1974, that was just an amazing feeling. When that buzzer went off at the end of Game 6 against the Bruins at the Spectrum and the scoreboard read 1–0, that was when it was finally real. It was at that moment that I was officially a champion. We were the underdogs, but we didn't know any better, I guess. We just played our hearts out. Guys like Bobby Clarke, our captain, just laid it on the line night in and night out. That leadership just made everybody else want to play as hard as they absolutely could. Nobody wanted to let anybody else down, nobody. We knew that we had to win one in Boston or we were dead. We lost the opener, but we came back to win Game 2 in overtime. I even got an assist on the game-winning goal, which was certainly a highlight for me personally. Our goalie Bernie Parent shut down Boston in Games 3 and 4 and then posted a shutout in Game 6 to clinch it. He was unbelievable. Without him we didn't stand a chance. What a thrill to win it on our home ice; our fans went absolutely wild.

"We were the first expansion team to win a Cup, which pissed off a lot of the old-school guys. Hell, we didn't care. We were having fun and changing the game at the same time. It was a different era. People would say, 'Oh, those Flyers just fought their way to the Stanley Cup...' That's B.S. We didn't fight our way to the Cup, we just got sick and tired of being pushed around and decided that we weren't going to take any more crap from anybody. We just made up our minds that we weren't going to be intimidated. And as soon as we did, things changed for us in a hurry. We earned some respect around the league, and teams started to take us seriously. Eventually they started to fear us, and that was when we knew that we were on to something. Yes, we were a tough team and we intimidated people, but we had some phenomenal talent. We were just a great hockey club. We played well as a team, we had great goaltending, and we had great leadership, from our owner, Ed Snyder, to our coach, Freddy Shero. We just had a great organization from top to bottom.

"Our attitude was that nobody was going to intimidate us. Period. We were proud of guys coming down with the 'Philly flu,' because that meant that they were intimidated before they even stepped foot in our building. Freddy paid me a great compliment one time when he said, 'Dave Schulze gives the Flyers courage on the road...' I took great pride in that because having courage on the road, that confidence that you could play against any team, anywhere, was a huge factor. We weren't going be intimidated at home, and damn it all if we weren't going to be intimidated on the road either. I used to hear stories from opposing players about when they would have to come into Philly to play us at the Spectrum. They would all be laughing and joking on the bus from the airport until they came to the Walt Whitman Bridge, then the entire bus would go silent. The big joke was that they would pull up to the arena and turn off the engine, but the bus would keep shaking.

"Intimidation went both ways, though. You don't think going into Boston to play the 'Big Bad Bruins' wasn't tough? I will never forget sitting in the penalty box and having Bobby Orr and Phil Esposito skate by and say, 'Hey asshole, the boys are going to get you tonight…' You don't think that was intimidating? There were times I had the 'Boston flu' too, trust me. Those guys were plenty tough, and we had some tremendous battles with them over the years, no question. I had a lot of respect for them, though. We kept each other honest.

"Then to win it again the next year? It was as if I had died and gone to heaven. Reggie Leach joined us that season, and that was a big addition; the guy could score goals at will. We certainly had a bigger target on our backs that year, though, everybody was gunning for us. So we had to step up our game and buckle down. For me, that meant more fights and more time in the box. I had to be smart about that stuff and I had to pick my spots, otherwise I would be letting my teammates down by taking stupid penalties that would put the other team on a power play.

"We beat Buffalo in 1975 in what would prove to be one of the wildest finals ever. We took the first two at home in the

Spectrum but then lost Games 3 and 4 up in Buffalo in the fog. Literally. Apparently, due to the heat and their lack of a decent refrigeration system, fog formed on the ice during the game to the point where we literally couldn't see the puck. It was insane. Then, if that weren't crazy enough, there was a bat that was flying around in the arena, and when he came swooping down by us, Sabres center Jim Lorentz whacked him out of the air with his stick and killed it. It was like an omen or something. Well, we wound up losing on Rene Robert's goal in overtime. We came back to win Game 5 in Philly, and then we clinched it back up in Buffalo for Game 6 behind Bernie's 2–0 shutout. Bernie played great, and our defense shut down their 'French Connection' line of Gilbert Perreault, Richard Martin, and Rene Robert.

"Winning that second one was very gratifying. It validated that first one too, which was a big deal to us because it shut up all the naysayers who said that we had just gotten lucky the year before. So this made it legit and proved that we were in fact a great hockey club. A lot of people forget, but we almost made it three in a row that next year too, but we came up just short against a very good Montreal team that would ultimately go on to win four straight Cups. It meant a lot to be a part of those two magical teams. It was awesome. You become a part of history in the National Hockey League, how incredible is that? It's something that nobody can ever take away from you.

"The people of Philadelphia have never forgotten what we did, and that means the world to me. Even now when I see fans and they are appreciative of what we did, that is wonderful. It was a rough time here in the early '70s, and we lifted this city up at a time when it needed some lifting. This city hadn't won a championship in years, and we changed all of that. Our fans embraced us and fell in love with us, and in turn we fell in love with them. They took pride in us, they embraced us. And once we won it, we had no idea what was coming next either. I mean, we had a couple of million people show up at our parade. How crazy is that? I will never forget them hanging off of telephone poles and climbing trees and hanging out of office building windows just to see us and to say thanks. It was a moment I will never forget. The whole Delaware Valley went wild. It was unbelievable.

"You know, even though I played for three other teams, I always consider myself to be a Flyer. I proudly wear my Stanley Cup rings every day. I even got inducted into the Flyer Hall of Fame in 2009, and that was such an honor. To see how the fans reacted and the way they treated me, I will never forget that. To know that my grandchildren can walk into the Wachovia Center and see my name up there forever, it's pretty awesome. It means a lot. I am just so thankful that I was in the right place at the right time. I genuinely feel bad for all the great hockey players who just never had an opportunity to win a Cup. I really do. It's a shame. So many phenomenal players with such outstanding careers never got to hoist it, and that's sad, because there's nothing like it. I wish everybody could experience it, friend and foe alike; it's what we all strive for as players. It's the pinnacle."

Dave Schultz
Philadelphia 1974 and 1975

"Winning it the first time, it was like a wave of emotions. A lifetime of dreams that started as a little kid, wishing for and imagining that moment one day when you would lift it over your head—it was overwhelming. So emotional. Then, at the same time, there was just this huge sense of relief. Just a gigantic release in realizing that you accomplished a goal that you had set for yourself so long ago. It's like the greatest dream come true, it really is. I was blessed to have won three of them, so each one was special and unique in its own way."

Brendan Shanahan
Detroit 1997, 1998, and 2002

"On May 24, 1986, my dream came true. I am sure you have heard it a million times, but yes, it was a dream come true. I can't tell you how many Game 7 game winners I scored in my basement and at the neighborhood rink, too many to count, I'm sure. So when I actually wound up scoring the game-winning goal against Calgary in the finals, it was beyond anything I ever could have imagined. As a professional, it's your goal and it's your greatest accomplishment, bar none. There's an old saying in this league that there are two types of retired players: the guys who won the Cup and the ones who wished that they did. I'm so grateful that I am among the former. I made it to four finals, and I am thankful I was able to win one; it means the world to me.

"We were young, but we had some outstanding players on that team. In fact we had eight rookies on our roster that season, but when you look at who some of those guys were you can see why we won the Cup. I mean, 15 years later several of them were still playing, including Patrick Roy, Chris Chelios, Stephane Richer, Claude Lemieux, and Brian Skrudland. I remember our GM, Serve Savard, having a meeting with some of the older

Brendan Shanahan reveals the sheer joy of winning the Stanley Cup after his Red Wings topped the Carolina Hurricanes in a five-game championship series in 2002.

players toward the end of the season. We were in serious jeopardy of missing the playoffs, and he was nervous. He basically said it was up to us as to what direction the team was going to go. It was a great wake-up call for us and we really responded. Thankfully we were able to pull it together and finish strong. We were a hard team to play against because we didn't give up many scoring chances.

"We lost Game 1 in Calgary and then won Game 2 in overtime, which totally swung the moment as we went on to win the next three in a row to clinch it. Our rookie goaltender Patrick Roy was just amazing and wound up winning the Conn Smythe as the MVP of the playoffs. What a wonderful run it was, just fantastic. I will never forget him stopping John Anderson in overtime of Game 7 against Hartford, our second-round opponent. He had a fabulous scoring chance to seal it for the Whalers, and Patty stopped him cold. Needless to say, we scored the game winner just a few minutes later. Without Patty Roy we don't win the Stanley Cup; he was the difference maker that season.

"I grew up in Ottawa, so to win it in Montreal was really special for me. What a class organization, Montreal. You know, we won our 23rd Stanley Cup in 1986, and I believe the Yankees had 22 World Series titles at that time, so the comparisons have always been there between those two iconic franchises. After we won they just rolled out the red carpet and basically handed us all the keys to the city. They even sent us all to the Bahamas after the season to say thanks. How classy is that? For me, though, it wasn't the parade, it wasn't the ring, and it wasn't my name on the Cup—it was just knowing that I won it and that I was a champion. That was it, that was honestly all I cared about. All that other stuff, sure it's nice, but to know that I had finally accomplished a lifelong goal that I had set for myself as a little kid meant way more."

Bobby Smith
Montreal 1986

"The first one was pretty special. It was quite a journey that I went through with my teammates for those couple of months, that's for sure. What a team we had. Wow. And what an honor it was to be a part of such an incredible organization. We were considered a dynasty in those days, and it was just a privilege to be a small part of it. There was another side of it for me too, which was unique, I think. There is such an intense elation at the moment you win it, almost a sense of euphoria, yet for me it went away right away. I know that sounds odd, but the reason it went away so quickly was because I immediately came to the realization that arguably the greatest time I have ever had in my life had now just come to an end."

Steve Smith
Edmonton 1987, 1988, and 1990

"Obviously it was a dream come true. As hockey players that is our ultimate goal, to get Stanley and raise him above your head. It was really an honor when I finally got to do it; it was pretty emotional. Just to think about it, wow, what a thrill."

Kevin Stevens
Pittsburgh 1992 and 1993

"To reach the pinnacle of anything you do in life is pretty awesome. What a great group of guys we had on that team; I just feel very fortunate to have been a part of that team. As time goes on you appreciate just how much it means not only to yourself and your family, but to the fans who were a part of it as well. It was amazing to win it, I just wish we could have won a bunch more, that's my only regret. I was pretty young in my career when it happened and figured that would be the first of many, but that was it. It's the toughest trophy in sports to win. As an active player it means a lot to you, but as the years go by and you are further removed from the game, you realize just how difficult it is to not only get to the finals, but to win it. The opportunities don't come around very often, so I am just glad that we were able to get it done in '89. As I sit back and reflect, it means an awful lot to know that my name is on that Cup. It's forever.

"Sadly, I never got to be out on the ice when we won it up in Montreal that year. I had broken my jaw pretty badly and had to watch it from the locker room. I really wanted to play, but I simply couldn't get medical clearance to do so, which was really disappointing. I remember practicing with my jaw wired shut. I couldn't get any oxygen and thought I was going to die; it was pretty crazy. Anyway, it was tough to not be out there on the ice with my team-mates, but the euphoria that followed once we won the game made up for it. What an unbelievable moment. My big regret was that I didn't run out there to have my picture taken with the team as they celebrated out on the ice. I think deep down I was sort of punishing myself. In some way I didn't feel as much a part of it because I wasn't out there contributing down the stretch. Plus, I always figured that because we were such a good team, that this was going to be the first of many, many Stanley Cups. Well, we all know how that turned out. So when you look at those dynasty teams of that era, Montreal, New York, and Edmonton, you really have to tip your hat to them. It was so tough to get back every year, so tough. Those were some very special teams.

"You know, we had some great fans up in Calgary. They were a big reason why the team got on a roll that season. They became known as the 'Sea of Red,' which was really amazing as a player to see how much your fans cared about you. They were a huge part of our success that year, no question. They were demanding too, though. They expected us to win, and we felt that pressure. We didn't want to disappoint them. We had a special year that season; I just wish we could have given them a few more Cups along the way."

Gary Suter
Calgary 1989

"Obviously it was a dream come true. There were so many pickup games and street hockey games as a kid in Quebec where I imagined myself raising the Cup, so to actually do it for real was almost indescribable."

Max Talbot
Pittsburgh 2009

"What a thrill. I will always remember being in the dressing room in Montreal after the game and seeing how genuinely happy everyone was. From a management point of view, it was very satisfying. Seeing the emotion on the faces of Chuck Fletcher, our GM, and Glenn Hall, our goalie coach, and all the coaches—from Terry Crisp to Doug Risebrough, it was a very special moment. The players were so excited, yet so exhausted from the physical grind they had just gone through. It was a very unique snapshot in time, that immediate aftermath. I have a photo of me drinking out of the Cup in that visitors locker room, and that, along with my Stanley Cup ring, are perhaps the two things I cherish most in all my years in hockey. What a wonderful, wonderful time that was."

Tom Thompson
Calgary 1989 (Scout)

"Ever since I was a little kid, all I could think about was possibly winning the Stanley Cup one day. It was a goal I had set very early on in my life, and to achieve it was extremely rewarding. Truly a dream come true."

John Tonelli
New York Islanders 1980, 1981, 1982, and 1983

"I have been fortunate to have won six Stanley Cups as a player, but winning that first one in 1980 was the most memorable. I remember the exact moment like it was yesterday. I was on the bench between shifts, and I saw Lorne Henning pass to John Tonelli, who in turn passed to Bobby Nystrom, who shot it past Philadelphia goalie Pete Peeters for the overtime game winner. It was the greatest moment of my hockey career, without a doubt. When that red light went off I was officially a Stanley Cup champion.

"You know, I will never forget being an eight-year-old kid up in Saskatchewan watching Jean Beliveau raise the Cup over his head on *Hockey Night in Canada*. I knew right

John Tonelli celebrates a game-winning goal in the 1978–79 semifinal series against the Rangers. The Islanders came up short in this season's quest for a championship but went on to win four straight Stanley Cups, 1980–83.

then and there that I wanted to do that one day. So to finally touch it was beyond words to me. To finally be able to grab on to it and hoist it over my head and kiss it, wow, what a special moment. It was so heavy, yet light as a feather. You just feel validated, like you have earned it. I remember winning the Rookie of the Year award in 1976, and when I went to get my trophy some reporters asked me to stand by the Stanley Cup to have my picture taken with it. I said hell no, I wasn't going near that thing. I knew that you didn't dare touch it unless you've earned the right to do so. Well, four years later I earned it.

"Later, when we got back to the locker room, I remember rubbing my fingers across all the engraved names on it and imagining where mine would go. Then to drink champagne out of that beautiful silver cup, it had never tasted so sweet. What a moment. I just wanted to remember everything about it. I didn't want it to end. I would look up and study the faces in the crowd, focusing on them. My senses were so heightened, what I was seeing and hearing and smelling. I remember every moment from that day, minute by minute, it's just ingrained in my head. It's so vivid. Hard to believe that was 30 years ago. Wow.

"Then to go back to back the following year, and then make it three in a row the next, followed by the fourth straight to solidify us as a dynasty—what an amazing run that was. We were the kings of hockey back in the early '80s, no question about it. Once you won one and got that taste of victory, then it just made you hungry for more. That was what drove us, that feeling of being the best, to be champions. What a privilege to have played with so many great teammates and to have been a part of such a fantastic organization.

"We got close in 1984 but lost out to the Oilers in the finals. They were the next great dynasty in hockey and would go on to win five of the next seven Cups. What a great team they had, with Gretzky and Messier, just so many great young players. Anyway, I stuck with the Islanders as we went through the rebuilding process. We had our share of ups and downs, but overall I enjoyed my time there. Then, in 1991, I got the opportunity to join the Pittsburgh Penguins. They were an up-and-coming team, and I was due for a change of scenery. What a thrill that was to play alongside guys like Mario Lemieux, Paul Coffey, and Jaromir Jagr and to hoist the Cup yet again at

35 years old. And not just once—we did it again in '92. I wasn't sure if I would ever have that opportunity again in my career, so it was really special.

"My role changed in Pittsburgh, but I felt important to the team's overall success nonetheless. In New York I was in the front of the train driving the engine, whereas in Pittsburgh I felt like I was driving the caboose. I was keeping everybody on track and being counted on for my leadership experience. It was a lot of fun playing there, though; I really enjoyed sort of reinventing myself. And even though I was the old man of the bunch, they played the hell out of me and gave me a ton of ice time. They appreciated me being there, and my contribution was meaningful to the team's overall success, which was very gratifying for me. Working with Bob Johnson and Scotty Bowman was wonderful too; both were great coaches and great people. It was just a great situation for me, and the memories that I took away from my time with the Penguins are very meaningful to me."

Bryan Trottier
New York Islanders 1980, 1981, 1982, and 1983;
Pittsburgh 1991 and 1992;
and Colorado 2001 (Assistant Coach)

"At the end of the day it meant that my childhood dream had come true. It really hit me after the game when I was in the locker room with not only all the guys but all of our families as well. You just look around and see the joy on people's faces, and you start to think about your journey up until that moment in your life. It was sort of a backwards fast-forward, starting when I was a kid playing youth hockey and just every step of the way until I got to where I was right then and there holding the Stanley Cup. It was extra special for me too in that it had taken me 16 years to do it. I knew that I was getting close to being at the end of my career and really wanted to accomplish that goal that I had set out for myself so many years ago. So when it happened not only was it a celebration, it was also a huge relief."

Pat Verbeek
Dallas 1999

"It means everything. That's what you live for if you are a hockey player. That is why we go out and practice every day. When you look back and see how many great players have been so close to winning it but never did, you just appreciate it even more. So to be able to win that last game of the season and to lift it proudly over your head, it is just an amazing feeling. You are kind of in a bubble during the playoffs, tuning everything out. And then when you finally win it and you realize just what you have actually done, it's pretty overwhelming. I called my mom right away, and that's when it hit me. As soon as I heard her voice telling me how proud of me she was, I broke down in tears. That's when I realized holy-shmoly, this is really happening. You know, growing up in Sweden I didn't even start playing hockey until I was 13, so I didn't grow up like most kids in Canada dreaming of winning the Cup. I had always played soccer and thought that was going to be my thing. When I was about 17 years old, though, I had to make a choice between the two. I chose hockey, against the judgment of many people too. But looking back I think I made the right choice!"

Niclas Wallin
Carolina 2006

"For me, winning the Stanley Cup was the most important thing I accomplished in my career. It was a long journey getting there too, 14 years to be exact, before we finally won it. I went through a lot of tough seasons in Detroit before we were able to eventually get it right. So to look back now at what it means, I would have to say that it has clearly defined my career. The Cup is so special because it's so hard to win. That two months of playoff hockey after already going through six months of the regular season really wears on you. So when you are the last team standing at the end, that means you've survived and that you're the champion. I'm just extremely proud to have played my entire career in Detroit and that I was able to be a part of bringing three Stanley Cups to that great city."

Steve Yzerman
Detroit 1997, 1998, and 2002

CHAPTER 2

Life Lessons

Whenever a player accomplishes something as profound as winning a Stanley Cup, there will undoubtedly be many life lessons and practical wisdom to take away. Every player's journey is unique, based on his own distinct set of experiences, emotions, and memories. For some it is about hard work and dedication, while for others it is about taking advantage of that rare opportunity of a lifetime.

WHAT LIFE LESSONS DID YOU LEARN FROM WINNING THE STANLEY CUP?

"For me it's about the little things. When I first got to the Canadiens, the biggest thing that stuck out to me was how hard everyone passed the puck. I remember talking to some guys after my first practice with the team and asking them about it, wondering why guys were drilling the puck at me. They told me that they practice with a purpose in Montreal, and when they pass the puck they are going to pass it hard—like they know where it is going. It was a little thing—but an important thing—and a complete eye opener for me. They practiced with a purpose, that was the bottom line. In Montreal it was all about the little things. The entire organization made a commitment to winning that Cup, and that was why we did it. Each and every guy on that team bought into that commitment and was accountable to it. That was what was different about the Montreal organization, versus all of the other organizations that I had been around during my career in the NHL. As an organization, Montreal took away any excuse you could possibly have not to perform well. 'Your wife is having a tough time adjusting? No problem, we'll get her a tutor to help her learn French. You need help finding a home? We will set you up with a Realtor. You need a car? We will help you get one, today. What are the 10 things that are troubling you or causing you to lose focus? Great, we will handle all of that stuff, now go out and play hockey and do your job. Let us do the rest.' That was how it was up there. It was a complete commitment to excellence. It was pretty incredible."

Brian Bellows
Montreal 1993

"Nothing worth getting comes easy. There is a price to pay to achieve success in hockey as well as in life. The reward, however, is so worth the journey."

Rob Blake
Colorado 2001

"To me it's about realizing and celebrating just what hockey means to different people. I know what hockey has meant to me over the years because it has given me everything in life. Hockey afforded me the opportunity to get a full-ride scholarship to play at the University of North Dakota. That led to me getting my degree as well as meeting my wife, which has led to me ultimately having children. I was able to play in the NHL, where I was able to win a Stanley Cup in 2000. Now I work for the Minnesota Wild, where I make my living in the 'State of Hockey.' It's all from hockey, everything I have today. So I am a big believer in the life lessons that hockey can teach people. Hockey is more than just stepping out onto the ice for an hour or watching your favorite player score a goal. It goes far beyond that. Having grown up in Canada, I figured it was just unique to us north of the border. But now that I live in Minnesota I can see that the game's impact is far reaching. For instance, we host the Minnesota State High School Hockey Tournament every year at the Xcel Energy Center, the home of the Wild. The first time I saw the place sell out for a high school game I was just blown away. When you see moms and dads and grandmas and grandpas all hanging out over here, rooting on their kids and grandkids, you realize just how much hockey is a part of the fabric of life here. It's a really big deal."

Brad Bombardir
New Jersey 2000

"If you work hard enough in life, anything is possible. No matter what people say or how many times others say no, if you have a conviction and you have a work ethic toward achieving a goal, then it *can* be achieved. I wasn't the most gifted hockey player out there, but I was always complimented on my work ethic—and that is something I took a lot of pride in. I have carried that ideal throughout my life, and it has served me well, even in my career today as a radio analyst for the Penguins."

Phil Bourque
Pittsburgh 1992 and 1993

"The biggest thing for me is to just not quit. My story is different from other guys'. I was never drafted and never really given a chance early in my career. I stuck with it, though, and never quit. I kept on working hard at every level I was at until I finally got an opportunity. Once that happened, I just made the most of it. So to go from being completely written off to being a key piece of a Stanley Cup–winning team within just a few years was pretty humbling. Others gave up on me, but I never gave up on myself."

Dan Boyle
Tampa 2004

"Stick with what you believe in would be No. 1, and nothing comes easy would be No. 2. Stay true to your convictions and don't take any shortcuts along the way. Those are the two biggest life lessons that I took away from that season, and I believe strongly that if you follow that path, then you will find success in anything you do in life."

Rod Brind'Amour
Carolina 2006

"I think what hit home the most for me was something I learned from my peewee coach when I was a little kid, and that was that in order to be successful you have to play as a team. In New Jersey everyone contributed, regardless of their role or stature on the team. Nobody cared who scored goals, and nobody cared who got assists. Everyone just worked hard, and we played together as a team. That was it. We all worked toward a common goal of winning the Cup, and we did it."

Neal Broten
New Jersey 1995

"Sacrifice. In 1995 when I got traded from Tampa to New Jersey my wife was eight and a half months pregnant at the time. I was torn. Here I was living my dream of winning the Stanley Cup, yet I was neglecting my family. I mean, I think I saw my newborn son a total of three times from the day I was traded in March until I finally got home around the Fourth of July, which was really tough. I couldn't even really completely enjoy it because I felt so guilty. I just wanted to get home to see my family. I remember winning the Cup in New Jersey and then being in my car the very next morning at 7:00 AM to drive back. I just couldn't wait to see my kids."

Shawn Chambers
New Jersey 1995 and Dallas 1999

"Momentum and trust were the big things for me. Early in the playoffs you felt the pressure on you to produce, big time. You felt like it was going to get worse and worse, yet what happened was exactly the opposite. As you went along and won games and closed out series, you just gained more confidence. You would get into a rhythm or routine, and the team became like a well-oiled machine, with each guy doing his part to keep it all going. The momentum would just grow and grow as we kept winning and moving on. Trust was huge too. The trust that is required for teams to succeed is a big factor that we don't hear enough about, but it's a big deal. We hear a lot about talent and hard work, but before any of that can pay off you have to trust one another as teammates. You may not even like a certain guy, but you have to trust him and visa versa.

"We were all headed toward the same goal that year, and not only did we all trust one another, we all genuinely liked one another. That was a big factor in us winning the

Stanley Cup, without a doubt. Sure, teams have won championships with rosters full of guys who didn't get along, but it doesn't happen very often."

Tom Chorske
New Jersey 1995

"I don't think necessarily winning the Cup in itself taught me anything; I think that I can take away something from the dedication and the perseverance that I had to go through in order to be in a position to become a champion. I found it incredibly gratifying to know that all of those thousands of hours of work that I put in over the years were worth it. At the end of the day, when you realize that you were able to do something that not a lot of people were able to do, you just feel validated. One thing is for sure, there is a lot to be learned in the journey of it all, and I am certainly still learning as I go."

Ben Clymer
Tampa 2004

"I learned a lot about the importance of mental toughness. Anybody who is successful in any field is mentally tough. While the 2006 season was great for us and things seemed to go well on the surface, there were a lot of ups and downs and challenges that came up along the way. To be mentally strong and to believe in yourself in all of those tough times is the difference between being successful and not being successful, in sports as well as in life. I also learned a lot about dedication and about the power of focusing on a single goal. To be able to stick with that goal and not allow other little things to creep in, that is much easier said than done. If you can do that, however, you will

find success more times than not. As a group we were
lucky that year in that everybody was on that same page.
We had a unique bunch of guys in that seemingly everybody, regardless of age, had something to prove. Looking
back, I think that was the difference for our team. Whether
it was an older veteran proving that he could still play or a
younger guy proving that he could be a next-level player
or a guy who was a castoff from another team proving
them wrong for giving up on him—we just had this amazing mix of people who were all hell bent on proving themselves. It was unreal. If you look up and down that roster,
each guy was in a unique spot in his career where he was
really trying to prove himself. That hunger and dedication
was really evident in our locker room the entire year, and
that was the difference between us making the playoffs and
winning the Stanley Cup. We didn't have the most talented
lineup that year either, no way, we just had a bunch of
guys with chips on their shoulders. So the power of having
everyone focused on that one common goal was a life
lesson I will never forget. It has just always stuck with me."

Matt Cullen
Carolina 2006

"I don't think you can fully grasp just what it means until
your career is over and you can reflect back upon it. If I
had to pick one thing, though, all clichés aside, it would be
passion. If you have a passion for something and believe
in it with all your heart, then anything is possible. If you
don't have it, whether that's in sports or in business or in
life, you are just not going to get very far. You may do
okay, but you're not going to become a champion. To
become a champion requires passion, because that will
allow you to do all of the other little things, like sacrificing

and working harder than you ever thought you could work. Passion is the key to everything, and you either have it or you don't. You can't buy it and you can't fake it."

Ken Daneyko
New Jersey 1995, 2000, and 2003

"I learned just what a group of people can do when they believe in themselves. Anything is possible if you work hard and believe, no question. Nobody thought we were going to win the Cup in '95, nobody. We believed, though, and used that negativity as motivation until we were the last team standing."

Jim Dowd
New Jersey 1995

"As kids growing up we play for fun; at the time you don't really realize just what sports does for you down the line. I have been out of the game now a long time, and I see and hear more and more about how companies are seeing the value in hiring former athletes, professional as well as collegiate. They know that athletes are people who are used to working toward a common goal. They know that they are tough both mentally and physically. They know that they have sacrificed for something bigger than themselves. And they know that they know how to work well with others. Decision makers in the business world understand the importance of all of that and realize how valuable those people are to have on their own teams. So the life lessons learned on the sports field definitely translate to the business field as well. No question."

Bruce Driver
New Jersey 1995

New Jersey's Ken Daneyko celebrates the Devils' victory over the Anaheim Mighty Ducks in the 2002–03 Stanley Cup Finals.

"For me it was about striving to be the best. Montreal was such an extraordinary place to play. The expectations there were unlike any other place. Every aspect of that organization was perfection. It was having the best arena, the Forum. It was having the best coach. It was having the best general manager. It was having owners who understood their responsibility to not only make money as a business, but also to win and to be the best. It was having the best fans, who created an atmosphere that reminded you at every moment that what you were doing mattered. Accordingly, you had to do your job to the best of your abilities, so that it mattered. You just had no right to approach it in any other way. So what I took away from all of that was the reality when you are in the midst of people who really know how to do something right, and they continually strive to be the best, then that has a profound effect on everyone else. Playing in Montreal was about being the best. When you are surrounded by people who are the best at what they do and who know that if they don't find the best in themselves they will suffer. When you are the best at what you do and you don't win, it's your fault and you know it. You can't deny the feeling and you can't argue it. Collectively, we all wanted to be the very best."

Ken Dryden
Montreal 1971, 1973, 1976, 1977, 1978, and 1979

"The biggest thing for me was just the realization of just how difficult it is to do, to win it. You also need a lot of good fortune as well. I have been to four Stanley Cup Finals with three different teams, and it wasn't until the fourth time that it all came together and we won it. So it teaches you just how fleeting things can be. It's humbling."

Chuck Fletcher
Pittsburgh 2009 (Assistant GM)

"Nothing comes easy. Winning the Stanley Cup isn't easy, that's for sure. Anything that you really, really want in life you have to fight for and you have to work hard for. It's tough enough just doing your job out there, but then to realize that there are a bunch of guys on the other team that are trying to kill you in the process, well, that makes your job even harder! In hockey, those players who reach that level practice nonstop and are constantly working on not only improving their games, but also on the fundamentals—which are so important."

Peter Forsberg
Colorado 1996 and 2001

"Two things. First, for me it's all about the team. I wouldn't be anywhere without my 19 teammates helping me pull the wagon. Personally, I could never have played an individual sport. I needed that camaraderie. They made all of those fights and battles along the way worthwhile because we did it together. You can't even consider individual accolades when you talk about the Stanley Cup; your team's success is a total team effort. Second, thick skin was a big thing too. I learned how to be able to deal with setbacks and turn them into positives. It was the same thing when I got into the financial business after hockey. There were many days where I didn't want to go to work. I wasn't used to sitting behind a desk. I wasn't used to being on the phone for 12 hours a day making cold calls trying to talk to people I didn't know. Facing all of that rejection, day in and day out, it was tough. We had the same thing in hockey too, but you learned how to deal with it, and you learned how to turn those negatives into positives in order to become successful. Of course it was always nice in hockey to be able to beat the crap out of somebody every now and then too, to relieve a little stress—something I gotta say I missed once I got into the real world!"

Clark Gillies
New York Islanders 1980, 1981, 1982, and 1983

"Hard work. Plain and simple. There is just no substitute, especially for a guy like me who isn't necessarily blessed with incredible skills. I just have to work extra hard on my game, both on and off the ice. That's the biggest life lesson for me."

Alex Goligoski
Pittsburgh 2009

"I learned that there are going to be ups and downs along the way, like a roller coaster, but if you stay committed to something and work hard, then anything is possible."

Scott Gomez
New Jersey 2000 and 2003

"To me it was the preparation and dedication that was required in order to win it. The same is true in life and in business; if you want to be successful you have to have those same traits. I would also say perseverance is important too, to not get too discouraged when you lose along the way. To win it is such a grind, and you are going to have ups and downs. So to keep steady and to be able to rebound after a bad night is really important too."

Butch Goring
New York Islanders 1980,
1981, 1982, and 1983

"I've learned a lot from winning, especially how you will always accomplish more as a team than you ever will as an individual."

Bill Guerin
New Jersey 1995 and
Pittsburgh 2009

"Winning the Stanley reaffirmed for me what it means to work hard; what it means to conduct yourself as a true professional every day of your career; and what it means to sacrifice of yourself for your teammates. You know, after I won it I reflected back on what I had accomplished and really thought hard about it. I kept thinking about what if I had never won a Cup? Would my career have been complete? Everybody kept telling me that now that I had won it after all those years, that my career was 'now complete.' Well, looking back, I guess I don't really agree with that. Sure, I am sure that there are a lot of veteran players who have played 10, 15, or 20 seasons and never had the chance to win one who feel that their careers were incomplete. I get that. But I truly think that it should be just the opposite. If you really conduct yourself a certain way throughout your career, as a professional, and you are respected by your teammates for how you played the game day in and day out, then ultimately those are the things that matter in the end. That's what the NHL teaches you. Win or lose, if you play the game the right way, then you should have nothing to feel incomplete about when it's all said and done. In my eyes it's much more about the journey and about the life lessons along the way."

Bret Hedican
Carolina 2006

"To me it wasn't so much about winning the Cup but more about what I learned from the guys on that team. What a great bunch of teammates, so many outstanding players: Kirk Muller, Guy Carbonneau, Patrick Roy, John LeClair, Brian Bellows, and Mike Keane. Just to see how those guys handled themselves both on and off the ice was pretty eye opening for me, especially as a rookie. They taught me more about life than they did about hockey, and I will always remember that."

Sean Hill
Montreal 1993

"I learned that you need to attack your goals with a sense of urgency. You need to realize that the window for certain opportunities in your life is so small and comes around so rarely that if you wait around for it, it may never come to fruition. I figured I would win a whole bunch of Stanley Cups after winning that first one, as players we all feel that sort of confidence. But it doesn't always work that way, in hockey or in life. So you have to take advantage of those unique situations when you can, otherwise you are going to have regrets later on. You can't just say, 'It'll happen some day,' because it may not. You have to live in the now and seize the moment. If something is really important to you, then you gotta go for it a hundred percent. It's 10 years later and I'm still waiting to win another Cup. Who knows if I'll ever get another chance?"

Dan Hinote
Colorado 2001

"*Perseverance* is the first word that comes to mind. The second would be to believe, and the third would be to work as a team. If you can do those things then you can accomplish anything in life."

Rejean Houle
Montreal 1971, 1973, 1977, 1978, and 1979

"For me it's just to focus on the little things. Even though you may not be able to score a goal or get an assist every game, you can still do something that will help the team each night—a big pass, a big check, or maybe even getting into a fight. If everybody works hard and contributes in whatever way they can for the betterment of the team, then great things can happen."

Tony Hrkac
Dallas 1999

"Looking back, I suppose the biggest things I learned from winning it were a) that you should never take anything for granted, and b) it takes bloody hard work to win something as valuable and as memorable as the Cup."

Bobby Hull
Chicago 1961

"As a coach now, I can tell you that I learned about leadership as a member of the Edmonton Oilers. In my opinion it's so important to have your natural leaders as the captains of your team, not necessarily your top players. There is a big difference. Great players don't always make great leaders. In Edmonton we had both, and that was a big reason why I think we were so successful. Great leaders get everybody involved. Even though I was a role player, the '20th man' on the roster, as I used to consider myself, the leaders on the team made me feel very, very important. I really appreciated that, and as a result I wanted to work hard for them."

Don Jackson
Edmonton 1984 and 1985

"I learned that if you work hard enough and long enough at something then you can achieve it. You need to be stubborn about it too, you have to get it in your mind that you are going to do it, and then you have to hold yourself accountable to it. Once you do that, then anything is possible."

Nikolai Khabibulin
Tampa Bay 2004

"I learned that there is no one right way to accomplish your goal. I took a sort of roundabout way to get to the NHL, going the college route, but I made it. I was sort of a late bloomer, but there were some goals that I had set for myself that I wanted to achieve along the way. Some people questioned that early on, but I certainly have no regrets. To be able to get my degree and now have two

Stanley Cups under my belt just seven years into my career, I think I took the right path. I just never took my eyes off of my goal of making it in the NHL, and fortunately it has worked out for me."

Chris Kunitz
Anaheim 2007 and Pittsburgh 2009

"To me, raising the Cup meant that anything is possible. To have that dream as a kid and then to finally achieve it is so fulfilling. Afterward I truly believed that anything I put my mind to and really wanted to do, I could do. It was all about hard work, that was it. If you are willing to work hard and put in the time, then almost anything can be achieved in life. To be able to be in a position to win it, you have to be able to work through adversity too because it's not a cake walk to win the Cup. I think of the old cliché 'tough times don't last but tough people do,' and I think that really sums it up. You have to be tough, and you have to be able to persevere through a lot of adversity. If you continue to work hard, then things will get better eventually. I have been able to apply that to my life after hockey, no question. Chemistry is a big part of it as well. It is hard to define, but to actually experience it is pretty special. It happens when the top guys on the first line are pulling for the role players on the fourth line and visa versa. So from top to bottom you have an environment where everybody truly cares about each other—not only as hockey players, but as human beings. When teams have chemistry—and it is not easy to achieve—amazing things can happen."

Mike Lalor
Montreal 1986

"For me it is the belief that if you want something badly enough and you are willing to work for it, you can accomplish anything. Beyond that, I learned that in order to be successful in hockey or in life, you have to have a good group of people around you. You may not necessarily enjoy working with all of those people, but you have to be able to work together in a constructive way. Once that happens, anything is possible."

Jamie Langenbrunner
Dallas 1999 and New Jersey 2003

"To me it's the willingness to never give up. Sure, there are going to be ups and downs, but you gotta keep plugging away and going into the corners. It's not always fun, and you have to pay a price, but that's what it takes if you want to be successful. And you gotta play through pain because if you can't go, then somebody else is going to take your job. So you can just never, ever give up."

Dave Langevin
New York Islanders 1980,
1981, 1982, and 1983

"It's all about focus. Winning the Cup is so demanding both physically as well as mentally. It is so draining to go through the regular season and then the postseason. Each playoff game is like a mini-battle in the war. You win some and you lose some, but you have to stay positive. You can't get too high and you can't get too low—you just have to stay steady, otherwise you won't make it. Sure, you get those adrenaline rushes when you score big goals or win big games, but you can't get completely depressed when you lose in double overtime either. It's really a grind, and only the strongest survive."

Martin Lapointe
Detroit 1997 and 1998

"Winning the Stanley Cup teaches you about sacrifice, about how to stay focused on a goal, and about having to pay attention to every little detail."

Igor Larionov
Detroit 1997, 1998, and 2002

"The biggest thing for me is the fact that you really never know when opportunities will come, so when they do you had better take advantage of it. You just never know in life. When Scotty passed away after we won that first Cup, it was just unbelievable. I'm so glad he was able to go out on top the way he did, but what a tragedy that was. It really makes you think about how short life really is and about how you have to make the most of your opportunities when they present themselves. Beyond that, I learned that you have to give it your all so that you will have no regrets. I would have felt just horrific had we not won the Cup for Bob in 1992. So if there is a silver lining at all, it was that he went out on top of his game."

Troy Loney
Pittsburgh 1992 and 1993

"Work ethic is the thing that stands out for me. You won't achieve much in life without making a commitment to it and working hard. You have to make sacrifices if you want to get ahead in hockey and in business; it's the same thing. You are going to be faced with obstacles along the way, but you just have to deal with them as they come and keep working hard if you want to have success. In my opinion the difference between winners and losers is the way that they deal with those challenges that come up."

Kevin McClelland
Edmonton 1984, 1985,
1987, and 1988

"To me it's about how community goals are celebrated much more than individual goals. The thing that really stands out to me about that team was how everybody accepted their role on the team and just made the best of it. I am sure some guys could have been higher in the lineup on different teams or in different situations, but they accepted it and made the best of it in order to put the team first. That selflessness was contagious, and everybody just bought into it. We were a team in every sense, and everybody's collective sacrifice was the big reason we won it that year."

Brian MacLellan
Calgary 1989

"Respect is the big thing. You have to play with respect, and you have to earn the respect of your teammates. You depend so much on your fellow players, and it really takes a team effort to win a championship. I am a senator in Canada now, and the correlations between hockey and politics are similar for sure. At the end of the day to be successful in both you have to be able to work with people, and you have to be able to help those who depend on you. So you learn the value of teamwork and about being able to work together with others—regardless of your personal opinions. Beyond that, you have to be humble and appreciative. You know, there have been so many great players who have deserved to have won the Stanley Cup, but for whatever the reason were not able to do so. So I don't take anything for granted. I really appreciate the opportunities I was given and am just very grateful that I was able to have the kind of career that I did. I certainly couldn't have done so without so many great teammates and coaches though. No way. I was very fortunate, absolutely."

Frank Mahovlich
Toronto 1962, 1963, 1964, and 1967; Montreal 1971 and 1973

"The big thing for me is to just never give up. You never know how the momentum can swing in this game, and that's what makes it so exciting. You can be down three goals one minute and up three the next. If you stay positive, work hard, focus on the fundamentals, and have faith, then anything is possible I think."

Dave Maley
Montreal 1986

"I think it would have to be to appreciate the moment. Beyond that, it would be just plain old hard work and patience. If you can do all of them, then good things will eventually happen for you."

Greg Malone
Pittsburgh 1992 and 1993 (Scout)

"I learned that you can push yourself harder and farther than you ever thought you could. There are times in your life in whatever you are doing where you think I can't go anymore; I can't do anymore, but you just have to realize that you can always dig deeper and find a little more to give. That's the difference between winning and losing, right there, that little bit more. I mean, to win a Stanley Cup you have to go through the preseason, an 82-game regular season, and then four grueling rounds in the playoffs. By the end you are so mentally and physically exhausted that you can't even see straight. When it's all said and done though, you look back, and you realize that if you hadn't pushed yourself and played through adversity, it may not have happened for you. So when you can stick with something and stay positive and truly believe in what it is you are trying to accomplish, then anything is possible."

Todd Marchant
Anaheim 2007

"As it applies to business, I think the biggest thing for me is confidence. To know in the back of your mind that you were a part of a championship at that level means a lot. People always ask me about it, and I am very proud of it. I also think it helps you because people want to associate with others who have been a part of something like that. I mean, even though my role on that team was pretty minor, I was a part of it—which means a lot. I still work in the world of hockey today so to be able to be a part of that elite fraternity of players who have won it, it carries a lot of weight—especially with the younger guys who are just coming up."

Chris McAlpine
New Jersey 1995

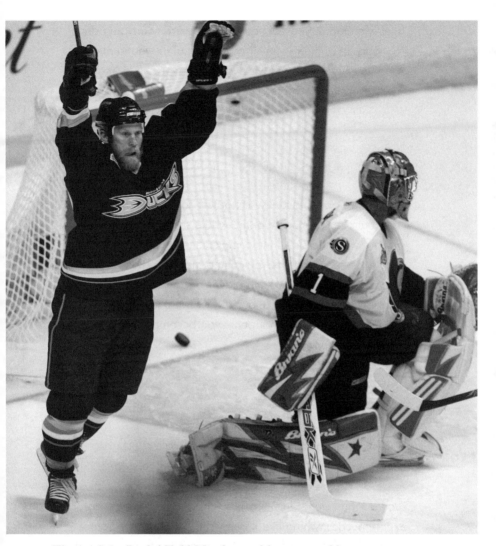

The Anaheim Ducks' Todd Marchant celebrates a goal by teammate Francois Beauchemin during Game 5 of the 2006–07 Stanley Cup Finals against Ottawa.

"I learned that if you put your mind toward something and you work at it, then you will be successful in whatever you do in life. Slackers don't win. You gotta work hard, really hard. That's the secret to success."

Ab McDonald
Montreal 1958, 1959,
and 1960; Chicago 1961

"For me it's about focus. And not just come playoff time, but over the course of the whole season. Eventually you start to understand the complexities of management putting the team together by getting the right chemistry of players. The roles of each player became much more magnified as you better understand what it takes to win at this level. Once that happens, you become a much better professional."

Marty McSorley
Edmonton 1987 and 1988

"I think the biggest thing for me was to realize just how much, mentally and physically, the body can take. To go 82 games and then go for another two months at such a high level of intensity is so draining. I have never experienced anything like it in my life. Nothing can compare to it. After a while, though, you realize that if you just hang in there, stay strong, and do your best, then anything is possible."

Mike Modano
Dallas 1999

"Winning the Stanley Cup gives you a confidence about yourself. It just reaffirms the fact that if you can persevere through all that adversity along the way, then you will be rewarded at the other end. Championship teams are different from other teams. When we were in the midst of winning those four straight Stanley Cups, we had achieved a level of confidence in ourselves that was totally unique. Teams that have won it have a certain air about them, almost like an air of invincibility. They have been there, they have been through it, and they know what to expect. Once you have achieved that and can just focus on the task at hand versus all of the other stuff, then winning becomes much easier."

Ken Morrow

New York Islanders 1980,
1981, 1982, and 1983

"The biggest thing I took away was to just really embrace the concept of focusing on what you do, not the result. What I mean by that is you shouldn't go out and try to score a goal; you should do all the little things that will eventually lead up to scoring a goal. So you really have to focus on the task at hand versus looking ahead at what the reward might be."

Kirk Muller

Montreal 1993

"You really learn a lot about yourself when you win the Cup. I know it's cliché, but you learn about commitment, about being a good teammate, about trust, about sacrifice, about hard work, and about what it takes to become a champion. You learn about how great things can happen when everyone decides to pull the same way, in the same direction. When it all comes together in the end and you are standing there with the Stanley Cup, that's what it's all about."

Joe Nieuwendyk
Calgary 1989, Dallas 1999,
and New Jersey 2003

"Winning the Cup teaches you so much about life. You learn firsthand about teamwork, character, sacrifice, and hard work. You learn pretty quickly that you can't get any-where alone."

Bob Nystrom
New York Islanders 1980,
1981, 1982, and 1983

"Sacrifice. I realized that sometimes you just gotta suck it up and play if it's important to you. After we won it I remember looking around at my teammates; they looked like the walk-ing wounded. The cuts, the bruises, the scrapes, the stitches, the wounds, the black eyes—it was crazy. Playoff hockey is such a grind, and when you're done you're literally exhausted. It's more of a sense of relief when it's over than anything else because your body can't physically take any more. So when you look at the Canadiens and Islanders and Oilers, those dynasty teams, you really have to tip your hat to those guys for being able to do that year in and year out. I personally couldn't even imagine going through that four years in a row. It's pretty impressive."

Joel Otto
Calgary 1989

What was your role on that Stanley Cup team?

"My role as a power forward was to get into the corners, forecheck hard, and to be around the net as much as possible to set up plays. Everybody's roles on that particular team overlapped. No one was above back-checking; no one was above blocking shots; no one was above going into the corners. Everybody did the little things, which collectively added up to big things. Nobody was doing anything just for himself, it seemed like. I mean, if we were up 3–1, then the purpose was to not score goals, but for everybody to play defense. It is kind of like the salmon swimming upstream together. That was us that year, all together, and that was why we played with so much confidence and were so difficult to beat."

Brian Bellows
Montreal 1993

"I learned about being a character guy and that you don't have to be a superstar to make it in the NHL. I was a fourth-line guy, and I understood my role on the team. I wasn't looked at to score goals; I was there to protect my teammates. I embraced it and they appreciated that, which made me feel great. There are a lot of working parts to the overall puzzle, and although my part wasn't very big, it was important for me to do my job so that my teammates would be able to do theirs. Beyond that, I learned a whole heck of a lot about the power of attitude, work ethic, and about never quitting. If you have those things, you can do incredible things."

George Parros
Anaheim 2007

"I think it's about trying to stay steady and just keeping it all in perspective. Look, the Stanley Cup is the hardest trophy to win in sports, no question. You're playing every other night. You're traveling. Emotionally you're a mess. Physically you are beat up and can hardly keep weight on because you're so exhausted. There are so many momentum swings. Your range of emotions is off the charts too because one minute you're on a huge high from winning an overtime thriller, then depressed the next minute from losing an overtime heartbreaker. The parity in the league is unbelievable too; I mean, anybody truly can win on any given night. You see No. 8 seeds beating No. 1s all the time, so you can never get too confident. While all of this is going on you have to try to keep it all in perspective. Sometimes it's truly overwhelming, but you have to try to stay steady. You just can't get too high or too low; you'll never make it to the end in one piece."

Mike Peluso
New Jersey 1995

"The big thing for me, I think, is to set your goals high, even if you don't think they are reachable or attainable at the time. If you work hard and you are determined then eventually your goals will become a reality for you. It takes a lot of sacrifice along the way, but if it is really important to you then it'll be worth it."

Frank Pietrangelo
Pittsburgh 1991

"The big thing I learned from being on that team was to just stay focused. No matter what happened that year, whether we had a guy get injured or we lost a bad game by six goals, we never lost focus of our goal—and that was to win the Stanley Cup. We were so even-keeled that year. We just sort of had this 'roll with the punches' attitude where nothing was going to phase us or deter us from our ultimate goal. We even had a mantra: nothing else matters. It was like we had the ultimate purpose. When things didn't go our way and obstacles arose, guys would just step up and assume different roles to help out. We had a lot of selfless guys on that team. In fact, I think there were 10 guys who were captains on that team—either with Dallas or with other teams. As a result, they weren't afraid to stand up and say something if they felt strongly about it. It created a very open dialogue among us, and that was very unique. So to have that kind of leadership on your roster is just huge."

Derek Plante
Dallas 1999

"I think the thing for me was that you don't have to be friends with everybody, but as teammates you have to be able to pull together at key times. It's the same in business. You just have to find ways to get along for the good of the team. We had a lot of big egos on that team, but we all managed to get along and come together for that common goal of winning the Cup. There is a lot of pressure to win it every year in Montreal too, way more so than any other franchise in the league. So for everyone to put their differences aside and come together was a really important factor in why that team won that season. That requires a lot of discipline and sacrifice, but that's what it takes to become a champion. Again, it's no different in the real world. There are times when you might want to do certain things, but you have to sacrifice that in order to make it work for your family or your company or whomever."

Larry Pleau
Montreal 1971 and New York Rangers
1994 (Assistant GM)

"Three things come to mind. First, you have to be smart enough to know that you're not that smart and surround yourself with great people. I try to surround myself today with great people, who in turn make me better. They are the ones who help me with my charitable foundation and with my business; without them I would be lost. Second, you have to have a passion and a love for what you do. Third, you have to be willing to work harder than the next guy in order to accomplish your goals. Those are my big takeaways from winning the Stanley Cup that I have been able to translate into my life after hockey."

Shjon Podein
Colorado 2001

"For me it was pretty simple: work hard and be patient...because you just never know when your opportunity will come. I was really fortunate to get my name on the Cup as the result of a last-minute call-up in the conference semifinals against the Islanders. Rejean Houle had gotten injured, and Scotty Bowman brought me in from the team's minor league affiliate in Nova Scotia to take his spot on the roster. I got to play alongside Bob Gainey and Doug Jarvis, which was pretty exciting for a rookie out of

Hibbing, Minnesota. Montreal was a dynasty team at the time, winning four straight Stanley Cups from 1976 to 1979, so it was a pretty big thrill to be chosen like that—especially considering the fact that they had four No. 1 draft picks that they could have selected ahead of me. Heck, I was never even drafted, but Scotty was after a certain type of player, and I apparently fit the bill. That's how Montreal was in those days, they didn't care where you came from or how high you were drafted, if you could help the team and could play a specific role then you were given a shot. One of the requirements to getting your name on the Cup is that you have to play at least one shift in the finals, and fortunately I was able to do so that year against the Boston Bruins, whom we swept in four straight to win it that year. To drink champagne out of the Cup afterward in the locker room with all of those Hall of Famers on that team was a moment I will always remember; what a moment that was. To be honest, I always felt kind of sheepish about getting my name on the Cup that way, especially when I think of guys like Jean Ratelle, who played 19 years for the Rangers and Bruins and never won one. That's hockey, though, and sometimes that's how it goes in a team sport like this, where you have to rely on 20 or so teammates to win a championship. On a side note, I later came close to winning another Cup in 1981 as a member of the North Stars, but we lost to the Islanders in the finals that year. So the life lesson for me was that if you just work hard, pay your dues, keep your nose clean, keep the faith, and don't feel sorry for yourself, then eventually good things will happen for you. It won't go unnoticed. Hey, the same is true in the real world too. You can't forget, the cream always rises to the top. Always."

Mike Polich
Montreal 1977

"Confidence. When we won it in Tampa Bay in 2004 a lot of people were doubting us. A lot. They simply didn't think we could do it. I can tell you this, though, in our dressing room we *never* doubted ourselves. Never. We believed in ourselves, and it simply never crossed our minds that we weren't going to win it."

Nolan Pratt
Colorado 2001 and
Tampa Bay 2004

"Perseverance. It's the old cliché: it's not a sprint but a marathon. Each game of each round is a battle. You can't get too high when you win or too low when you lose, you just have to remain steady and not get too ahead of yourself. So certainly that same logic applies to the real world as well with regard to not looking too far into the future but rather first focusing on accomplishing the task at hand."

Rob Ramage
Calgary 1989 and Montreal 1993

"There are so many clichés surrounding what success really is these days. But one of the things that is very apparent is that it rarely happens by accident. To win the Stanley Cup you have to go through an 82-game schedule and then play at the highest level for another two and half months of playoff hockey—which is such a grind. When the playoffs start it's a totally different mind-set. It's two and a half months of living like a monk. You play, you sleep, you wake up, you have a training meal, you practice, you sleep, you wake up, you play, and then you do it all over again. You become so aware of everything you put into your body, everything you thought about, and how you took care of your body.

"In 1994 we had two of our four playoff series go to seven games, with a couple of games going into double overtime. To survive all of that, to stay healthy and focused, requires a lot of preparation as well as a little bit of luck. Aside from that, you have to be able to get past tough losses almost immediately. You can't dwell on that stuff, it will kill you. Great teams can overcome tough losses and rebound the next night. It requires discipline and it's tough, both mentally as well as physically, but it's paramount to success. You have to be internally motivated at this level; that is what separates those who have success and those who don't. Skill only gets you so far in this game, it requires perseverance, dedication, and focus—all things that you learn over time. Make no mistake, though, they are absolutely vital to success—not just success in hockey either, but in life.

"The satisfaction is proportional to how difficult it is too. Nothing is given to you in this league, nothing. You have to work so hard, day in and day out. You have to apply yourself with everything you have or else you can not expect anything to go your way. That's when it becomes so compelling, when you are pushed to your limit, and then you have to push just a little bit farther. That is the difference, right there, between winning and not winning the Stanley Cup. The real satisfaction for me was being able to make those sacrifices for my teammates and being able to overcome those challenges. Putting yourself physically and emotionally at risk, that is when you grow as a player and grow as a person. To be able to perform at such a high level, consistently and with intensity, is so demanding. You have to be able to learn how to control what you can control: how hard you work, how much discipline you bring to your game, and how you prepare. You can't control anything else out there; you just have to trust your teammates and coaches and believe that they will do the same. Winning a championship is a fantastic thing, but being pushed in order to fulfill your potential is really the more satisfying thing at the end of the day."

Mike Richter
New York Rangers 1994

"In hockey and in business you have the top guys, you have the middle guys, and you have the low-end guys. The top guys have to set the table and score goals, but they can't do their jobs unless the middle and low-end guys do theirs. The point being that it takes everybody to do their job, regardless of the role, for the team to have success. We had Mario Lemieux on those two Stanley Cup teams, arguably the best player in the game at the time, but he wouldn't have been able to do a thing out there had it not been for the third- and fourth-line guys who went into the corners and made the sacrifices for the betterment of the team."

Gordie Roberts
Pittsburgh 1991 and 1992

"The big takeaway for me about that year was about how everybody needs to buy into the same system. It has to be a team effort. I have been on other teams over my career where it hasn't been that way, and this was usually the reason why. In fact I have been on other teams that were better talentwise than that '95 Devils team but fared much worse. So if you have everybody working together and all focused on the same goal, then that is the recipe for success—both on and off the ice."

Brian Rolston
New Jersey 1995

"The biggest life lesson for me is that if you work hard and make sacrifices for your team, then you will get rewarded. My story of how I got my name on the Cup is rather unique, to say the least. It started the year before, around the end of March 1985, when I had just finished playing out my senior season at Providence College. The Canadiens, who had drafted me, called and said that they wanted to sign me for the final few games of the year. I was thrilled. Here I was about to get to play with guys like Larry Robinson and Bob Gainey, guys I had looked up to as a 13-year-old kid. So I told my agent that I would love to sign a contract. The only stipulation, however, was the fact that I was getting married on April 13. So I told him that before I signed the contract I needed him to make sure that it was going to be okay for me to be excused that day should the team advance into the playoffs. Yeah, yeah, sure, sure, no problem. Right? Well, I headed up there and played in the last three games of the season. They wanted me to stick around for the playoffs, which was great, but it also meant that I was going to be cutting it close with my wedding. Luckily for me, our first-round opponent was none other than the Boston Bruins, and Boston was not too far from where my wedding was. Fully expecting the whole day off, I was instead told to enjoy my wedding day, and they would look forward to seeing me in uniform that night. I was just happy that I didn't have to miss my own wedding, which would not have gone over too well with my wife—believe me! So I got married, cut the cake, did the dance, and then ran off to the game—complete with a state trooper escort from the reception to Boston Garden. I showed up with my tux on and ran down to get dressed. I was so nervous to play in my first-ever playoff game, but the adrenaline took over, and I wound up scoring a goal on my very first shift. Well, that sacrifice by me didn't go unnoticed by management. They appreciated it, and they rewarded me the following year when they did something pretty amazing. You see, to get your name on the Stanley Cup, you have to play in at least 40 regular-season games *or* at least one game in the finals, not just the playoffs, but the finals. Well, I got hurt midway through the season and wound up playing only 38 games. I then sat out our entire playoff run until Game 5 of the finals against Calgary. Behind our rookie goalie Patrick Roy, we won 4–3 that night to clinch the Cup, and I was in the lineup. Wow. Our coach, Jean Perron, and our GM Serge Savard, the guy who drafted me, rewarded me that night in a way I never could have imagined: I got to hoist the Cup afterward with my teammates, and it remains one of the greatest thrills of my life. What a statement! I will never forget it for as long as I live."

Steve Rooney
Montreal 1986

"There is a fine line between winning and losing in this game, and in my opinion it comes down to the little things, like perseverance. That's the one word that comes to mind for me, *perseverance*. I believe that if you persevere and

pay your dues in hockey or in life, then good things will
eventually happen to you. It's easy to give up and quit, but
champions persevere and keep going even when they
don't want to. If you do that, then you will have no regrets
when it's all said and done. I always tried to prepare
myself as best as I could; I respected the game; I believed
in myself; and I always played hard. That was it. I never
wanted to show any weaknesses, and I always stood up
tall. I wanted my teammates to know that they could
always count on me, no matter what. Whether I was
injured or just down, I wanted them to know that I had
their backs. So, if you do those things, and you can persevere, then you have a great chance for success I think."

Patrick Roy
Montreal 1986 and 1993,
Colorado 1996 and 2001

"Winning the Cup was certainly a gift, but the pursuit of it
was the life lesson in my eyes. I would also say that even if
I hadn't ever won it, it wouldn't any less justify my commitment and dedication to that pursuit. I mean, what if I
wasn't on the 'right team' or I wasn't in the 'right place at
the right time?' Would I say that all of that hard work
wasn't worth it? Of course not. So I was very fortunate to
have worked hard and was rewarded by being a part of
three incredible Stanley Cup–winning teams."

Brendan Shanahan
Detroit 1997, 1998, and 2002

"I think you learn more from your failures than from your successes. I remember when I was with Minnesota in 1981 and losing to the Islanders in the finals. I had a terrible feeling afterward that we hadn't given it our best. We were the underdogs that year from the get-go, having to start out each series on the road in Boston—a place where we had never won before in our franchise's history. We battled them, literally, and were thrilled to finally get that monkey off our backs and get a well-deserved series sweep. From there we knocked off Buffalo, followed by Calgary, until we made it to the finals, where we had to face the defending champion New York Islanders, a team that was about to win number two of four straight Stanley Cups. Going in I got the feeling that we all sort of thought, 'Hey, if we don't win it this year we'll win it next year.' All of our best players were in their early twenties, and we figured this was probably going to be the first of many, many trips to the finals. We had this 'we're just happy to be here' kind of attitude, and that was exactly how we played. It was extremely disappointing to lose that year.

"Flash-forward five years later, and I am now a member of the Montreal Canadiens. It is the night before we open the finals against Calgary, and we are in the hotel at a team meeting. Our coach, Jean Perron, is addressing us. He says that because there are several players on the roster who have already won Stanley Cups that it would be nice if they would say a few words. So Bob Gainey says something, followed by Larry Robinson, and Mario Tremblay. It was great, very motivational. Then when they were done, I asked Jean if I could have the floor for a moment to please address the team. He agreed. With that, I stood up and said, 'Gentlemen, I am the only guy in this room who has been to the Stanley Cup Finals…and didn't win. So we should play tomorrow as if we were all going to retire next week. That should be our attitude going in, because I can guarantee you without a doubt that not everybody in this room is going to get a chance to win again…and maybe none of us will.' Needless to say, we beat Calgary four games to one to win the Cup. Coach Perron even wrote a book afterward and wrote in it that a big reason why we won that season was because of my speech, which really got through to our guys. That meant a lot. It's interesting to note too that I got back to the finals yet again in both 1989 and 1991, only to lose both times. So I guess you just never know in this game. When you have your chance you better go for it, because you just never know. That's why the Stanley Cup is the most elusive trophy in all of sports, it's just so tough to win it."

Bobby Smith
Montreal 1986

"Winning the Cup made me realize that the team is bigger than the individual, and the individual's success comes from team success. The old adage 'the harder you work, the luckier you get' really resonates with me for this too. Winning the Cup taught me about how when you work hard, good things will happen. It also taught me about perseverance, about being a good teammate, about humility, about how to deal with adversity, and about never giving up. Everybody had a role on those teams, and regardless of the size of that role it was important to the overall success of the team. There was a reason we won all those Cups—we had a group of players and coaches who all believed in these things and worked hard to achieve them."

Steve Smith
Edmonton 1987, 1988, and 1990

"Discipline. That was the big thing for me. Without it you can't accomplish very much, but with it you can do anything. After that, it's about working together with your teammates as a unit. There's no room for anybody to be selfish in hockey, and teams that are able to win it all do so with unselfish players. That was what we had in Pittsburgh those two years, a bunch of unselfish, disciplined players."

Kevin Stevens
Pittsburgh 1992 and 1993

"I learned about what plain old hard work can do for you. Sure, it takes talent and it takes getting a couple of breaks along the way, but without working your tail off it will never happen. When you realize what you can accomplish together as a member of a team, when everybody has one goal, that is a pretty powerful thing. Hockey isn't an individual game; it's the ultimate team sport that requires everybody to come together and to work hard. That's what it's all about."

Gary Suter
Calgary 1989

"When you win a championship you earn that label of being a winner, and that is life changing. It changes your mind-set, and it gives you confidence both on and off the ice. People respect you and want to associate themselves with you too, which is very humbling. Then the more known and respected you are, the more things you can do with that, such as charity work or even being looked up to by young kids who emulate you as a winner. It opens doors for you, and you can parlay it into other things. You just have to make sure you choose the *right* things and the *right* people to associate with, otherwise it can get you into trouble."

Max Talbot
Pittsburgh 2009

"I learned that there is just no substitute for hard work. Beyond that, I learned that when you are fortunate enough to be able to play with a group of guys who have the energy and the passion to win, and that you know you can trust, then anything is possible. I am in sales nowadays, and I think there were a lot of correlations between the two. You need the guys to be able to buy into a style or system, and that was what Al [Arbour] was able to do. He sold us on winning and we bought in. We believed in him, and because of that we were able to win four Stanley Cups. In sales too, every year your slate is wiped clean. You have to start over and hit your numbers all over again. The same is true in hockey, where you have to do it all over again and persevere."

John Tonelli
New York Islanders 1980,
1981, 1982, and 1983

"I have learned so many life lessons along the way. I learned about teamwork, about discipline, about setting and accomplishing goals, about learning to work with others, about accountability, about having strong mental fortitude, about friendships, and about having a deep commitment to something. I learned that when you apply all of those characteristics, then great things can happen. Sure, obstacles are going to come up, but as long as you work hard and follow your heart, then eventually you will find success. Stanley Cups are nice, but it all comes back to having passion. Hey, nobody has ever handed me a medal for being a dad, yet it's my favorite thing in life."

Bryan Trottier
New York Islanders 1980, 1981, 1982, and 1983;
Pittsburgh 1991 and 1992;
and Colorado 2001 (Assistant Coach)

"For me it was about persistence and never giving up on your dream. It took me 16 seasons to finally win the Stanley Cup, but I finally did it thanks to a whole lot of hard work and dedication to a sport I absolutely love. Beyond that, I would say that little things turn into big things. In hockey it's about all the little things, or details, that transpire through-out the course of a game. Whether it's a big hit or a faceoff win or winning a battle for a loose puck in your zone or sacrificing to block a shot—all of those little things add up. At the end of the day, those are the things that are often-times the difference between first and second place."

Pat Verbeek
Dallas 1999

"The big thing for me is to be well rounded, in hockey as well as in life. If you are a goal scorer, then I think you should work on your defense; if you are a defenseman, then you should work on scoring goals. Things like that are really important. You can't just be a one-dimensional person and have success; you have to be well rounded and wear many different hats."

Niclas Wallin
Carolina 2006

Steve Yzerman and his Red Wings teammates celebrate Detroit's first Stanley Cup since 1955 after sweeping the Flyers in the 1996–1997 Finals.

"Determination. It takes a lot of determination to reach your goals, whether they are in hockey or in life. To become a champion in hockey you have to pay a price. The Stanley Cup playoffs in general are really a test of your will. They are a test of your ability to stay strong and to deal with adversity. If you can do those things and persevere then you will be successful. It won't guarantee you a championship, but it will guarantee you an opportunity."

Steve Yzerman
Detroit 1997, 1998, and 2002

"My big takeaway was realizing that almost anything is achievable in life as long as everybody within the group is willing to subordinate their individual interests, goals, and agendas for the good of the group. Whether it's in hockey or in business, unless everybody on the team is committed to that, you will rarely, if ever, achieve success."

Bill Clement
Philadelphia 1974 and 1975

CHAPTER 3

Winning as a Team

There are reasons, specific reasons, as to why teams are fortunate enough to win the Stanley Cup: hard work, perseverance, timing, staying healthy, or even plain old luck. What's fascinating about that, however, is how those reasons vary from player to player. Each player sees that path to victory through his own unique pair of glasses. Those special intangibles, those difference makers, are oftentimes the difference between first and second place. Here is what some of the players had to say.

WHAT WAS SO SPECIAL ABOUT YOUR TEAM THAT ALLOWED YOU TO WIN THE STANLEY CUP THAT SEASON?

"We were so mentally strong that season. In fact, we won 10 playoff games in overtime during our Cup run that season, and that's an accomplishment that may never be repeated. Patrick Roy was amazing. What I learned from Patty Roy was that your leader has to be strong, and he has to be confident, yet he still has to be humble and down to earth enough to relate to everybody. I remember being in the locker room before one of our playoff games that season. Patty stood up and said, 'Boys, just get me one goal. They will not score tonight.' He didn't say it with a sense of cockiness either; he just said it very matter of factly. He led by example and we followed. He carried us that season, and it was pretty incredible. I remember being in a slump one time that season. I led the team with 40 goals, but I hadn't scored in like five or six games. I was pretty down. After practice one day he came over to me and said, 'Brian, don't get undressed. Let's go back onto the ice, and you can shoot pucks on me.' I was blown away. I mean, here is arguably the best goalie in the world, telling me he wants to stay after a really tough practice to work with me for an hour on the fundamentals. Patty knew that if we were going to win the Cup, then I needed to break out of my slump and get my confidence back. It is one thing for a teammate to say something to try to help you; it is entirely different when he actually means it and is willing to get dirty and work with you. Big difference. That's why he was such an amazing leader."

Brian Bellows
Montreal 1993

"I will never forget the day our coach, Robbie Ftorek, was let go. There were just eight games left in the regular season, and we were boarding a bus to play out on Long Island. Just as we were about to leave, our GM, Lou Lamoriello, came on board and said that he had to let Robbie go. He was not happy. We were shocked. Then he told us that the reason he was let go was pretty much on our shoulders. He told us that we were there to win the Stanley Cup. Period. That was our sole purpose, and anything short of that was not going to be accepted. Needless to say, we got the message. Our assistant coach, Larry Robinson, then took over, and from there we just went on a magical run through the postseason. Led by guys like Scott Stevens, Martin Brodeur, and Claude Lemieux, we really came together and rallied behind Larry. It was a huge wake-up call for us and really got the momentum swinging in our direction."

Brad Bombardir
New Jersey 2000

"For starters, we had a great group of individuals who put the team first. Beyond that, I think we were really hungry—especially the older veteran players such as myself who had never won it before. There was a sense of urgency for us, and I think the younger players responded to that. Players aside, though, I think that at the end of the day our group of guys just wanted it more than everybody else that season. It seemed like every series there was a huge moment that swung the momentum back for us. It looked like we were down and out so many different times, but we somehow were able to keep rallying back time after time. It's kind of like the old cliché 'it's just meant to be.' That was how I felt at times when things just kept going our way. It was incredible. Everything came together for us in the end, and thankfully we were the last team standing."

Rod Brind'Amour
Carolina 2006

"Winning the Cup is such a long process. It's months and months of extremely hard work. To go through the regular season and then to have to go through another couple of months in the playoffs, it's so draining. We had a magical season that year in Tampa; it was such a neat experience. I will never forget Game 7 of the finals against Calgary. We had a great pregame skate. We didn't need a pep talk. The focus was there, and you could just tell that the guys were ready to go. From there we went back and had our pregame meal. It was the same exact routine as the other 100 games we had played that year, except this time it was entirely different. The volume and the focus that day was turned up to just an incredible level. Nolan Pratt and I then headed back up to our hotel room to try to get in a pregame nap. Of course I couldn't sleep, though, being so nervous, and I looked over at Nolan, and he was wide awake too. So we got up and went down to our team room, where we had TVs, video games, and food. We walked in, and there were Marty St. Louis and Freddy Modin hanging out. A half hour later about 10 guys showed up, and an hour after that maybe 20 guys were in there. We were all so amped up, nobody could sleep. We all just sat around and talked, it was surreal. It was as if we knew we were going to win that night, I can't explain it. We then all got dressed and walked over to the arena. It was June, and I remember sweating through my suit because it was so hot and humid. I just remember thinking that we were not going to be denied that night. I had worked so hard and put in so much for so long, it just wasn't going to be an option. As I would later find out, most of my teammates felt exactly the same way. We were all so determined to win; it was unlike anything I had ever seen before. Sure enough, we came out on fire, and thanks to Ruslan Fedotenko's two goals we were able to jump out to a quick lead. Nikolai Khabibulin then played great down the stretch, and we were able to hold them off, 2–1, to win the franchise's first-ever Stanley Cup. What a feeling. I can't even imagine how those guys from Calgary felt on the plane ride home. I felt for them, I really did. If that were me, to have lost by one goal in Game 7 of the finals, I honestly can't even put it into words. Needless to say, it would be one very, very tough summer. I'm just glad we came out focused and finished the job we had started all those months earlier."

Ben Clymer
Tampa 2004

"One of the most important guys on our team that year was Mike Peluso, our enforcer. We had a lot of big-name stars on our roster, but without Mike I don't know if we could win it or not. His job was to not only protect his teammates out on the ice but also to keep guys in line. Teams that win the Stanley Cup have guys like Mike Peluso; they are really vital for the team's success. If someone got out of line, it was his job to straighten them out—for the betterment of the team. That wasn't an easy job, either. I remember one day in the locker room I was in there with Mike and Scott Stevens and Claude Lemieux. All of a sudden Scott and Claude just started going at it in the locker room like two bulls; they wanted to kill each other for whatever reason. Well, luckily Mikey broke it up and got them separated. Those guys were really competitive players, and sometimes those things happen, but out on the ice they were teammates, and they were all business. They put their differences aside and did what they could to help the team win. That was how it was on that team, the farther we went in the playoffs, the closer we got as teammates."

Jim Dowd
New Jersey 1995

"It was a really memorable season for a lot of reasons. For starters, it was a shortened season due to the lockout, and we really didn't get going until after the holidays, which was odd. I mean, we only wound up playing a 48-game schedule that year. So being locked out, that fall we had to practice every day on our own to try to stay in shape. Players would come and go and just try to stay upbeat and positive for when the season started. Nobody knew when it was going to get started, which was tough. It was even tougher for me because at the time I was the team's player rep, so I was right in the middle of that whole firestorm. As a result, it was my responsibility to keep all the players informed about what was going on with the collective bargaining agreement. It was stressful, but eventually we got things sorted out.

"We had a pretty good year, but we limped into the playoffs as the ninth seed, which meant we had to start out on the road against Boston. I can't explain what exactly clicked, but if I had to point to one single moment that season it would be at the practice just before we opened the first round of the playoffs against the Bruins. It was the most crisp practice that we had all year. Every pass was tape to tape, and the guys just seemed really confident. We went out and won that next night, and things just snowballed from there. Then, after beating Pittsburgh in round two, we met up with Philly in an extremely physical conference finals. Again we played great on the road, and from there we advanced on to the finals against Detroit. Luckily, we wound up playing our best hockey of the season when it mattered most, and we wound up sweeping the Red Wings to win the Cup. We were the ultimate road warriors that year, literally. In fact, we still hold the record to this day for the most wins on the road in the playoffs with 10, which still boggles my mind. It was just an unbelievable experience, to go through all of those tough years and then to finally hoist the Cup.

"Everybody played great, and we just had great chemistry. Guys like Neal Broten and Shawn Chambers, who were brought in that year, fit in really well, and each made big contributions. Then we had Claude Lemieux, who won the Conn Smythe that year after scoring 13 goals in the play-offs. Each one was big too, seemingly coming at key times in every game. It was incredible. We were a team built on four lines, which was huge too because we were always fresh. Our fourth line, the 'Crash Line,' with Bobby Holik, Randy McKay, and Mike Peluso, was without a doubt one of the greatest fourth lines in history. Their role was to go out there and forecheck and create havoc and just make it miserable for the other team. Those guys were tough too, really intimidating. Opposing players had to think twice about turning back to go get pucks deep into the zone, which created offensive opportunities for us. Thanks to those guys doing the dirty work, we just wore teams out.

"I will never forget when Mike Peluso got so caught up in the moment toward the end of Game 4, when we were about to win it, that he literally couldn't go out and play anymore. I mean, here is this huge tough guy, our enforcer, just weeping because he was so emotional. It was just an amazing sight; I will never forget it. It just showed Mike's heart and Mike's character. What a selfless player he was. He loved the game so much, and it meant so much for him to be able to win the Cup that he just lost it. It just hit him at that moment, that he was going to win the Stanley Cup after such a long journey, and it was just too overwhelming for him. What a sight, it was wonderful. I remember all of us just comforting him on the bench, to sort of shield him from the crowd in this really intimate, special moment. I will always treasure that memory."

Bruce Driver
New Jersey 1995

"Obviously it was a very talented hockey team with a lot of terrific young players on it—starting with Sidney Crosby and Evgeni Malkin, two of the league's top players. It was a three-year process. Over those three seasons what happened with that team was that it transformed from a collection of talented young hockey players into a team of talented, hardworking, purposeful hockey players. There were a lot of lessons learned over those three years, good and bad, and all of those players matured and learned the things that were necessary to compete and beat good hockey teams. It took more than talent, and once those guys figured that out, great things started to happen. They rose to the top pretty quickly too. I mean, three years before they had made the playoffs for the first time in many years and then lost in the first round. The next year they made it all the way to Game 6 of the Stanley Cup Finals, and then the following season they won it all. The way they did it too, coming back from being down two games to none against the Red Wings, it was just amazing. They had an outstanding coach too, in Dan Bylsma, who planted a lot of seeds that came to fruition on that June day in 2009. Dan is a very passionate person and was able to inject some enthusiasm and some optimism in that club. He and his staff were able to keep them focused on the task at hand, and thanks to a lot of hard work and preparation, they were able to get to that next level. So there was a process that everybody needed to go through

Young Penguins captain Sidney Crosby reacts with joy after being handed the Cup on June 12, 2009. Pittsburgh had just won a hard-fought seven-game series over Detroit.

in order to learn what it takes in terms of work ethic, commitment, defensive accountability, and controlling your emotions, to finally raise the challis.

"If I had to pick one defining moment from that team's Cup run, it would be in Game 6 against Philadelphia in the first round of the playoffs. We were up three games to two and really wanted to end it that night. The game was in Philly, and they were up 3–0 early, and it was looking like we were headed to Game 7. Midway through the game one of our players, Max Talbot, challenged Philadelphia's tough guy, Dan Carcillo, to a fight. Now Max was not a fighter, but he saw this as an opportunity to swing the momentum to pick up our guys. Well, Dan won the fight as expected, but Max's act of courage really motivated us, and sure enough we rallied back to win the game and the series. I think that really brought us together. Max was the spark-plug that crystallized our resolve, and we just went on from there. It showed that we weren't going to go meekly into the night and that we were prepared to stand and battle. Sometimes it is the most unlikely of heroes who will inspire others, and that night it was Max. It certainly had a lasting impact on the club."

Chuck Fletcher
Pittsburgh 2009 (Assistant GM)

"We went through a lot down the stretch that season, start-ing with our coach, Robbie Ftorek, being replaced by Larry Robinson with only eight games to go in the regular season. As a wide-eyed rookie at that point, I quickly real-ized that nobody's job was safe in this business. I mean, we were in first place at the time, but Mr. Lamoriello, our GM, wanted to make a change, and that was what he did. It was a huge wake-up call for us and we responded. We swept Florida in the first round and then started building momentum from there. We had so many great players on that team; it was just an incredible experience to be a part of it. We had a special bond, we really did."

Scott Gomez
New Jersey 2000 and 2003

"The first Cup in 1980 was tremendous, but the second one in 1981 has always had a little more value for me. I say that because I joined the team midway through the season in 1980 and didn't know the guys that well. The organization had gone through its share of hard times and setbacks in the years prior too, and I wasn't a part of that whole process. I mean, here I was coming in and joining this all-star lineup and winning the Cup right away, and getting all the gravy without having to pay my dues. So to win it again the next year was more meaningful to me personally because I was a part of it from start to finish. It was much more enjoyable, for sure. From there, winning the third and fourth were just incredible. To be a part of a dynasty like that is just indescribable."

Butch Goring
New York Islanders 1980, 1981,
1982, and 1983

"That team was all about hard work, about character, about teamwork, and about no egos. It was a brotherhood that we had, just a super special group of guys down there. We had all the ingredients to being champions that year, and fortunately it went our way. When we lost to Detroit in the 2002 finals I decided right then and there that I was going to re-sign with them. I just knew that this team had a chance to win. Four years later we accomplished our goal, and I couldn't have been happier or prouder."

Bret Hedican
Carolina 2006

"We had such a great team that year with so many solid players. They made it fun to come to the rink every day. The biggest thing, though, was Patrick Roy, who was just unbelievable for us in goal that season. He would basically tell us to worry about scoring goals and that he would take care of the rest. When you have a goaltender with that kind of attitude, it just rubs off on everybody. It's like the old saying 'confidence breeds confidence,' and he was the catalyst for all of that. Once the season got rolling along you could just sort of tell that good things were going to happen. We just gelled together as a team, and it all came together for us."

Sean Hill
Montreal 1993

"We had such a tight-knit group that season. I had been on tight-knit teams before, but this was different because this time we were surrounded by Hall of Fame players. Now, usually when you have a bunch of superstars on a team you would expect there to be a bunch of huge egos. These are people who have always been the very best players on their teams, so one would expect there to be conflicts and politics and drama. Not here. It was crazy. None of these guys was like that at all, and we're talking about a who's who of the hockey world that season: Joe Sakic, Peter Forsberg, Ray Bourque, Patrick Roy, and Rob Blake. These guys were the ultimate team players, completely selfless. No egos whatsoever. And as much as everyone wanted so badly to win the Cup for Ray, it was never about any one individual that year. It was never about him, and he would never want it to be about him. No way. All Ray did was to give us that one thing that we could grasp in our quest for the Cup. He just made it that much more real. Here was a guy who had spent his whole career being one of the best, if not *the* best defensemen, to play the game. Well, he came to us in his last season because he so desperately wanted to win a Stanley Cup. We were like, 'Wow, one of the best ever believes in us, so we need to step it up and deliver this season.' So for a team to be that tight knit and that good at the same time was very rare. There was so much pressure on us to win that year, too. I mean, we were the favorites from day one. Yet we played at an extremely high level from game No. 1 all the way to game No. 82 and beyond into the playoffs. It was just a magical ride. I was a young guy on that team and had to pinch myself every time I walked into the locker room. What a privilege to be a member of the 2001 Colorado Avalanche."

Dan Hinote
Colorado 2001

"I had come from Edmonton the season before and was new to the team, but you could just tell from day one of training camp it was Stanley Cup or nothing. That was the mentality from top to bottom, all business, and we were determined to win it that season. The team had lost to Detroit the year before in the conference finals, and they were not happy about it. I can't explain it, but as a team we were just so focused and so confident. We weren't going to accept anything but the Cup. Even getting to the finals wasn't going to be acceptable; it was to win the championship. So to see it all come to reality was pretty amazing."

Tony Hrkac
Dallas 1999

"Goaltending and defense. That was the key that year for us. We had a helluva goaltender that year in Glenn Hall, he was outstanding. We also had five veteran defensemen in Jack Evans, Al Arbour, Dollard St. Laurent, Elmer Vasko, and Pierre Pilote. If we didn't have that group of guys back there we never would have won the Cup. No way."

Bobby Hull
Chicago 1961

"Nobody would have picked us to win the Cup that year, no way. When we started the season we had seven rookies, myself and Patrick Roy included, as well as a rookie head coach—clearly a 'rebuilding year' by most of the veteran's standards. We just came together at the right time. For those two months of the playoffs we were better than everybody else. The timing was perfect, and things just fell into place for us. There is some luck involved too, absolutely. We were just an average team during the regular season, but something clicked in the playoffs. We had a lot of confidence during that postseason run, and that was the difference for us. Patrick Roy was just amazing in goal for us, and he gave us so much confidence as a team. For whatever reason, we just weren't capable of looking beyond the series or the round that we were in. We knew that if we worked hard, then we could win. So it was a day-by-day approach.

"We played Boston in the first round, and because we had had success against them during the regular season, we were confident playing them. It was a good matchup for us, and we swept them. We beat Hartford in the next round with that same approach. That one went seven games, however, and we wound up winning in overtime. It was close, but nobody looked beyond that series, and I think that kept us in it. We weren't cocky at all; we were just happy to be there and happy to have a chance to compete. From there we faced the Rangers in the conference finals. They had upset Washington and Philly to get there and were in a similar situation that we were in. Nobody expected them to be there, either. So that gave us confidence too, and we wound up beating them four games to one.

"Next up were the Calgary Flames for all the marbles. They had just upset the Edmonton Oilers, who were the powerhouse of the '80s and had just won two straight Cups and were on the verge of winning a total of five Cups in seven years. Nobody gave us a shot to beat the Flames either, but we just believed in ourselves and were able to somehow pull it off. It was the first all-Canadian finals in like 20 years, so there was a lot of interest coming into the series. We lost Game 1 but then came back to win Game 2 in overtime thanks to Brian Skrudland, who scored the game winner just nine seconds into the extra session, which was a record for the quickest overtime ever. That just swung the momentum in our favor, and we never looked back. From there we won the next three straight and were able to secure the Cup. It was incredible. Everybody worked hard and everybody had a role; mine was to be a steady stay-at-home defensive defenseman. We all bought into the system, and we came out on top. It was just a wonderful experience. I will never forget it."

Mike Lalor
Montreal 1986

"I think all teams that win championships have a closeness about them that other teams don't. Winning certainly creates that type of culture too, where you create bonds with your teammates. My first Cup came in Dallas in 1999, and that team was really tight. The guys genuinely liked each other, and it showed. We had a lot of talent on that team with a lot of pretty special players. Beyond that, sometimes you can have all the talent in the world, but you need to be a little bit lucky too. We were able to avoid a lot of big injuries that playoff run, and we caught some breaks here and there as well. When we finally won that classic game up in Buffalo to give us the Cup, it was just an amazing feeling. I will never forget it. I was lucky enough to win it again with New Jersey in 2003, and that was a similar situation. I was new to that team, having come there the year before, but we had a nice chemistry on that roster. It was a great group of guys who really played for each other. They knew how to win too. They had just won it all a few years prior, and they were hungry to do it again. I just came along for the ride. It was pretty special."

Jamie Langenbrunner
Dallas 1999 and New Jersey 2003

"We were a team that year. We were close, and we genuinely liked each other. It was a total team effort; everybody contributed that year, regardless of their role. Sure, we had Scott Stevens and Scott Niedermayer and Marty Brodeur and Neal Broten, but we were not a team of superstars by any means. From top to bottom we were a very good hockey team, though, just a lot of solid players. We won a ton of games on the road that year too, which says a lot about our makeup and about how we dealt with adversity. I remember losing to the Rangers the year before in seven games in the Eastern Conference Finals, and that really drove us too. We were ahead in that series three games to two, and that was when Mark Messier made the guarantee that they were going to win the series. He then scored a hat trick in Game 6, and from there we lost Game 7 on Stephane Matteau's goal in double overtime. That was so tough. To watch those guys win the Cup and to celebrate in New York City, right next door—we wanted that. So to come back the next season and win it the way we did, beating a heavily favored Detroit team, was very satisfying. We learned a lot from that loss in '94, and that really helped us, I think. It brought us closer. In some regards I think that you almost have to lose it before you can win it. So to finally win it was just an incredible feeling, especially for us original Devils—myself, Kenny Daneyko, and Bruce Driver. We were there with the franchise through the lean years, and to see how far we had come was very satisfying."

John MacLean
New Jersey 1995 and
2003 (Assistant Coach)

"Chemistry. Even though we had several big-name super-stars on those teams—Gretzky, Messier, Coffey, Lowe, and Kurri—they treated everybody with respect and never acted like they were better than anybody else. They made me feel just as important as anybody else on the team, and I really appreciated it. They welcomed me aboard in '84 via a trade from Pittsburgh, and they made me feel so welcome. I just did whatever I could to fit in on that team and did whatever was asked of me. If guys on the other team started running around and getting after Gretz and Mess, then I would take care of it. I knew my role as a mucker and grinder and had no problem whatsoever dropping the mitts either, hell no. I enjoyed my role and really relished it. We were the type of team that could play any type of game. If teams wanted to play us physical, then I got more ice time and did what I needed to do. I remember at one point we had a line of myself, Dave Semenko, and Marty McSorley. It might have been the scariest line in NHL history. We just terrorized opposing teams, it was hilarious! We would put pucks deep and then crash and bang. Nobody wanted to be out there with us, nobody. Everybody kept their heads on a swivel because we were looking to get a piece of anybody we could. If teams wanted to play more of a speed and finesse game, then I sat back and waited for my opportunities to come. I was ready for anything and was more than happy to be a role player and just contribute any way I could. Luckily I was able to play all the way through to the finals too, which was a real compliment. A lot of role players aren't so fortunate, and I never took that for granted. It drove me to work as hard as I could because I didn't want to let anybody down."

Kevin McClelland
Edmonton 1984, 1985,
1987, and 1988

"That was a unique team. We had a lot of guys who were coming into their prime all at the same time: Al MacInnis, Doug Gilmour, and Joe Mullen; a good group of young guys in Joe Nieuwendyk and Gary Roberts; as well as some solid veterans in guys like Lanny McDonald and Rob Ramage. We were deep and we had good size, which really helped us to be physical down the stretch. We had good chemistry too. I will never forget going into Game 7 against Vancouver in the opening round of the playoffs.

We were heavily favored to beat them coming into the series, and here we were in a Game 7 we weren't even supposed to be in. So we were all pretty uptight before the game. I will never forget getting ready and Jamie Macoun put in the movie *Slap Shot.* Everybody just started laughing and quoting lines, and it really loosened us all up. It cut the tension and I believe actually proved to be a momentum swinger for us, I really do. Here we are about to play the biggest game of our lives and guys are just laughing their heads off, it was great. Sometimes little things like that can go a long way. Needless to say, we went out and won the game. From there we swept L.A. and beat Chicago four games to one before beating Montreal in six games to win the Cup. What a run. And to do it in Montreal was pretty special too. In fact, I believe we were the first visiting team ever to clinch the Cup on their home ice. The thing I remember most was how the Montreal fans treated us after the game. Even though their team had just lost, they all stayed and cheered for us. It didn't even feel like we had won it on the road. It was one of the neatest moments and just speaks volumes about those fans up there. Very classy and very respectful of the game. They especially showed a lot of respect for Lanny, who would retire after that, but not before scoring that iconic goal against Patrick Roy in Game 6. I will never forget that one, just amazing."

Brian MacLellan
Calgary 1989

"From top to bottom, we were a *team* that year. A team. Sure, we had a great mix of goal scorers and role players, as well as an element of toughness that allowed us to do some different things out on the ice. But most important, we cared about each other. I honestly believe that everyone on the team genuinely cared about everyone else. There was no jealously, and there were no ulterior motives between players. You wanted to go out and work as hard as you could and sacrifice and do everything you possibly could for that guy across from you. And you knew that he was going to do the same for you, which built trust and chemistry on that team."

Todd Marchant
Anaheim 2007

"We had a unique team in Edmonton. The coolest thing about it was the fact that we all cheered for each other. Everybody was pulling for you, regardless of your role on the team. They praised you when you did your job well, and they supported you when you didn't. That was rare. I have been on plenty of other teams in this league where guys were worried about their jobs and wound up against one another. In Edmonton we cared about each other, and that was why we had such a great run up there. Even when we won the Stanley Cup, the veterans couldn't wait to get it into the hands of the rookies or free agents who had never won it before. They enjoyed that moment when he would hoist it for the first time because they knew how wonderful it felt. The older guys helped out the younger guys too, even if it meant sharing ice time. Case in point, Dave Semenko was very good to me. He mentored me and taught me things at a time when some thought I was trying to take his job. He was selfless, though, and he wanted to help me out because he knew that in the big picture it would ultimately help the team. I really appreciated that so much. As a result, I wanted to pay it forward to the next guy, and so on. When you get that type of chemistry on a team, good things are going to happen. That's why the Cup is so special; it's truly a team trophy that celebrates the accomplishments of the entire team, not the individuals."

Marty McSorley
Edmonton 1987 and 1988

"There was something special about that team. You could tell even in training camp, there was just an aura about it. There were going to be no excuses, and nothing was going to deter us from reaching our goal of winning the Cup. It was a complete team with four really solid lines, a good defense, and a great goalie. We had a good mix of veterans who had won before and been through the battles, as well as a lot of young legs. We even had good special teams and penalty killers, not to mention a great coaching staff. So we just had every aspect of the game covered. We had a great season and then stepped it up even more in the playoffs, which is the key. Everybody has to elevate their game in the postseason or you can't get it done. We were hungry and we worked hard, and we were rewarded in the end. It was very satisfying."

Mike Modano
Dallas 1999

"Winning that first Cup was just amazing. It was such a whirlwind for me too, having just come off of winning the gold medal at the 1980 Olympics. In fact, our last game against the Finns was on February 24, and I was playing with the Islanders just six days later. I was just trying to keep my head above water; to tell you the truth, it was all just a blur. I remember we went on an undefeated run at the end of the season and were able to carry that momentum into the playoffs. We had traded for Butch Goring, and the team really responded. From there we went through some really tough battles in the postseason. Then to finally win it was just incredible. To go from winning the gold to winning the Stanley Cup in less than three months was pretty surreal. From what I understand I am the only American to have ever done so, which is something I am very proud of.

"The second Cup, in 1981, was a totally different experience. We were the favorites coming into that season, and we had to defend our title, which meant we had a big target on us the whole year. We had a lot of confidence about us, though, and we were able to come together in order to repeat as champions. We wound up beating Minnesota in the finals, and it really validated our first Stanley Cup. Nobody could say it was a fluke; we were for real.

"The third Cup was probably our best season in that whole dynasty era. We really were a juggernaut at that time and simply dominated in the playoffs. We swept Quebec in the semifinals and then swept Vancouver in the finals to win it. It was pretty incredible. That stuff doesn't happen very often, so you have to just look at that and appreciate the magnitude of what we had accomplished.

"The fourth one was really fulfilling in that we were able to beat the up-and-coming team in the league at the time in Edmonton, which of course was led by Wayne Gretzky. We were getting a little run down, with all the wear and tear, at that point, but we were able to hold it together to beat those guys. A lot of people thought that they were going to upset us, and I think that really motivated us to prove them wrong. It worked too, because we swept them in the finals to make it four in a row—firmly establishing our dynasty. They were a really young team, and our experience had paid off for us. It made them hungry, though, and they were able to use that to come back and beat us the next year in the finals to get revenge. They would then of course go on and win five Cups in the next seven years, establishing their own dynasty in the process."

Ken Morrow

New York Islanders 1980, 1981, 1982, and 1983

"We had such a special team that year. I was on a line with John LeClair and Brian Bellows, and it was just a fantastic group of guys all the way around. We were so resilient. I mean, we won 10 overtime games that year. We were loose and just had fun. From our epic water fights at hotels to just hanging out with each other, we were a close group. Our coach, Jacques Demers, kept us loose too—even when he wasn't trying to. You see, Jacques spoke in a pretty thick French accent, and sometimes he would get his words messed up. I will never forget his big pregame speech for us right before we took the ice against L.A. in the Stanley Cup Finals. We were all so nervous, and he wanted to give us this big pep talk. So he comes in and says, 'This is it, this is what we've all been waiting for! This is what separates the men from the boys. So let's go, boys!' We all just started laughing. His big motivational speech was lost in translation, but we didn't have the heart to tell him. If anything, it loosened us all up and set the tone for us to go out and have fun. Sure enough, we got the job done and won the Cup."

Kirk Muller

Montreal 1993

"My first Cup came in 1989 in Calgary. I was 22 years old and just a pup. So seeing guys like Lanny McDonald, who had waited a lifetime to raise the Cup, had a big impact on me. I will never forget the goal he scored on Patrick Roy in Game 6 of the finals against Montreal in the Forum. It would turn out to be his last goal ever because he retired after the season. What a storybook ending for such a classy player. The emotion that came out afterward, especially from the older guys who had waited their entire careers for that moment, was pretty intense. I will never forget it. Being 22, you are kind of like, 'Woo-hoo, this is fun! This was easy!' You're sort of clueless at that point. Well, it took me another decade to win another one, this time in Dallas, and at that point I had grown up quite a bit. In fact, I went 10 years without even getting past the first round, which was just brutal. So to win it again was really meaningful. And to win it in Dallas, a football town, was neat too—to be able to steal a little bit of the Cowboys' thunder. To build that franchise up from nothing in the late '90s was just an incredible experience. It was so different from when I had won it in Calgary, where hockey is just everything. I was older and in more of a leadership role at that point, which made it very rewarding. Then to be able to win one more on the tail end of my career like that, where I was more of a role player at that point, that was just icing on the cake."

Joe Nieuwendyk

Calgary 1989, Dallas 1999,
and New Jersey 2003

"I was blessed to have won four Cups in my career, but certainly winning that first one in 1980 against Philadelphia was the most memorable and exciting. I mean, to score the game-winning goal to give us the Cup

Joe Nieuwendyk (right), Ed Belfour (center), and Guy Carbonneau celebrate the Stars' 1998–99 Stanley Cup at the foot of Reunion Tower in downtown Dallas.

was just magical. It was a thrill of a lifetime, it really was. It changed my life from a business standpoint too. Then to win it the second time, it just validated what we had done the year before, I think. It proved that it was no fluke. The third was amazing as well, but I think it was the fourth one that was the most satisfying to me. We beat Edmonton that time and held them to just six goals over four games, which was pretty amazing. They were the up-and-coming team at that point and had just incredible firepower with Gretzky and company, so to beat them was pretty special. Looking back, I think we played our best hockey in that series and really rose to the occasion."

Bob Nystrom
New York Islanders 1980, 1981, 1982, and 1983

"We won it because we all bought into the same message, and a big part of that message was toughness. Our GM, Brian Burke, really championed his fighters. Our attitude was that we weren't going to be intimidated by anyone—and we certainly weren't, as evidenced by the fact that we led the league in fighting majors. A lot of comparisons were made between us and the old Broad Street Bullies that year, which I thought was pretty neat. You can't argue with the results; it worked for us. A couple teams tried to emulate that same physical style the next year, but it didn't really work out for them. We just had the right mix of talent and toughness, I suppose. Beyond that I think that we were all pretty hungry. Scotty Niedermayer was the only guy who had won a Cup prior to that season, and we all wanted to experience it as well. We wanted it pretty badly and that drove us."

George Parros
Anaheim 2007

"That team had such heart. We believed in each other and it showed. We were really confident too, as evidenced by the fact that I think we set a record for road wins that year. Everything just came together for us at the end. We got hot and just rode Martin Brodeur all the way through the finals. It was amazing. To watch John MacLean, Ken Daneyko, and Bruce Driver all get to raise that Cup at the end, that was amazing. Those guys had been with the organization for so long and had been through a lot of lean years. And Neal Broten too, what a great addition he was for us that year. I was in awe just being out there with Neal, to be honest. I grew up idolizing the guy in Minnesota and firmly believe that he's the best U.S.-born player ever to play the game. We just had so many great guys on that team, and it was such an honor to be a part of that. Bill Guerin and Stephane Richer played great, as did Scotty Stevens, who shut down Eric Lindros in the conference finals against Philly. It was a total team effort, it really was.

"As for me, my job was to look after my teammates. If that meant dropping the gloves, then so be it. I enjoyed fighting; I was pretty good at it. I just tried to do my part; I knew my role. I skated alongside Randy McKay and Bobby Holik, and we were known as the 'Crash Line.' Our job was to wreak havoc out there, to intimidate and to try to create turnovers. We brought energy to our teammates and physically punished the opposition. Not only did we go out there and hit guys, but we also drew a lot of penalties as well, which put our team on the power play. Those are big momentum swingers, and we looked for that stuff. We were pretty well rounded, though. In fact we were plus-71 at the end of the season. So we contributed a ton on offense too, including in our playoff run. I would even go so far as to say humbly that there will never, ever be a fourth line in NHL history that will contribute the way we did. I just felt very fortunate to be in the lineup every night during the postseason. A lot of times enforcers are scratched at that point and replaced with skill players, but I was well rounded enough to keep my roster spot, and that was something I'm very proud of. I've seen a lot of heavy-weights over the years raising the Stanley Cup out on the ice after the game is over, only they're wearing suits and ties—meaning they didn't get to play down the stretch. Well, thankfully Jacques [Lemaire] believed in me, and I took great pride in raising Stanley with my full gear on out there with my teammates."

Mike Peluso
New Jersey 1995

"What a team we had that year. Winning aside, just look at the Hall of Fame lineup of guys we had: Joe Sakic, Peter Forsberg, Patrick Roy, Rob Blake, and of course, Ray Bourque. What a thrill to be out on the ice with those guys. What I learned from each and every one of them was that everybody has a different view and a different take on life. Take a guy like Joe Sakic, who may be one of the greatest players ever to play the game, yet in my mind he is, even more important, the best family guy and best dad that I have ever played with. Peter Forsberg was another guy who will rank among the best ever to play this game, yet when I think of my time with Peter I will always remember that we never talked about hockey. We talked about our passions for life, for travel, for food, and about the enjoy-ment of the journey through life.

"Patty Roy, meanwhile, was the greatest competitor that I ever played with or against. Bar none. He would put everything to the side in order to win. I remember in practice one day where I scored on him on kind of a bad goal. He looked over to me and said in his thick French accent, 'That's it, Big Poads, no one is scoring on me again today!' Sure enough, he didn't give up one goal for the next 45 minutes, I kid you not. It was incredible. I was just waiting and watching too, so I could go over and rub it in as soon as somebody scored on him, but he stayed true to his word. It was without a doubt one of the greatest exhibitions of goaltending I have ever seen. Rob Blake, what a tremendous defenseman. I learned so much just from watching that guy. He was a man of few words, but when he spoke, guys listened. He was a very respected player both on and off the ice.

"And last but not least, Ray Bourque. Are you kidding me? He may be the classiest professional I was privileged to play with. A great player, sure, but what a great human being. Every year on the last day of the Stanley Cup Finals I call Raymond and ask him if he remembers by chance what he was doing back in 2001 at that moment. We have a great laugh and relive a great memory every year like clockwork. It's awesome. I still think about what a classy gesture it was on Joe Sakic's part to hand the Cup directly to Ray so that he could be the first to raise it. Commissioner Bettman handed it to Joe, and as the captain it was his right to raise it first, but he wanted Ray to experience that feeling so he selflessly passed it to him. Ray had waited his entire career for that moment, and Joe didn't want him to have to wait another second more. Amazing. I will never forget that moment for as long as I live. There wasn't a dry eye in the house. We all wore hats that season that read 'Mission 16W,' meaning the team needed 16 wins to get Ray his Cup. Ray never took that thing off. I remember that last shift before the final buzzer went off in Game 7. We all wanted Ray to be out on the ice, and it was getting close, so Rob Blake came flying over to the bench to come off and then screamed at an exhausted Ray to get out there for the last few seconds of the game. He hopped over the boards and got to enjoy the moment. It was classic. Just classic."

Shjon Podein
Colorado 2001

"Winning my first Cup in 2001 with Colorado was such an amazing experience for me. Everybody had a role on that team, and they all did their jobs well, night in and night out, so it truly was a total team effort that season. We had so many outstanding players too: Joe Sakic, Peter Forsberg, Adam Foote, Rob Blake, Patrick Roy, and of course Ray Bourque—who was such a motivating factor for all of us that year. We so wanted for him to raise the Cup. It was our mission. I remember being in the locker room just before Game 6 of the finals against New Jersey. We were down three games to two, and it was pretty much do or die at that point. Ray stood up and said, 'This is it for me, boys. I'm not playing anymore after this so we *have* to win tonight!' What a moment. Nobody else could say something like that and have the same effect or outcome. Nobody. He commanded so much respect from everybody, and it really got to us. I will never forget just looking at him and thinking about how long he had played and how much he had sacrificed to get to that point right there. We were all ready to go to war for him on the spot. Needless to say, we won that game and then won it all two nights later. So to see him raise that Cup out on the ice, that was a moment I will never, ever forget. Truly epic.

Ray Bourque (raising Stanley), captain Joe Sakic, and the rest of the Colorado Avalanche celebrate their 2000–01 Cup victory over the New Jersey Devils.

"Three years later I was fortunate to win my second Cup, this time with the Tampa Bay Lightning, and the experience was completely different. I was much more involved this go around, right down to being on the ice for the last minute of the game. What a thrill that was. The way we did it too was so incredible. Being an expansion franchise in the Deep South, it was a completely different experience for all of us, including our fans. It's hard to explain, but it's so physically demanding, and your body is taking such a beating for those two months, but it's also so fun and so rewarding, and there is nothing you would rather be doing. Every minute of it was just a thrill. Once the puck drops for the playoffs the level of play just amps way up. So many rallies and comebacks, what can you say? Traveling to New York and then going to Montreal, maybe the greatest place of all time to play playoff hockey, and then to Philadelphia, where they had the Orange Crush going—it was so memorable. Our fans were so into it, I think we took hold of the city during that magical run, and they really got behind us. Everyone talked about Calgary being the noisiest building in the league for the playoffs, but I would stand behind Tampa any day of the week, saying we had the best fans going that year. Then to win it in seven games the way we did—it was everything I had ever dreamed of as a kid growing up playing hockey. What an incredible, incredible experience."

Nolan Pratt

Colorado 2001 and Tampa Bay 2004

"Winning the Cup in 1992 was pretty emotional for all of us. Losing our coach, Badger Bob Johnson, to cancer that year was so difficult. He had coached us to the Stanley Cup in 1991 and then fell ill shortly after the season. I will

never forget seeing him for the last time in the hospital,
that was so tough. We had a pretty touching moment with
him just before he died at our team's ring presentation late
that summer. We set up a live video feed into his hospital
room, and when each guy went up to get his ring from
our GM, Craig Patrick, he would look into the camera
and say a few words of thanks to Bob. It was extremely
emotional. He died, of course, just a few months later.
Well, we went through a lot of ups and downs that season
and really only came into our own during the playoffs.
Scotty Bowman had taken over as coach, and once we hit
the postseason it became obvious why he is the winningest
coach in NHL history. He was amazing. We kicked it up
to another level, and things just fell into place for us. We
had also made a pretty big trade that year too, where we
got Rick Tocchet, Ken Wregget, and Kjell Samuelsson in
exchange for Mark Recchi and Paul Coffey. I don't think
we would have won it had we not made that deal. We
had a great balance of veterans and young guys too,
which really helped us."

Gordie Roberts
Pittsburgh 1991 and 1992

"We didn't really have any superstars on that team, and I
think that was what was special about it. We had a lot of
veterans too, which certainly provided a lot of solid leadership. We also had great goaltending in Martin Brodeur, as
well as good team defense—which was a hallmark of all
Jacques Lemaire–coached teams."

Brian Rolston
New Jersey 1995

What was your role on that Stanley Cup team?

"My role was to be a defensive shut-down guy. I took pride in bringing that physical, nasty presence every time I stepped onto the ice. My job was to keep my goaltender, Marty Brodeur, protected and to look out for him back there. If I could block the odd shot for him or move someone out of his way, then that was what I was going to do. I understood that sacrificing my body in order to help my teammates was just something I was going to have to do, and I embraced it. Sometimes that led to the occasional scrum, and that was okay. For me it was about being disciplined and knowing when to take a penalty. Hey, fighting is definitely part of the entertainment during an 82-game schedule, and let's face it, we're in the entertainment business. But once the playoffs start, you've really got to bite your tongue if you get a whack. Believe me, it was hard, but you take that hit and maybe bide your time until next year. One penalty, one mistake, could cost you a playoff game. Look at our 1995 Stanley Cup team. Our fourth line had some guys who liked to mix it up, Mike Peluso and Randy McKay, but they played fantastic hockey in the playoffs. That's what it's all about, choosing your spots so that you don't put your team into a shorthanded situation that could ultimately cost you a game.

"As a stay-at-home defenseman, I didn't get the opportunity to score that many goals. I did get one against Dallas in the finals back in 2000, though, which was a huge thrill for me. My teammates really got pumped up over that one too, which was neat to see. You know, when a guy like me gets a goal that can really swing the momentum on the bench. It's not expected, it's just a bonus. They were all pulling for me, and they could see how excited I was out there, which in turn got them going. Hell, they were even more excited about my goal than I was, and that really brought us together as a team, I think. We won the game, and that set the tone for the whole series, which we wound up winning in six games. The bottom line is this, you can't win the Stanley Cup with six Bobby Orrs and nine Wayne Gretzkys. You also need role players to do the dirty work and to protect your goal scorers."

Ken Daneyko
New Jersey 1995, 2000, and 2003

"All three Cups were special and all were unique in their own way. It's weird, but I can remember every goal from each of the finals. It's funny, I can barely remember scoring any of my own goals, but I remember all of those. They are just still as plain as day to me. We had so many great players on those teams: Wayne Gretzky, Mark Messier, Paul Coffey, Jari Kurri, Glen Anderson, Esa Tikkanen, and Grant Fuhr, to name a few. There are so many wonderful memories too. If I had to pick one big moment, however, it might be in 1990 when we rallied back to beat Winnipeg in the playoffs when we were down three games to one. Gretzky was gone at this point to L.A., and the Canadian press was saying that we weren't good enough to win anything without him. That really motivated us, and we rallied back to beat them and just kept on going from there, all the way to our third Cup in four years."

Steve Smith
Edmonton 1987, 1988, and 1990

"We had some great teams in Calgary in those days, really great teams. We figured we were going to win a whole bunch of Cups during that stretch, so in some regards it's disappointing that we only won one. Don't get me wrong, I'm thrilled we got the one, but when you look at the talent we had in those days, we could have really had a dynasty team. Certainly Edmonton was in their heyday back then, and that was their time. Those 'Battle of Alberta' games against those guys were always memorable, though. I think we really brought out the best in each other."

Gary Suter
Calgary 1989

"We had such good chemistry on that team. We had all been playing together for a while, and we had gone through our fair share of ups and downs, which really brought us together. Management made a coaching change midway through that year to shake things up, going from Michel Therrien to Dan Bylsma, and they made some trades too, bringing in guys like Chris Kunitz, Bill Guerin, and Craig Adams—which gave us a big boost. I think we were able to use that momentum to carry us through the playoffs. We started believing in each other at the right time, and we had that swagger about us. From there we got hot, and we just rode that all the way to the Cup. Facing Detroit in the finals was tough, though; they had a great team.

"For me personally, I took great pride in just doing what-ever I could to help the team win. Whether it was going into a corner to pass a puck to Sidney Crosby or scoring goals or getting into fights, I just wanted to chip in. I fought a bunch of guys who were twice my size that year, usually getting my ass kicked in the process, but I didn't care. That's part of my game, my character. Hey, I don't play in the NHL because of my stick-handling skills, I play because I will do anything to help my teammates win. Anything. I think my teammates really appreciate that too. Hey, if I can give them a little courage and get them pumped up, then mission accomplished. It's the little things, like fighting a guy or blocking a shot or finishing a check, that make a big difference in the end."

Max Talbot
Pittsburgh 2009

"The first Cup was amazing because it was the first. I had dreamed of that moment all my life, and when it happened it was indescribable. So much hard work goes into it, and when it finally becomes a reality it is such a relief. You have such an appreciation for your teammates at that point too, because you are forever bonded through that achievement. You all went through that same sacrifice in order to achieve that goal, and to be able to share that is just so rewarding. Afterward, it made me even hungrier. I wanted so badly to win it again, it was like a drug. So winning the second one was almost like the beginning of an obsession. It was like we were addicted to winning. We just wanted to keep that amazing feeling going. Eventually we just expected it. We knew what it was going to take—all the hard work—and it became like second nature. Going into the third one we had the experience, and we had the confidence. From there we just kept rolling along until everyone started talking dynasty. There is something different about the mentality of a team that wins four straight Stanley Cups, especially in those days when we did it with pretty much the same core group of guys. Sure, there were ups and downs along the way and some new blood was brought in from time to time, but overall we were determined to be the best...and for those four years we were."

John Tonelli
New York Islanders 1980,
1981, 1982, and 1983

CHAPTER
4

Playing Hurt

Part of the unwritten code of honor in hockey is that players must play through pain and hardship. They don't have to, of course, but they all do. It is just understood. Hockey players, perhaps more so than players in any other sport, are expected to suck it up and "play through" their injuries. That is the culture of the sport, to sacrifice your body for your team and to lay it all on the line. Professional hockey is all about the team, and players will do whatever it takes to help their teams win. If that means playing with a broken arm, so be it. If that means getting your mouth quickly stitched up between shifts with no Novocain, then so be it. If it means losing seven teeth during a game, then so be it— which was exactly the case for Chicago defenseman Duncan Keith, who was "spitting Chiclets" after blocking a shot against San Jose in the conference finals in May 2010. Incredibly, Keith missed only five minutes of ice time and was back out taking a regular shift. Amazing. That's not rewarded behavior, though, it's expected behavior. There's a big difference. It is a state of mind unseen in any other professional sport.

Playing hurt is a mentality that has been handed down from generation to generation, starting with guys like former Montreal Canadiens winger John Ferguson, one of the toughest S.O.B.'s who ever played. When Ferguson went on to become the general manager of the New York Rangers, he was notorious for insisting that his players suit up at all costs. Any injury, Ferguson used to contend, could be cured with "a little tape and aspirin." The guilt and peer pressure was overwhelming. Players simply did not want to let their teammates down, no matter what, and Ferguson played into that. For instance, if a player came off the ice with a sore leg, Ferguson would say to him—just loud enough for his line mates to hear—"Your leg is bad? Gee, that's a long way from your heart."

When you play pro hockey, you belong to one of the toughest fraternities known to man. Being "soft" is unacceptable. Pussies are simply not allowed into their frat house. Like soldiers with an unwavering allegiance to their cause, hockey players at times possess an almost superhuman tolerance for pain and suffering. To them it is all about "we and us" versus "I and me." It is all about the responsibility they feel toward one another in an effort to help their team in any way possible. For most, it would simply take an extraordinary set of circumstances to keep them off the ice. This iron will to "play at all costs" is especially heightened come the playoffs, when the stakes are at their highest. It's even got a name, "playoff makeup." Hockey's version of the color wheel features bruises that come in a variety of colors, including black and blue, yellow and purple, or even blood red—which looks great contrasted against the freshly painted, bright white ice. The longer your team plays, the prettier you get. Black eyes, stitches, and facial cuts all tell the story, and that doesn't even include all of the unseen welts, bruises, and lacerations that are covered up under layers of protective equipment. Collectively, those wounds are seen as badges of honor to these men and are something they actually display with great pride.

And there won't be any whining or complaining about those injuries either. No way. That would be dishonorable and is not tolerated. They will suck it up and hit the ice like they have done a million times before. The hockey player's threshold for pain is unimaginable, and most outsiders probably couldn't stomach a locker room scene from a typical NHL game. Sure, they might see broken fingers being taped up, or perhaps they might see some bruised ribs being wrapped, and they will for sure see players trying to numb up their groins and deep thigh bruises with bags of ice. What they won't see, however, are players getting shots of cortisone with giant needles placed deep into their knees, hips, ankles, shoulders, and wrists. That all goes on in secret closed-door training rooms that are off limits to the press and anybody else who wanders in.

Why, you might ask? Because if word got out via a member of the media or someone else who just so happened to be in there at the time, then that player's safety would be seriously compromised. Injuries in hockey are on a "need to know" basis, and other than the coaches and trainers, nobody else needs to know. Period. You see, every team has a role player, otherwise known as an "agitator," and it is his job to hack and whack opposing players who might be injured. If he finds out through the grapevine that a player has a separated shoulder, then that body part instantly becomes a target. The agitator will swarm like a killer bee, waiting to feast on that tender piece of meat. He will wait patiently and then swoop in at just the right time, maybe while finishing a check in the corner, to slash it, grab it, or bend it—all in an effort to take that player off his game. He knows that if that player is thinking about protecting his shoulder then he is not totally focused on doing his job. That's an intangible that can have a big impact on the outcome of a game.

That's why if a player has an ankle injury, it might very well be reported as a "lower body" injury. That way that filthy agitator won't have a bull's-eye to focus in on out on the ice. That's why most hockey injuries are listed as something generic, like a "groin injury." It's a basic, vanilla ailment that every player suffers from time to time, except it is one that is nearly impossible to exploit. Whack a guy "downstairs" and you will get what is coming to you ten times over. That's a major code violation, and the repercussions will be swift and severe.

You also might not see a player having stitches removed back in the locker room either, but they quite often are prior to games to prevent those same agitators from trying to bust them open again out on the ice.

"You know a guy has a broken wrist, you hammer him there a few times and you don't have much trouble with him for the rest of the night," wrote Punch Imlach in his memoir, *Hockey Is a Battle*. "It's nothing personal. I'd do it myself."

And just why are there so many injuries and so much carnage in hockey? The short answer: physics. Just as Sir Isaac Newton said centuries ago, when you have large masses moving at great speeds and colliding with one another, there is going to be some friction. Hockey has been described as a "nuclear" game, with explosive and unpredictable power. You have 12 grown men skating around at speeds up to 30 miles per hour on a 100-foot-by-85-foot ice surface, wielding carbon composite sticks that can launch a rock-hard vulcanized rubber puck as fast as 110 miles per hour. You do the math. Hockey is all about kinetics and high-velocity movements, with players constantly coming on and off the ice by "changing on the fly." Violent collisions aren't the exception to the rule in this sport, they *are* the rule.

Part of the reason for so many injuries in the sport has to do with its confinement. The enclosed, claustrophobic environment that the players compete in lends itself to a more intense atmosphere, conducive to violence. Hockey, unlike football, baseball, basketball, or soccer, is the only game that is completely closed off, with no open spaces. Those sports have escape routes, so to speak, whereas in hockey once you are out in that pit of dasher boards and Plexiglas, you are trapped. Many contend that with no place to duck and hide, the hitting becomes even more ferocious. Even the basketball court has no defined boundaries and at least offers the illusion of openness. And a scrambling quarterback can usually dive out of bounds in order to elude the clutches of a linebacker out to rip his head off. Not so in hockey. When a guy is bearing down on you in the corner, it doesn't matter how fast you are, you are going to get hit hard. Period. And with the players seemingly always getting bigger, faster, and stronger every season, the rinks appear to be shrinking.

Hockey has created a culture that breeds athletes who feel as if they can overcome almost any injury in order to play. From coaches to teammates to team doctors, nobody is going to tell a player, "Sure, sit this one out tonight. That cut above your eye needs some time to heal." No way. Most believe that if you can walk upright and have a pulse, then you can suit up and play. Many contend that this play-at-all-costs mentality is a learned behavior that follows the simple adage of "leading by example." The grizzled veterans mentor the young guns, and so on and so forth, until it becomes a generational thing—passed down like a treasured heirloom. When your respected team captain laces 'em up no matter what, then his teammates will do the same. That is the ultimate sign of respect, to be there for your comrades in battle. All for one and one for all. It is the essence of the warrior code.

There are countless legendary stories too, almost like folklore, of players displaying incredible acts of courage in leading their teams to victory. Like tall tales or ghost stories, they have been embellished over the years, to enhance their dramatic impact. Hockey is all about momentum and courage, and both can swing a game to one team's advantage in a heartbeat. Just as a crushing body check that flattens an opponent can swing the pendulum of emotion, so too can an act of bravery where a player gives up his body for his team. Coaches will tell their players when they are down that there have been many losses that have been miraculously transformed into wins over the years thanks to the heroic efforts of players who were willing to sacrifice their bodies in order to break their opponents' spirits.

Players young and old have all heard about how Montreal star winger Maurice Richard was knocked out cold during Game 7 of the 1952 Stanley Cup semifinals. After colliding with Boston defenseman Bill Quackenbush late in the second period, he was carried out on a stretcher. He came to, though, and demanded to return to the ice. He then rejoined his teammates with just under four minutes left on the clock and proceeded to make history. With the score tied, Richard, with a bloody bandage covering six fresh stitches on his face, pulled off one of his signature end-to-end runs, skating around three Bruin defenders before scoring the thrilling series-winning goal. That was the day Maurice became "The Rocket" in many fans' eyes.

Or how about Detroit's Marcel Pronovost, who showed up to each game of the 1961 Stanley Cup Finals on crutches. The Red Wings defenseman would play each night on his severely broken ankle and then have his cast put back on after the game—only to take it off all over again the next evening. You just can't make that stuff up.

Or take Toronto Maple Leafs defenseman Bobby Baun. The story of how he scored the game-winning overtime goal in Game 6 of the 1964 Stanley Cup Final on a broken leg is epic. And if that weren't enough, Baun actually hid from team doctors after the game, refusing to have his leg X-rayed for fear of them putting a cast on it. He then showed up already dressed just moments before the start of the deciding Game 7 and snuck onto the bench. How did he do? He wound up playing a regular shift that game, having his leg "frozen" after every period to numb the pain, en route to leading his Leafs to the Cup title. That is how respect is earned in the National Hockey League.

And it isn't just about heroic games either. Most players just go about their business and keep their mouths shut. Amazingly, the goalies might be the toughest of them all. Take Hall of Fame net minder Glenn Hall, who once played more than 500 consecutive complete games without a mask. Or the "Gumper,"

Gump Worsley, who was on the receiving end of more than 1,000 stitches to his pretty mug. For goalies of that era, getting cut was just part of the job. The late Montreal keeper, Lorne Chabot, who played between the pipes back in the 1920s and '30s, even used to shave right before he hit the ice. Said Chabot: "I stitch better when my skin is smooth."

The transitions in the game are also a reason for more injuries. Hockey is such a fast game with so much speed and constant transitioning from offense to defense. Unlike football, basketball, and baseball, where teams can only make substitutions after a whistle, hockey players change "on the fly." Guys will skate hard for a one- or two-minute shift and then dump it in and head to the bench, where they catch a breather while the next line goes out and does the same. The action turns on a dime, with players skating forward on the forecheck and then instantly skating backward on the backcheck. On the gridiron, only after an interception or a fumble does the shift from penetration to protection come into play. In hockey this happens nonstop, and that is what makes it so exciting.

Lastly, players are bigger, faster, and stronger nowadays. Thirty years ago the average NHL player was 5'11" and about 180 pounds. Today that number has grown by two inches and 20 pounds. And that's just an average. The prototypical players have that rare combination of speed and power, guys like Eric Lindros, Mario Lemieux, Derian Hatcher, or Chris Pronger, who are all at least 6'5" and 230–250 pounds. There are some giants out there though, like Minnesota Wild enforcer Derek Boogaard, who comes in at 6'7" and 275 pounds. Or Boston Bruins defenseman Zdeno Chara, who towers over his competition at 6'9" and 260 pounds. Those guys are scary. It is no wonder people think that the rinks have gotten smaller.

Plus, these athletes are better conditioned on year-round programs with state-of-the-art exercise and weight-training equipment. And the player's gear has gotten more high-tech with newer, lighter, and stronger materials being used to help them achieve great speeds while maintaining a high level of protection. Add all of those factors together, and it is no wonder guys are getting hurt. Head injuries are on the rise big time, and the days of guys getting their bells rung are over; now they understand much more about the epidemic of concussions and post-concussion syndrome—a situation that is keeping way too many players out of the lineup these days.

Success in hockey comes down to the little things. You see it all the time in instances such as overtime, when it is all on the line and a single player makes a mistake or doesn't properly execute his job, and it has catastrophic consequences. Yes, the margin between a win and a loss in hockey can be razor thin. Sometimes the teams are so evenly matched that it just comes down to the tiniest of things that can make all the difference in the world. Sometimes it is another man's desire to succeed that will win out. Sometimes the team with the most courageous players gets the victory. Sometimes it's the team with the most disciplined players, the ones who sacrifice their bodies by taking a hit or finishing a check or going hard into the corner to dig the puck out or even going down to block an incoming slap shot.

Shot blocking might be the most courageous element of hockey because guys know that they may take a puck in the face in order to save a potential goal from going in. It is an art form, to be sure, based on perfect timing and judgment. Go down too soon and the player can go around you or pass off; go down too late and you either miss the puck or take it right in the face. The code honors shot blockers for their courage, selflessness, and vulnerability in the line of fire.

To win in hockey you need role players, muckers, and grinders. They are the fourth liners, the guys with heart—they are the difference makers in this game. Sometimes, just sometimes, the best players—with the fat contracts and all the talent in the world—can't hold a candle to the guys with heart. That is the great equalizer in this game. Some guys have it and will play through the pain, while others simply don't. Those who do, they are usually the ones who are the most respected and revered on their teams. You never really know when they are hurt because they don't let anybody know; they just play. They just do whatever they can to help their teams win. Most will tell you that they're the real heroes in hockey. Here's what some of the players had to say about playing hurt.

PLAYING HURT IS PART OF HOCKEY'S SACRED CODE. WERE THERE ANY INJURIES THAT YOU HAD TO OVERCOME EN ROUTE TO RAISING STANLEY?

"I broke three ribs at the end of the first round, which forced me to miss the first two games of the second round against Buffalo. I came back after that and just sucked it up for the next month. I would get shot up before each game and then again after the second period to keep it numb. I wore a big band on it while I was out there, which helped, but it was tough. Every team's opposing agitator knew about it, which was not a lot of fun. I will never forget when we were playing the Islanders, and Stevie Thomas just drilled me square in the ribs. The pain was excruciating, but what are you going to do? Everybody is hurt in the playoffs, everybody. So you just deal with it the best you can. Jacques [Demers] knew that I was doing this and that I could barely move the next morning after games. So he just let me rest during the day and basically let me skip practices. I really appreciated that."

Brian Bellows
Montreal 1993

What was your role on that Stanley Cup team?

"I was proud of the fact that I was able to play several different roles on the various teams that I have played with over my career. In Detroit, for instance, we had an advantage over our opponents in that we had some good players who weren't afraid to mix it up. Many of our opponents had to sit their tough guys when the playoffs started, but not us, and that gave us a huge advantage. Teams had to play us honest, and they couldn't run around out there. Getting physical and dropping the gloves to me wasn't so much about laying a beating on somebody who was smaller than me, it was more about following the code and fighting with honor. I learned that from my brothers when I was a kid. I always fought for a reason. If an opponent broke my code against what I believed in or they broke a team code against one of my teammates, then I was going to get involved. Hey, I enjoyed it. In fact, looking back, if I could have I would have done it a whole lot more. I never got any joy out of starting a fight with a guy who I knew I could easily beat, though. I always got a thrill out of fighting heavyweights, guys who were known for being real fighters. I liked the challenge, I really did. Anyway, in Detroit we had some really tough players, and I was just happy to play whatever role I could in order to help the team win. If that meant dropping the gloves, then so be it. You just do whatever it takes. That's what playoff hockey is all about."

Brendan Shanahan
Detroit 1997, 1998, and 2002

"I played three rounds with a broken hand during our Cup run. It happened early in the second round, and I played 18 games with it. What can you do? It was tough, but hey, that's playoff hockey. I had to get it frozen or shot up every game so that I could play. I led the team in ice time that season, though, and there was no way I was going to sit out. That just isn't in my nature. I had to keep it secret too, in order to make sure opposing agitators didn't start harassing me. Luckily it worked out, and in the end I was able to raise Stanley."

Dan Boyle
Tampa 2004

"When we won it in 1999 in Dallas, we were the walking wounded. We had so many guys beat up during that play-off run that it's amazing as I look back to think we were still able to win it. We had guys getting IV fluids between periods—it was nuts. I remember Mike Modano was play-ing with a busted wrist and had to get shot up just so he could take faceoffs. Brett Hull had something torn in his leg, and he could barely skate. Everybody was hurt. I was get-ting my knee drained after every single game; it was just brutal. It's war. You don't think about it at the time, though, you just play. Even now as I am retired, I still get chills watching playoff hockey on TV just knowing what it takes to get through those games. Everybody steps it up a notch, and the hits are just a little bit harder and meaner. Every shift there is just a little bit extra pain, and over time it adds up. I mean, to play upwards of 28 games during the playoffs, usually every other day, with all the blocked shots and crushing checks—your body just takes a pounding. You basically live with ice bags 24/7. Looking back, I don't know how the hell we did it, I really don't. It's insane. I think that the grind of it all is a big reason why so many teams struggle the following season after winning it. They call it the 'Stanley Cup hangover,' and it makes sense. Case in point, we missed the playoffs the next year after winning it in 1995 in New Jersey."

Shawn Chambers
New Jersey 1995 and Dallas 1999

"I actually broke my jaw that season after taking a slap shot to the face. Ouch. I knew instantly it was broken too, because by the time I got to the bench my face was just massively swollen. It was hideous. I remember flying home the next day after spending the night in the hospital. I looked like a freak show walking through the airport. It was like something out of a cartoon. They had wrapped white tape around my head to keep my jaw from coming loose, so I was basically frightening children as I walked by looking like the old ghost from *The Christmas Carol*. What a sight I must have been. Luckily I healed up pretty quickly and was able to play in the playoffs."

Matt Cullen
Carolina 2006

"I had shoulder surgery that year, which was tough, but I rehabbed it and eventually worked my way back into the lineup. When you are out with an injury at this level there is someone just as good if not better ready and waiting to take your roster spot, so you learn pretty quickly to do whatever it takes to stay in the lineup—otherwise you are going to be out of a job."

Jim Dowd
New Jersey 1995

"The 1981 playoffs were just brutal for me. I will never forget breaking my finger on literally the first shift of the postseason against Toronto. I had to get it frozen and shot up before every game, which was tough. I could barely shoot the puck. I was not going to sit out though, no way. Then, if that wasn't bad enough, I took a skate blade to the face against the North Stars in the finals. My tongue even got sliced open; it was pretty bad. I took about 50 stitches on my chin in that one. The hardest part about that wasn't the injury, though, it was the fact that I lost about seven pounds due to the fact that I couldn't eat. I had no energy. I just hung in there, and my teammates picked up the slack. Hell, everybody was beat up at that point. That's playoff hockey. So when I was awarded the Conn Smythe Trophy that year after we won the Cup, it was extra special. [The Conn Smythe Trophy is awarded annually to the player judged most valuable to his team during the playoffs.]

Butch Goring
New York Islanders 1980, 1981, 1982, and 1983

"I was a mess in the playoffs that year. Heck, we all were. I mean, welcome to the Stanley Cup playoffs. I was getting by all right until Game 1 of the finals against Edmonton, however, when I blew out my labrum in my hip. My hip would actually pop out of the socket every time I took a shift, and then I would have to sort of shove it back in when I got back to the bench. After the game I had to get it drained because so much fluid had built up in there. So they rushed me to the hospital, and they stuck a needle in there that was about four feet long, I think, and it was absolutely excruciatingly painful. I remember when they stuck it in the hip the fluid just shot out. When they finally finished draining it they then shot it up with cortisone, which allowed me to play out the rest of the series. Then, if that weren't bad enough, I ripped the ligaments off of my thumb in Game 3 after checking a guy in the corner. So I had no thumb the rest of the series—which, by the way, went seven games. It was brutal. Then, after we won it and were all back in the locker room celebrating with the Cup, I just lost it. I fell to my knees next to my locker and just heaved my guts out. I think I had literally left every ounce of energy I had on the ice that day, and I was just completely spent. I had nothing left. Nothing. Mentally and physically I was toast. That's what it takes, though, if you want to win the Stanley Cup. Even when you are convinced that there is no way you can play, you just have to dig deep and find a way, no matter what, so that you don't let your teammates down. Needless to say, I had to have surgery on my hip and thumb shortly after the season."

Bret Hedican
Carolina 2006

"I was hurting, sure, but you just had to deal with it. We were all hurting. I mean, everybody is dinged up at that time of the year. If you're not, then you're not playing hockey— you're sitting on the bench. As long as you can get your skates on and grab a stick, then you played. That was it. You just didn't want to let your teammates down. If that meant playing hurt, then that was what it meant. You didn't make a big deal out of it, you just did it. I remember getting eight stitches in my face during a game one time and feeling pretty woozy. I didn't want to keep playing, but I did and even wound up getting the game-winning goal. My teammates appreciated that, and that meant a lot to me."

Gordie Howe
Detroit 1950, 1952, 1954, and 1955

"I got checked pretty hard in Game 4 of the opening round against Edmonton and suffered a concussion along with four busted ribs. I had to miss the next two series, which really sucked, but I eventually got to come back and

Hurricanes defenseman Bret Hedican raises the Cup as he exits a joint session of the North Carolina legislature recognizing the team's 2005–06 NHL championship.

play in the finals. I finally couldn't take it anymore and practically begged our trainers to let me wear a flack jacket so I could play. Luckily they agreed because I don't think I could've taken another day of not being out there with my teammates."

Tony Hrkac
Dallas 1999

"It's amazing what guys go through, especially in the play-offs, it really is. Playing hurt is just a part of the culture of this sport. It's pretty much just expected; it's a part of the gig. You don't even know who is hurt and who isn't until after the season, when teams roll out the list of guys who have to go in for surgery. As an assistant GM today I see that all the time. Teams that win it every year seem to have players who rise above and inspire others. Those players are the glue that binds their teams together. Their injuries, their pain, and their sacrifices are what makes winning the Stanley Cup so unique. You just don't see players in other sports playing under those same conditions. Just look at the players right after they have just won it, they look like hell. They're green, they're gaunt, they're cut and scarred, and they look like they have just been beaten up in a street fight. And do you know what? That's what it takes. That courage, that will and determination, that sacrifice—that's what it's all about. That's why it's so special. That two-month saga of going through the playoffs to win the Stanley Cup is the most demanding quest in all of sports, bar none. I'm sorry, but nothing compares. Nothing. People in Canada know this and live this, but most people in the U.S. don't have that same appreciation, for whatever the reason. There are pockets in the U.S. where hockey is fully appreciated, in the north and in the east, but not nearly enough. We need more. So I hope this book helps to spread the word because more people need to know about this wonderful game."

Tom Kurvers
Montreal 1986

"I remember in 1999 with Dallas, of the 20 guys who dressed each night, probably eight of them had to take needles before every game. It was nuts. The playoffs are a

two-month grind, just a battle. You are always going to
have injuries, that is just the nature of the beast. If you are
lucky your injuries won't keep you out of any games, but
you just never know. Mike Modano had a broken wrist for
that entire playoff run, so how he was able to play every
night was just amazing. It is pretty remarkable when you
think about it, about what guys are willing to put themselves through in order to win the Cup. The sacrifice is just
insane, it really is."

Jamie Langenbrunner
Dallas 1999 and New Jersey 2003

"When we won our fourth Stanley Cup over Edmonton my
knee was just about shot. I remember getting hit behind
the net in the second round against the Rangers, and
afterward I was told I would never play again. The doctor
told me it was one of the worst he had ever seen in his
career. My knee at that point was basically just being held
together with skin; everything structurally was gone. Well,
I didn't want to retire so I started rehabbing it and building up the muscle around the knee. I missed the next
round but was able to get back into the lineup against
Edmonton in the finals. I was in constant pain. After the
games I would have it drained, and then I would have to
be helped to get on the bus because I could barely walk. I
never got injected, though; I didn't want to do that. I could
play with pain, that was not a factor. I would just ice it all
day long. It was just a matter of whether or not I could
physically play. I really wanted my dad to see me raise
the Cup for the fourth time, and thankfully he did. We
even got to drink out of the Cup together afterward, which
was such a special moment for me. Sadly he passed away
the next year as we tried unsuccessfully for our fifth one.

Needless to say, I have since had my knee replaced after having seven surgeries on it. But hey, I got my four Cups, and that's all that matters."

Dave Langevin
New York Islanders 1980, 1981, 1982, and 1983

"I had hernia surgery right at the end of that 2007 season, which was really a tough thing to go through. The recovery time was supposed to be about 10 weeks, but I rehabbed hard and got back on the ice after four weeks so I could rejoin my teammates in the conference finals. It was rough, but I played through the pain. I just didn't want to let my teammates down. In retrospect, it was one of the best decisions I have made in my career."

Todd Marchant
Anaheim 2007

"I wound up breaking my wrist during our Cup run in 1999, and it was tough. You just do whatever you have to do to play through it. I mean, everybody at that point is banged up, some guys worse than others, but nobody is a hundred percent. You just realize that you have to push yourself, sometimes to a place you never thought you could get to, and then you push some more. That's the difference between winning a Stanley Cup and not winning a Stanley Cup. You find out a lot about yourself when you are hurt, I think. The bottom line for me was that I did not want to let down my teammates. I had a role on that team, and my teammates were depending on me to do my job. Plus, I really wanted to win it. There are no guarantees in this game, and you never know when you are going to get another opportunity. You just have to make the most of them whenever they present themselves, regardless of your physical limitations."

Mike Modano
Dallas 1999

Mike Modano—followed by teammates from the 1999 Cup-winning Dallas Stars—carries Stanley during festivities at the 2007 NHL All-Star Game in Dallas.

"I remember tearing the muscle right off my collar bone after getting hit by Mike Ricci on my very first shift of our opening playoff series against Quebec. It was awful. I had to freeze it pretty much every game from then on in, which was so tough. I am not a big fan of needles, and I got pretty sick of seeing them every night. There was no way I was going to sit out though, no way. If you want to make it to the top then you need to pay the price. Needless to say, when that stuff wore off after every game…*ouch*! Not fun. It felt a lot better when I was able to lift the Cup up, though, that was for sure."

Kirk Muller
Montreal 1993

"To me, playoff hockey is by far the most intense of any sport. Everybody is hurt, and there is just no time off to heal up, so you have to just suck it up and play. I was fortunate to have not had too many injuries throughout my career, but to watch so many of my teammates play hurt was pretty inspiring. I will never forget one year watching Kenny Morrow getting his knees drained on the training room table before every single game; it was unbelievable. That is so painful. The guy still walks with a limp to this day. What a gamer."

Bob Nystrom
New York Islanders 1980, 1981, 1982, and 1983

"By the time the finals roll around, literally everybody is hurt in some way. It's like the walking wounded in the locker room before and after games at that point. We're all banged up, some guys more so than others, but what are you going to do? Complain? Sit out? No way, so you just suck it up and play. I had broken ribs and a concussion, but some of my teammates were way worse off than me.

Everybody has to push their bodies through that adversity at that stage of the game, it's just expected. If you want to raise the Cup, that's what it takes. You have to sacrifice your body for the betterment of your team, that's the bottom line."

Shjon Podein
Colorado 2001

"I had hurt my back pretty badly just before the playoffs started in 1998, and that was pretty painful. I missed the first few games of the opening series with spasms, but I just sucked it up and played after that. I remember seeing chiropractors and specialists after every game; it was tough. I tried cortisone shots, massage, and even acupuncture, but I just couldn't shake it. After a while I got so frustrated that I was ready to see a voodoo doctor. I mean, as a player it's hard to not be at a hundred percent out there. What are you going to do, though? It's the playoffs, and everybody is hurt. That's just the way it is."

Brendan Shanahan
Detroit 1997, 1998, and 2002

"I had shoulder surgery just prior to the season, and it gave me problems all year. I battled through it, though, because in the end I would gladly trade my shoulder for a Stanley Cup any day."

Max Talbot
Pittsburgh 2009

"When it comes to playoff hockey, all bets are off. I tore some ligaments in my knee at the end of the season and actually had to miss the first series of the playoffs that year against Edmonton. I was supposed to be out for much longer but said no way, I wanted to play. Everybody is dinged up at that point of the season, everybody. I mean, we had at least a dozen guys who were injured in some way to the point where during the regular season they would have had to sit out. Mike Modano was playing with a broken wrist, and Brett Hull and Benoit Hogue had torn ACLs in their knees. We were all hurting, but nobody wanted to let anybody down, so we just did what we had to do so that we could be out there and contribute. That's just the nature of the beast at that stage of the season."

Pat Verbeek
Dallas 1999

"You play such a long season, and you are going to get banged up along the way. Everybody goes through it. Then the playoffs come around, and it's so intense, with so many games in such a short amount of time, so you suck it up and play. You don't want to let your teammates down so you just do what you have to do. You figure out ways to get ready for the next game by whatever means necessary. Once you get through that one, then you do it all over again for the next one. That is the mentality at that stage of the season. I have certainly had my fair share of injuries throughout my career, from spinal fusion to numerous knee injuries. In fact one of those knee injuries came in 2002 during our Cup run, and it was extremely difficult to play, but luckily I got through it. Hey, there were a lot of guys worse off than me, so what are you going to do?"

Steve Yzerman
Detroit 1997, 1998, and 2002

The genesis of a great rivalry

Fans love drama, and there is no greater drama for sports fans than a storied rivalry—especially in the playoffs. In hockey, perhaps more so than in any other sport, there is an abundance of simply outstanding rivalries. Because the NHL has roots that go back so far, and because its original franchises were begun in such relatively close proximity, generations of fans have been able to watch those rivalries grow over time. Not only were they able to see great games, great players, and great goals being scored, they were also able to see the carnage and bloodshed firsthand as well. Great rivalries are usually synonymous with great battles.

When their teams won, the fans rejoiced. And when their teams lost, their hatred of their arch nemesis just grew and festered. As the years went by, the politics and the soap opera antics only added fuel to their fires. Yes, great rivalries are—to those of us who follow them—actual living, breathing entities. We mark those dates on our calendars as soon as the schedules are released, and we then wait in eager anticipation. We want to be there when history is made; we want to say that we were at that game, and we want to believe that our presence made a difference. Special rivalries are just that intense.

Among the NHL's greatest all-time rivalries are two common denominators. The first is geographical proximity, because teams that are located near each other tend to hate each other because of bragging rights, and the second is whether or not they were members of the storied "Original Six" franchises: Boston, Chicago, Detroit, Montreal, New York, and Toronto. When you look at the league's first great rivalries, both factors are prevalent. For starters you've got Toronto versus Montreal, which goes deep due to their cultural differences: English-speaking Ontario versus the French-speaking inhabitants of Quebec. Then you've got Chicago versus Detroit, which goes back to the 1930s as well. More recent geographical rivalries include Wayne Gretzky's Edmonton Oilers versus the Calgary Flames in what is known as the "Battle of Alberta." Others include interstate rivalries, such as the Philadelphia Flyers versus the Pittsburgh Penguins, as well as the New York Rangers versus the New York Islanders. Boston also had great rivalries with both Philly and Toronto back in the 1970s too. Many rivalries have come and gone, such as the Chicago Blackhawks versus the Minnesota North Stars, who moved to Dallas, but the memories remain forever ingrained in the minds of the fans who rooted for them in the old Norris Division.

Physical confrontation and intimidation come to the forefront in rivalry games. A big hit or a big punch can swing the momentum in a big game, and that might be the catalyst that sparks the home team to victory. Everybody has to get involved, including the unlikeliest of heroes, whomever that might be. In the most intense rivalry of the past 20 years, that unlikely hero was Detroit Red Wings goalie Mike Vernon, who duked it out with Colorado Avalanche goalie Patrick Roy on March 26, 1997, en route to leading his team to what would ultimately be a pair of Stanley Cups. That single incident has become the poster child for the toughness and guts of the modern-day rivalry.

All great rivalries have a checkered past, complete with vengeance, retribution, and violence. They also feature a genesis and a history chock full of storied chapters. And that history almost always starts with a flashpoint, an incident that sets the wheels of retaliation in motion. The Colorado-versus-Detroit flashpoint actually transpired a year earlier, in the opening game of the 1996 conference finals, when Detroit's Slava Kozlov shoved Colorado's Adam Foote head-first into the boards. As a result, Foote suffered a nasty cut to his face that required nearly two dozen stitches to seal up. In an attempt to seek justice for his fallen comrade, Avs agitator Claude Lemieux retaliated by decking Wings winger Kris Draper from behind into the boards a few nights later. Widely viewed as a deliberate cheap shot, Draper wound up suffering severe facial injuries that required plastic surgery. Even though Lemieux was suspended for two games, his Avs went on to win the series and the Stanley Cup.

That next season the teams met three times with no incidents of retribution. Many were upset that Lemieux showed no remorse or offered no apology to Draper, which only fueled the fire. Finally, on their fourth and final meeting of the regular season in Detroit, all hell broke loose. Wing's enforcer Darren McCarty, anxious to seek revenge for his friend and teammate, pummeled Lemieux into a bloody mess that night. Lemieux, who later claimed that he had been sucker punched, wound up turtling and didn't fight back. Pretty soon mayhem broke out at Joe Louis Arena, and everybody was pairing off, old school. The crowd was going absolutely insane, and before you knew it, both goalies, Roy and Vernon, came skating out of their creases and squared off in a fight at center ice. Roy was bloodied by Vernon, who got the best of him. More fights broke out periodically throughout the rest of the game, with nearly 150 penalty minutes being racked up. The game was tied 5–5 and ultimately went into overtime, where McCarty, of all people, scored the thrilling game winner. It was a game for the ages. It had taken a whole year, but justice had been served.

The teams met again in the Western Conference Finals, with the Wings beating the Avs in six games. The series was full of drama, complete with questionable hits by Draper on Peter Forsberg, as well as by Mike Keane on Detroit's Igor Larionov—both of which took the respective players out of the game. So pissed was Avs coach Marc Crawford at one point that he even scaled the glass separating the two benches to hurl obscenities at Detroit coach Scotty Bowman. Detroit, meanwhile, would go on to win their first Stanley Cup title since 1955. The Red Wings would later confess that they were unified and inspired by their huge brawl. It had a profound effect, to be sure, as a demoralized Roy would later say that "the Wings won the Cup that night." After the series Lemieux extended his hand to Draper, but Draper was upset that Lemieux wouldn't make eye contact with him, so he refused to shake it.

The drama continued that next season as well, when the two teams met again early in Detroit. Lemieux, who was viewed as Public Enemy No. 1 in Motown, salvaged his pride during the opening faceoff when he answered the bell by dropping the gloves with McCarty. He even switched places with Avs enforcer Jeff Odgers just so he could line up across from McCarty and get it over with right out of the gates. Detroit went on to win their second straight Cup that season, but the subplots with the Avs kept on coming. There was yet another rare goalie fight, this time between Roy and

Detroit goaltender Chris Osgood. Other drama included Detroit's Kirk Maltby breaking Valeri Kamensky's forearm with a slash as well as Colorado's Peter Forsberg shoving Brendan Shanahan into the glass in Game 1 of the 1999 playoffs, giving him an extra 40 stitches for good measure. McCarty and Lemieux continued to battle that season too, with McCarty ultimately refusing to shake Lemieux's hand after Colorado won their playoff series.

All of those little things go into making a great rivalry, and that is why this one will forever be remembered as one of the best. Sadly, with free agency the way it is nowadays, and so many players changing sweaters every season, rivalries will never be like they were back in the day. So when a special one like that one comes along every now and then, the fans really savor it.

CHAPTER 5

Defining Moments

In every Stanley Cup playoff run there is without a doubt a "defining moment," an incident that has a major impact on the outcome of any one particular game or series along the way. They call them "momentum swingers," and they are like shots of adrenaline. It might be a thrilling double-overtime goal, a big fight, a bone-crunching check at center ice, or maybe a player blocking a shot and losing some teeth. They are the types of things that will get guys on the bench to stand up and bang their sticks on the dasher boards to salute a selfless act of sacrifice.

Playoff hockey is like an entirely different season, it really is. Everybody digs deep and elevates his game in the postseason. Everybody. Otherwise you are a healthy scratch watching from the press box. Players know that they have to step it up in the run for the Cup and do the dirty work that nobody wants to do. They know that they have to go hard into the corners or in front of the net, which will almost always lead to severe consequences. That doesn't matter, though, because in the playoffs it is all about the team. Everybody is willing to pay that price, regardless of the outcome. Everything is different when the playoffs get going. It is not uncommon to see players getting cuts sewn up on the bench so they won't miss a shift. Players finish their checks in the postseason, and superstars will drop the gloves if they have to. And everybody blocks shots. Everybody. Guts and passion are just synonymous with the postseason. It's like the old saying goes, "In the playoffs, will beats skill."

Who could forget watching Detroit's Dallas Drake block blistering slap shot after blistering slap shot during the '98 play-offs? He was blocking them from the point, head-on, from his knees, not on his side, sliding legs first—which is much safer. The 39-year-old knew that this was his last chance to raise the Cup, and he was willing to do whatever it took to help his team win, regardless of the personal sacrifice. His body was so bruised that he could hardly walk at times, but he didn't care, he was on a mission. He had all off-season to heal, and this was all about winning right now because there were not going to be any more second chances. This was it. That type of inspired hockey is otherwise known as being "in the zone," and it's rare. After they won, the championship team captain Nick Lidstrom rewarded Drake by handing him the Cup first. It was the ulti-mate show of respect for the guy who had played more than 1,000 games without ever having reached the finals prior to that. He retired shortly thereafter, satisfied and vindicated.

Sometimes that big momentum swinger will come in the form of a dumb penalty that leads to a power play. Such was the case in 2010 when Philadelphia, down three games to none and on the brink of elimination in the first round of the playoffs, rallied to tie Boston and force a Game 7. There, down 3–0 early, the Flyers rallied again to tie it up. Late in the third period the Bruins got a penalty for having too many men on the ice. Simon Gagne's ensuing power play goal then acted as the catalyst to lift the Flyers to an improbable 4–3 win. Coaches can deal with physical mistakes, but mental mistakes? No way. Heads will roll. It was a crushing defeat for the heavily favored Bruins, who with that loss became just the third team in NHL history to lose a series after winning the first three games. That momentum didn't stop there, though, it propelled Philly all the way to the finals that season.

Defining moments are the essence of what playoff hockey is all about. Here are a few that resonated with these players.

WAS THERE A DEFINING MOMENT DURING THAT PLAYOFF RUN THAT SWUNG THE MOMENTUM YOUR WAY?

"For me it was when Eric Desjardins scored the overtime game winner in Game 2 against the Kings. That was huge. The key to that was when Marty McSorley got a penalty for having an illegal curve on his stick. We capitalized and came out on top; it was pretty incredible. Jacques had the ref measure it with like 90 seconds left in the game, and sure enough, it was illegal. We scored to tie the game and then won it in overtime to even the series, which we eventually won in five games."

Brian Bellows
Montreal 1993

"In 1992, against Minnesota, the one particular moment that really stands out was something that never even took place on the ice. It was after Game 3, when they were up two games to one, and we read in the newspaper about how some of their players had already started talking about parade routes and about the size of the diamonds that they were going to get in their rings. We felt so disrespected at that point, we couldn't believe it. Needless to say, they never won another game in the series. That was a big momentum swinger for us, I think; it rallied us together and we responded.

"Then, afterward, when we flew back to Pittsburgh we were met by a mob of about 50,000 fans at the airport. It was nuts. We ended up taking some school buses from there over to Tommy Barrasso's house to start the festivities. We partied over there until six in the morning, and then we had to get back to the airport to go get our cars. So Frank Pietrangelo, Jimmy Paek, and I all hopped on one of the school buses and started toward the airport. We are chugging along and wouldn't you know it, the bus runs out of gas. Not deterred, I jumped out and hitchhiked to the airport. I literally put up my thumb along the side of the highway and just started walking. Eventually a guy stopped and picked me up; he couldn't believe his eyes. It was crazy.

"Then, in 1993, I would have to say that my most memorable moment would have to be Mario Lemieux's game-winning goal in Game 1 against Chicago in the finals. We were down early, and we rallied back to win it in the final seconds. Mario got a rebound out front and buried it. It was amazing. That was as loud as I have ever heard Mellon Arena. Ever."

Phil Bourque
Pittsburgh 1992 and 1993

"Winning the Cup in 1999 with Dallas when we beat Buffalo was such a thrill. To win the way we did in overtime, and in such a controversial way, on Brett Hull's infamous 'toe in the crease' goal, it just adds to the lore of it all. I was on the ice when he scored, and I even have that puck hanging on my wall as we speak. I skated over after he scored and grabbed it out of the net. How cool is that?"

Shawn Chambers
New Jersey 1995 and Dallas 1999

The Stars' Brett Hull scores his legendary Stanley Cup–winning "toe in the crease" goal against the Sabres' Dominik Hasek in June 1999.

"One of the most defining moments for me came on the team flight back to New Jersey from Detroit. We were up two games to none at that point to the heavily favored Red Wings, and I remember sitting next to Marty Brodeur on the plane. We were sitting there talking, and I said, 'Man, I can't believe we're up 2–0 in the Stanley Cup Finals, can you?' He just looked at me and said very matter of factly, 'It's over. Trust me, this thing is over. The way you guys are playing and the way I am seeing the puck, it's over.' I couldn't believe my ears; I was just in shock that he would say that. He was so confident and had such conviction, it was incredible. Well, sure enough, we swept them a couple nights later. Amazing. That guy just put us on his back and delivered. He will go down as maybe the best goaltender of all time; the guy is just unbelievable."

Tom Chorske
New Jersey 1995

"I will never forget those games against Detroit; we had such a rivalry with them in those days. We swept Florida in the finals, which was incredible, but to beat Detroit in the conference semifinals was even more sweet in some ways because of that intense rivalry. They had such a good team that year, and we were just very fortunate to beat them. Those were some extremely physical games, so tough. Once we got past them we knew that we had the confidence to go all the way. I will always remember scoring a hat trick in Game 2 of the finals, which was certainly a highlight for me personally.

"In 2001 I don't have too many good memories from the playoffs because I had to miss them after having my spleen removed just before we faced Los Angeles in the conference semifinals. I remember it was maybe two hours after the

Focus

"Sorry, I can't hear you. I've got two Stanley Cup rings in my ears!"

The perfect one-liner from Colorado goaltender Patrick Roy
to Coyotes center Jeremy Roenick, who was trying
to get under his skin by yapping at him in front of the net

game, and I wasn't feeling well so they took me to the hospital. About an hour later I was having emergency surgery. That was extremely difficult to go through. The timing was horrible, but there was nothing I could do. I will always remember watching Ray Bourque raise the Cup though; that was so special. We all wanted to win it for him so badly. When Joe [Sakic] handed it to him, wow, what a moment. I got to come down to the bench for the last minute of the game, and to see him crying those tears of joy was something I will never forget. Everybody was so happy for him."

Peter Forsberg
Colorado 1996 and 2001

"There were two defining moments. The first came against Los Angeles in the Western Conference Semifinals. It went to seven games and it was tight. Rob Blake had just gotten traded to Colorado from L.A. at the trade deadline that year, and there was a lot of tension there with him going home to play the team he had been with for 12 years. There was a lot of pressure on him, and the fans were really riding him hard. Now, Rob is a Hall of Fame defenseman, just a great player. He plays hard every shift and is very steady. Overall he is just a very well respected, nice guy. There is a whole other side to him, though, that I wasn't aware of, what I would call 'Mad Blakey.' Mad

Blakey came out in this series, and it was really fun to see. Sometimes that guy's wires cross and he goes nuts. It's so much fun to watch and so much fun to be a part of because he goes out with reckless abandon and just hammers people. It's so out of character for him too because he is quite possibly one of the nicest humans on earth. He would give you his house if he thought you needed it, that is the kind of guy he is. Well, his wires crossed against the Kings in that series, and especially in Game 7, and he turned it up a whole other notch. It was incredible. He was running around like a madman, just leveling guys out there—including their star player, Ziggy Palffy, who he practically terrorized. Our guys would stand up on the bench when he was out there, we were just feeding off of his momentum. I had never seen anything like it. He completely inspired us and put us on his back.

"The second defining moment came in the finals against New Jersey. We were tied at one apiece and just about to head onto the ice for the third period when Ray [Bourque] stood up and said, 'I'm going to get the next one, boys, so don't worry.' Sure enough, he buries the game winner top shelf past [Martin] Brodeur. We just went nuts, all of us jumping up and down on the bench and hugging each other. That kind of thing in sports gives you the chills. I mean, for a guy like Ray, who is very quiet, to say something like that in the first place was rare. Then for him to actually go out and do it was just amazing. For him to 'call his shot,' so to speak, with the pressure on...come on. The guy was superhuman. That was a turning point for us as we obviously went on to win it in seven back at home."

Dan Hinote
Colorado 2001

"The big moment for me was when we beat the Montreal Canadiens in triple overtime behind Murray Balfour's game-tying and game-winning goals. To beat the defending champion Canadiens, who were *the* team in hockey in those days, was something special. That was the night that we knew we could win the Stanley Cup. That was the night we got our confidence. From there we went on to beat Detroit to win the Cup. What wonderful memories those are."

Bobby Hull
Chicago 1961

"I had a few overtime game winners, which are about as good as it gets, but the one game that really stands out was Game 6 in Colorado of the 1999 conference finals. We were down, and I was able to score a couple of goals in that one to help us go on to win that series. That was pretty neat. Then in the 2003 conference finals against Ottawa when I was with New Jersey, we were down 1–0 in Game 7, and I scored two goals to give us the lead and eventually the win. That too was pretty amazing. It's like the old saying goes, the harder you work the luckier you get. I was just in the right place at the right time, I suppose. Those were a couple of great teams, and I was just lucky to have been able to have been a part of them."

Jamie Langenbrunner
Dallas 1999 and New Jersey 2003

"I will never forget when Darren McCarty scored the game-winning goal in the finals against Philadelphia in 1997 to clinch the Cup. It was a fantastic finesse goal where he came in across the blue line, faked out a defenseman, cut back, and then beat [Ron] Hextall. It was totally unexpected from a guy like that. Darren was a grinder, a tough guy, a player who was not known for scoring goals. He contributed in other ways. But when he stepped up and not only scored but netted the game winner, it really lifted the entire team up. It was a big momentum swinger for us. So to see him elevate his game like that at such a key point in the game and in the season was pretty amazing. He earned a lot of respect that day from his teammates for the way he rose to the occasion, no question. It was certainly a defining moment for us."

Martin Lapointe
Detroit 1997 and 1998

"The defining moment for us came in Game 5 of the conference finals against Detroit. I will never forget it. We were down by a goal with less than a minute to go, and we had pulled our goalie. Scott Niedermayer skates in from the point, shoots the puck, and it ricochets off of Nick Lidstrom's stick and up and over Dominik Hasek's glove. It was insane. I mean, it was like one Hall of Famer shoots the puck off of another Hall of Famer's stick and it goes over a Hall of Famer goalie. Talk about surreal. Then Teemu Selanne scored the game winner in overtime shortly thereafter to give us the thrilling 2–1 win. We all just looked at each other like, 'Okay, this stuff doesn't just happen, this is destiny or something.' The momentum swung for us that night, and we closed it out at home two nights later. It was huge. That confidence really propelled us into the finals as we were able to beat Ottawa four games to one to win the franchise's first-ever Stanley Cup."

Todd Marchant
Anaheim 2007

"I think my best moment came in 1984, the year we actually lost to the Oilers to end our four-year dynasty. We were playing the Rangers in the first round of the playoffs, and I wound up getting the game-winning goal in Game 5 to win the series. It was pretty incredible. That rivalry between the Islanders and Rangers was so intense in those days, and to make it even more compelling for me was the fact that Herb Brooks was the coach of the Rangers at the time. Herbie, of course, was my coach on the 1980 'Miracle on Ice' team that won gold in Lake Placid. So that was probably my biggest thrill, despite the fact that we wound up losing to Edmonton in the finals."

Ken Morrow
New York Islanders 1980, 1981, 1982, and 1983

"The big moment in the finals that year that really swung the momentum was when Marty McSorley got busted for using an illegal stick. The Kings had beat us in Game 1 and then were up on us in Game 2, 2–1, late into the third period. Our coach, Jacques Demers, suspected it was an illegal curve so he called for a measurement. It was this big dramatic moment as we all waited to see what would happen. Sure enough, he was guilty and got a two-minute minor for unsportsmanlike conduct. Jacques then surprised everyone by pulling our goalie, Patty Roy, to give us a six-on-four advantage. Thank God for Eric Desjardins, who scored from the point with just seconds left to tie the game at two apiece and force overtime. Desjardins then scored his third goal of the game about a minute into the extra session to complete the hat trick and give us the thrilling win. It was at the Forum, and our fans just about went through the roof. It was incredible. The momentum was with us at that point, and we just cruised from there all the way to the championship."

Kirk Muller
Montreal 1993

"My most memorable moment probably came in the first round against Minnesota, when I got into a scrap with Derek Boogaard during warm-ups. He decided to cross-check Chris Pronger at the red line, so I raced over and we got into a big scuffle. Our guys fed off of that, and it really set the tone for the entire series. We played really physical that game and were able to neutralize them. We just rode that momentum all the way to the finals; it was pretty amazing."

George Parros
Anaheim 2007

"I will never forget getting ready to face Boston in the opening round of the playoffs that year. We were putting together a game plan to shut down Cam Neely so we had our assistant, Red Gendron, put on a yellow jersey and become Cam for the day. Claude Lemieux, whose job it was to shut down Cam, then chased him around all practice and basically beat the shit out of him. After a while Red got pissed and let him have it, and the two of them went at it for a while. It was pretty hilarious. That was Claude, though, an agitator through and through. He could get under guys' skin and get them off of their games, whether it was yapping at them or hacking at them. Nobody was better. Hell, I remember lining up against him one time in a faceoff when I was with Ottawa. He started talking shit to me right out of the gates, about me being a stupid goon—real personal stuff, right at the jugular. Right when the puck was dropped he stepped on my stick blade and snapped it just like that. Then before I could grab him he was outta there. That's just his nature, that's how he plays the game. His teammates loved him and opposing teams hated him. It's funny but I used to think he was such an asshole, but once I got to know him he is actually a really nice guy. Needless to say we beat Boston four games to one that series, and Cam—as great of a player as he is—wasn't a very big factor."

Mike Peluso
New Jersey 1995

"I remember having an emotional breakdown right after Game 5 of the finals against New Jersey, thinking this is it, this is my last shot to maybe win this thing that had eluded me for my entire career. I just kept thinking that this was it, that I would never have another opportunity to get back to that point, and about how many people I was going to be disappointing if I didn't win it. I just lost it. Then the next night, before Game 6, I remember sitting down with Ray Bourque, and he told me that he was going to retire at the end of the season and about how important it was to him to win that game. I just got chills sitting there talking to him. Well, we went out and won that to force a Game 7, and from there the rest is history. What an incredible run. I was so drained. You know, when people ask me about that season all I can say is that it was a lot more fun when it was over. Getting to that point was so draining, emotion- ally and physically, that afterward I was completely spent.

So seeing Ray hoist that Cup means so much to me because I got to be a very small part of it, which is something I will always look back on fondly."

Shjon Podein
Colorado 2001

"The defining moment of our 1980 Cup run was in Game 2 against Boston in the second round of the playoffs. The 'Big Bad Bruins' thought they could pound on us and knock us around, so they really tried to intimidate us that series. The benches cleared and all hell broke loose. It was mayhem, just really intense, and it went on for at least a half an hour. Some of the fights that went on got scary. Terry O'Reilly fought Clark Gillies several times. Bobby Nystrom fought John Wensink, and I remember Wayne Cashman and Garry Howatt going like three rounds. The worst was when Bobby Lorimer, who was not a fighter at all, got pummeled by Stan Jonathon. Stan was a monster, and when he hit him in the eye, blood squirted out about six inches. Oh, it was ugly. I even got into the action along with Smitty [Billy Smith] after their goalie, Gerry Cheevers, had come out and slashed Duane Sutter. We had all four goalies going at it at one point, it was crazy. There weren't enough officials to break them all up. Well, the period finally ended, and we went in to sort it all out for the third period. I will never forget Bobby Lorimer, with his eye completely swollen shut at this point, patting guys on the back and encouraging us to hang in there. It spoke volumes about how far our team had come over the past few years, and it really got us fired up. So we went back out there for the third period and wound up getting some timely goals to beat them. Once we got past those guys we knew that we had the confidence to go all the way. We stood up for ourselves and showed the rest of the league that we simply were not going to be pushed around. It was just an epic game; I will never forget it."

Chico Resch
New York Islanders 1980

"Winning the Cup in 1994 in New York was amazing. We had such a great team that year with so many talented players. Our work ethic, our talent level, and our experience was all there that season. We all wanted to win for each other that season. It was a unique team. We were all friends, and we genuinely cared about each other. That doesn't always happen in sports either, which is why that team was so special. We beat a very good Vancouver team in seven games, and it was a classic in every sense. We were up 2–0 early and they rallied back. Mark Messier got the game-winning goal, and he just put everyone on his back that season. He was our captain and our leader. It was amazing. The guy had won several Stanley Cups before, and it clearly showed. What a guy.

"I think the best memory for me would have to be when the final buzzer went off and everybody came racing over and we all just embraced. What a relief. Wow. It was almost an odd feeling, to sort of let go at that point. Up until then it was so intense. There was no tomorrow up until that point. Now it was finally over, and you could relax and come up for air. Then it sinks in: you have just fulfilled a childhood dream of winning the Stanley Cup, and you are all of a sudden overcome with emotions. It's crazy, it really is. Just indescribable. What a feeling. You just want to share it with everybody. Being in Madison Square Garden at that moment felt like being with 17,000 of your closest friends. Everybody was hugging and crying and singing and cheering. I wanted the moment to go on forever, I really did.

"Afterward I will never forget Mark [Messier] taking the Cup over to the glass and letting the fans see it and touch it. Who can forget him jumping up and down with that priceless joker grin, like a little kid with so much emotion, as he got to hoist the Cup amid the backdrop of all that ticker tape falling from the rafters in the Garden. He understood that the Cup belongs to the fans, especially the fans in New York, who were with us every step of the way. That is who we played for. That is what makes the Cup so special too, I think, the fact that the fans really understand its rich history. They get to see it out in the community afterward, and they get to celebrate with it just like the players do. It's the people's trophy, it really is. There is such an attraction and love affair with it too. I remember having the Cup at my apartment in Manhattan, and one morning I was going to take it with me to a party. So I went down to the street to hail a cab. I was just standing there on the sidewalk, minding my own business, holding the Cup. Before long everybody saw me and started smiling and staring. As I was waiting there, this guy came over and was just in awe. He said, real tentatively, 'Is that the Stanley Cup?' I said, 'Yes it is.' He said, 'I'm not a big hockey fan, but that is just the most amazing thing. Can I please touch it?' I said sure, and he very delicately and respectfully leaned over and put his hand on it. He smiled and said, 'Thank you.' Then he walked away, smiling. That was it. It was a pretty powerful moment for me. I felt pretty proud to have earned it that day and was even prouder to be able to share it a little bit as well."

Mike Richter
New York Rangers 1994

New York fans cheer as Rangers goalie Mike Richter hoists Stanley skyward during a ticker-tape parade down Broadway celebrating the team's 1993–94 NHL championship.

A trio of classic comebacks

The "Easter Epic"
The "Easter Epic" was a four-overtime Game 7 playoff thriller between the Islanders and Capitals played on April 18, 1987, at the Capital Center in Maryland, which started on Saturday evening but did not finish until the early hours of Easter Sunday. This record-setter was decided when Pat LaFontaine beat Washington net minder Bob Mason on a slapper from the blue line to give his Isles a 3–2 victory.

The "Miracle on Manchester"
The "Miracle on Manchester" took place in the opening round of the playoffs between the Kings and Oilers on April 10, 1982, at the Forum in L.A.—which is situated on Manchester Boulevard. In it, the Kings completed the largest comeback in NHL playoff history, rallying from being down 0–5 to win the game 6–5 in overtime on Daryl Evans' wrister that beat Grant Fuhr.

The "Monday Night Miracle"
The "Monday Night Miracle" was a Game 6 playoff game between the Flames and the Blues that took place on May 12, 1986, at the St. Louis Arena. What made this one so memorable was the fact that the Blues were able to overcome a three-goal deficit with just 12 minutes remaining in the third period and then ice it in overtime on Doug Wickenheiser's game winner.

"Winning the first Cup in 1997 was pretty special. The most memorable moment for me was the first two minutes of the opening game against Philadelphia. We knew that we were going to win the Cup in those first two minutes. Seriously. Everybody thought that they were going to walk all over us too, because they were so much bigger and stronger than we were. We came out flying, though, and took it right to them. Once we had our first shifts under our belts, literally in the first few minutes of that opening game, we all just knew that we were going to crush them. I can't explain it. It was really unique and something I had never experienced before. It was pretty amazing. We not only had more skill and speed than they did that night, but physically we were crushing them. We didn't come into it feeling that way either. We had seen the clippings and read what the media was saying about the [Eric] Lindros line and about how dominant the 'Legion of Doom' was. I remember the commentators talking about how Philly had beaten Pittsburgh, and afterward, during the handshake at center ice, Mario Lemieux had told Lindros, 'Now it's your time,' which sort of meant he was 'passing the torch.' Then they talked about how Lindros had manhandled Mark Messier in the next round against the Rangers. I mean, everybody picked these guys to win, but we totally destroyed them. It was pretty intense. Beyond that, I will never forget getting the double-overtime game winner against the Ducks in round two to eliminate them. I picked up some garbage around the net and shot it in to give us the win. It was a thrill of a lifetime, it really was.

"Winning the second Cup in 1998 against Washington was pretty special too. My most memorable moment from that series was probably the big come-from behind win in Game 2 at home. It looked like the Capitals were going to tie the series with a 4–2 lead in the third, but we rallied late to tie it up and send it into overtime. Kris Draper scored with about four minutes left in the first overtime, and we wound up winning 5–4 to take a two-games-to-nothing lead. I remember Esa Tikkanen missed a wide-open net that could have iced the game for them, but we hung in there and just grinded. It was a big momentum swinger for us, and it really set the tone, as we went on to sweep the series.

"The third Cup came in 2002, when we beat Carolina. I think my most memorable moment from that postseason was our first-round win against Vancouver. We had gotten beat in Games 1 and 2 in Detroit, and everybody had written us off. Game 3 was a must-win for us, and we played like it. Our goalie, Dominik Hasek, had to stop a penalty shot late in the third, and we all just fed off of that. Had they scored, it probably would have been lights out, but we rallied from there and didn't lose again in that series."

Brendan Shanahan
Detroit 1997, 1998, and 2002

"For me the defining moment of our playoff run came in that epic overtime Game 7 against Vancouver in the first round of the playoffs. We finished well ahead of them during the regular season, and nobody really expected that series to go seven games. I will never forget when Stan Smyl skated down in overtime and had a great opportunity to end it, but our goalie, Mike Vernon, somehow got his 5'3" body sprawled out to make an unbelievable kick save on his slap shot. The momentum swung, and a couple of minutes later Joel Otto skated in and scored. That was a huge turning point for us. A lot of times teams will go through adversity or they have a big scare like that, and it proves to be the kick in the pants that really propels them to a championship. Certainly that was the case for us because that series was a huge wake-up call for us."

Gary Suter
Calgary 1989

"For sure my biggest moment was scoring both goals in our 2–1 Game 7 win against Detroit in the finals. That was pretty exciting. To score the game winner in the finals was something I had done in my head many, many times before as a kid up in Quebec. What a thrill. I guess I was in the right place at the right time and got lucky. I just wanted to do whatever I could to help my teammates win, and thankfully we were able to close it out that night and raise the Cup."

Max Talbot
Pittsburgh 2009

"The single biggest defining moment on the way to winning the Cup that year came in the first round when we beat Vancouver in Game 7. Joel Otto got the overtime game winner, and that was without a doubt one of the most thrilling moments in my hockey career. 'Otto from Peplinski and Loob at 19:21 of the overtime.' I will never forget it. Winning that first round was a big, big obstacle for us that year, and it really propelled us toward winning the franchise's first Stanley Cup."

Tom Thompson
Calgary 1989 (Scout)

"I would have to say that my most memorable moment came in Game 6 of our first Stanley Cup Finals against Philadelphia. It was overtime, and I wound up going in on a two-on-two alongside Bobby Nystrom. Lorne Henning had hit me with a perfect pass through traffic in the neutral zone, and as soon as I got the puck Bobby and I criss-crossed, which was something we had practiced together many, many times. Their defenseman got hung up for just a split second at the blue line, and Bobby got past him. As soon as I saw him get open I decided to pass it over as he broke in toward the net. Sure enough, he redirected it past their goalie, Pete Peeters, and with that we were the Stanley Cup champions. We just dove on each other, and all hell broke loose. It was such an amazing moment, I will never forget it. You know, I coach kids today, and the one thing I always tell them is about how important it is to pass the puck."

John Tonelli

New York Islanders 1980, 1981, 1982, and 1983

CHAPTER
6

Championship Coaching

There are many different ways to get from Point A to Point B in hockey, and good coaches understand that. Their philosophies on team building, leadership, and motivation vary widely, yet all have one common goal—to win championships. For Philadelphia Flyers coach Freddy Shero, it was a simple saying on a locker room chalkboard just before Game 6 of the 1974 finals against the Boston Bruins: "Win together today...and we walk together forever." Simple, yet profound. For Toronto Maple Leafs coach Punch Imlach just prior to Game 7 of the finals against Detroit in 1964, it was placing a mountain of cash—$10,000 in small bills to be exact—on a table in the middle of the locker room as both an incentive and visual reminder for the guys about how much their collective bonuses were if they won that night. Needless to say, both motivational tactics worked. Here are what some of the players had to say about what they learned from their coaches, each of whom was able to lead them to the promised land.

HOW WAS YOUR COACH ABLE TO MOTIVATE YOUR TEAM TO VICTORY THAT SEASON?

"Badger Bob and Scotty Bowman were completely different personalities. Total opposites. Badger was so incredibly positive about the game of hockey and about life in general. He didn't necessarily buy into the philosophy that you had to kick your guys in the butt when they were down. That just wasn't his thing. His motivational style was more about stroking guys in a positive way, rather than being negative. He would critique you and correct you when he felt you were doing something wrong, like a teacher. He was so different from any other coach I ever had. Scotty, on the other hand, was all business and much more to the point. He wasn't as engaging of a personality as Badger was. His philosophy was more 'I'm the coach, you're the hockey player—and that's that.' There were clear lines with Scotty, and those lines didn't cross. So, as players, going from Badger in 1992 to Scotty in 1993 was a hard adjustment. We went from Bob, who was outgoing, positive, and engaging, to Scotty, who was more of a thinker, a strategist, and a task master. It took us a while, as players, to gel with Scotty, but eventually we figured out his style. Both led us to the Cup, though, which proves that there are many ways to achieve success in this game. Both were great guys and great coaches, they really were."

Phil Bourque
Pittsburgh 1992 and 1993

"John Tortorella was a great motivator. That was his best asset as a coach. With 82 regular-season games to play it can be tough to get up for games sometimes, but he found ways to motivate each guy individually and just always was able to say the right things in order to get you to play hard. He prepared us well and got us ready to play. Then in the playoffs we didn't need any motivation. We were ready to go, and he knew that."

Dan Boyle
Tampa 2004

"Peter Laviolette's uniqueness was his ability to get us to believe in each other. He brought a family kind of an atmosphere to the team to where you got to care not just about the guy you were playing with, but also his family. You play harder for people you care about, and Peter instilled that in us, which was a big reason why we won the Cup that year."

Rod Brind'Amour
Carolina 2006

"Jacques Lemaire was a really good coach. He was very patient. He focused on the fundamentals too; that was really important to him. As long as you played defense and played smart, then you were going to be okay with Jacques. He was just very different from any other coach I'd ever had. He had much more of a hockey mind, or intelligence, than a lot of the other coaches I have had over the years. I mean, the guy won almost two handfuls of Stanley Cup rings, so how can you argue with that?"

Neal Broten
New Jersey 1995

"Peter Laviolette was a great coach. He gave me opportunities and he really believed in me, and as a player that is so important. That gave me so much confidence too, to know that I didn't need to worry about making mistakes or to be afraid to attack the net. He gave me a lot of freedom to be an offensive-minded player and encouraged me to go out there and just make things happen. Almost every time I would jump over the boards to take a shift he would say either 'shoot the puck' or 'be dynamic.' He wanted me to be offensive and to attack, which was a fantastic role to have. It was great to have a coach who trusted me and gave me that freedom to be creative out on the ice. He never gave up on me either. I remember at one point during the year I went 19 games without a goal, yet he always had faith in me. I just appreciated that so much."

Matt Cullen
Carolina 2006

"Jacques [Lemaire] taught us about just what it was going to take to become champions. He had already had so much success up in Montreal, and we were just hoping that was going to rub off on us. He got us all pulling the rope the same direction. He reminded us that we can say it in our heads all day, but until we feel it in our hearts it will never happen. That really hit home with us, and sure enough that next season we won our first Stanley Cup. I learned more from Jacques in the first two months he was there than I had in the previous 10–11 years in the league. His understanding of the game on a technical basis with regard to positioning and game planning and efficiency, it was off the charts. The guy is a genius. His passion for the game was so unbelievable. I just have the utmost respect for him."

Ken Daneyko
New Jersey 1995, 2000, and 2003

"Jacques [Lemaire] taught me about the importance of preparation. If you were prepared to do your job with Jacques, then you would have success. If you weren't willing to buy into his system, then you weren't going to have a job. That was just the bottom line with him."

Jim Dowd
New Jersey 1995

Marty McSorley on the role of the enforcer come playoff time and on the power of the "Code"

"I took great pride in the fact that I was able to take a regular shift when the playoffs rolled around. Most tough guys weren't able to say that, and that meant a great deal to me. I worked very hard on being a well-rounded hockey player, and as a result of that I was rewarded in the postseason with ice time. Teams don't want to risk having enforcers out there in crucial games if they think they are going to be a liability and take a stupid penalty. One shorthanded power play goal in the playoffs can swing the momentum in a heart-beat and cost you your entire season. So I had to be very disciplined and not get goaded into doing anything stupid, which was tough at times. Having an enforcer on your bench in the playoffs is a luxury most teams wish they could afford but simply can't, although we are seeing more and more of it. Look at Anaheim, who won the Cup in 2007; they led the league in fighting majors that season. It's rare, but if you can have enforcers out there delivering big checks and looking after your star players, then that is a huge advantage.

"My job was to enforce the code. The code, to me, was what we as hockey players lived by. The code was a sort of living, breathing thing among us. It changed and evolved as the rules changed and evolved, and it kind of took on a life of its own. With the code there is the basic premise that you have to answer for your actions on the ice. You learn that pretty early on in your hockey career, and it doesn't take very long to figure out just how important it is. The code says that you play hard and physical in order to get yourself more space out on the ice, but you don't take advantage of guys who aren't in a position to defend themselves along the way. I enjoyed playing the game very physically. I was always under the assumption that you stood up for your teammates no matter what, but it wasn't so much about intimidation for me as it was about just playing honest.

"The most important aspects of the code, bar none, are honesty and respect. Because without those things it is just the Wild West out there, which is no good for anybody. If players don't play honest and with respect, then there is a price to pay in this game. That is just the way it is. Hockey is a game that polices itself, and there is a lot of honor behind that. It is something we as players take very, very seriously. If opposing players wanted to take liberties with my guys, then they would have to answer to me. That kept things honest, and that is the basis of the code in its purest sense.

"Most fans will be shocked to hear this but it's true: almost every time two heavyweights get into a fight, they didn't start it. It escalated from something way down the line and finally wound up on their laps. Maybe a rookie trying to show he belongs by doing something stupid or an agitator carrying his stick too high; it could be anything, really. And everybody on both benches knows it's coming too, that is just the way it is. A series of events led up to that point, and we would have to end it so the game could calm down again. That's how the code works. And when the fight was over, it would have a sobering effect on the guys back on the bench, who could then get back to playing good clean hockey. So that is what we did, we made sure guys played clean because if they didn't, things were going to get ugly.

"I think that the toughest thing about fighting was that your hands and body would get so beat up, and then you would have to go out there and try to play a hockey game. I mean, it is tough enough to do one or the other, but to combine them both night in and night out, that was a constant battle for sure. Sometimes you were just so exhausted, both mentally and physically, and it could have an effect on how you played the game.

"Fighting is all about deterrence. Hopefully my presence out on the ice would deter dirty play and disrespect toward my teammates. I tell you what, though, fights settle the game down and clean them up. I've seen it happen a million times. And most of the time it didn't even come to that. Things were settled with words or by us just being visible on the end of the bench.

"I will never forget when I was with Edmonton and a game would get chippy. Dave Semenko, one of the toughest guys around, would skate over and just look at the agitator who had been stirring it up or pissing off one of our finesse guys like Gretzky or Messier. He just had this way of looking at him, and then he would very calmly say, 'Okay, somebody is going to get hurt out here.' And that was the end of whatever was going on, guaranteed. Nobody wanted to mess with that guy. He cleaned up the game way more than people will ever know. Nobody wanted to piss him off, nobody.

"The mere presence of a tough guy will usually deter any scrums, cheap shots, unnecessary obstruction, or little intimidation tactics, and that ultimately keeps the game flowing freely. That veiled threat of knowing a fight could happen at any moment really cleans up the game. You have to remember this about tough guys. The real tough guys, the respected ones, go after the guys who need to be addressed. If not, your better players are going to get hurt, and the fans are never going to see their abilities out on the ice because they would be on the shelf.

"So why do we do what we do? We are hockey players, and we all have roles to play on our teams. Not everybody can be Wayne Gretzky, that is just a fact of life. Football teams need offensive linemen and hockey teams need enforcers; that is how teams win, with role players. Some guys fight out of fear, some guys fight out of insecurity, some guys fight because it is the right thing to do, and some guys fight because they just like to fight. For whatever the reason, fighting in hockey is a necessary evil and something that actually protects the game's best players from injury and acts of disrespect.

"You know, hockey enforcers are typically the nicest guys on their teams. They are the most approachable and the most fun to hang around with too. They usually accepted that role because they care about their teammates so much. In fact, it might just be the most selfless job in all of professional sports. They are good people. They are like the cop on the beat or like your protective father looking out for those who might not be able to look out for themselves. Some people like to paint horns on them and call them animals, but when you get to know most of them you will see that it couldn't be further from the truth."

"Jacques Lemaire was a player's coach. You had to play both ends of the rink with Jacques, and you had to be accountable. He was the perfect combination of being a motivational guy as well as a teacher. He was a great teacher, though, for sure. The way he taught us things and the way he got us to commit to his style of play was amazing. Jacques had a plan, and he needed everybody to buy into that plan, no matter what. Yet he was always willing to listen to any suggestions that the players made too, which was why we respected him. That just speaks volumes about the kind of person that he is."

Bruce Driver
New Jersey 1995

"Marc Crawford did a great job leading us to the Cup in 1996. He was a young coach, but he was smart in that he brought in some great assistants in Jacques Martin and Joel Quenneville, who were both outstanding as well. Marc was a good motivator and was able to get the players to play hard for him. It was tough for Marc that year too, in that we were new to the community and had all new surroundings to get used to. There were a lot of distractions that year. We had brought in Patrick Roy and Claude Lemieux that season though, both proven winners, and that helped a lot."

Peter Forsberg
Colorado 1996 and 2001

"Al [Arbour] was a great human being, just a really fun guy to be around. He was good at figuring out each player's unique personality and motivating him accordingly.

Everybody had to have his buttons pushed a different way, and Al was able to figure that out. That was probably his biggest attribute in my eyes."

Clark Gillies
New York Islanders 1980, 1981, 1982, and 1983

"Al Arbour had the unique ability to be able to read and understand his players. As a result, that ability allowed him to get whatever he needed to get out of each player. He treated everyone differently. I don't mean that in a negative sense either; I mean in it in a positive one. He was always trying to figure out what it was that motivated each player. He wanted to find out what was best for him and what it was that would get that player to play as best as he could. Everything he did was always in a team concept, but he motivated us as individuals. It's hard to explain, but he was a tremendous motivator and just an outstanding coach."

Butch Goring
New York Islanders 1980, 1981, 1982, and 1983

"Jacques Demers wasn't a huge Xs and Os guy, but he was a great players coach. He really respected us and did what he could to make us all feel comfortable. You just knew that he would do anything that he could for you, whether it was on the ice or off. He was one of those guys who you just wanted to play so hard for because you know he genuinely cared about you. As a result, the players really wanted to play hard for him. He motivated us with respect."

Sean Hill
Montreal 1993

"Ken Hitchcock was our driving force. He prepared us unbelievably on what we had to do in order to be ready for the opposition. He kind of let the veteran guys assume a lot of the leadership role too, guys like Guy Carbonneau, Craig Ludwig, Pat Verbeek, Dave Reid, and Brett Hull, to name a few. He continually reminded us that over the course of those nine weeks of the playoffs that we were going to have ups and downs and wins and losses, not to mention injuries, but that we needed to stay focused and not get too high or too low. The guys really bought into that 'long journey' mentality, and it paid off for us."

Tony Hrkac
Dallas 1999

"Glen Sather was a great coach. I remember when I first got to Edmonton and was worried if I was going to be able to keep my spot on the roster. One day after practice Glen came up to me and said, 'As long as you look after your teammates, then you can have a job on this team.' I took those words and defined them myself. He never once told me to fight anyone; he never had to. If somebody was taking liberties with Wayne [Gretzky] or Mark [Messier], then I knew that I had to get involved. And it wasn't just those guys either. I turned it into my own little philosophy where I had to convince opposing teams that Kenny Linseman and Glenn Anderson, both notoriously chippy players, were allowed to do whatever they wanted to out on the ice! And if anybody messed with them, then I had to go out there and back them up. My teammates appreciated me doing the dirty work and so did Glen, which was why we got along over the years."

Don Jackson
Edmonton 1984 and 1985

"Ken Hitchcock was my coach in Dallas, and he was an extremely smart guy. He understood the game, and he had systems that he demanded we all follow. I think teams that win have a good structure in place, and we certainly had that. Beyond that, the players all held each other accountable, which was important to Ken as well. It can't just be the coach who does everything; the players have to buy into it and help keep everybody honest. Then in 2003 with New Jersey, I learned a lot from Pat Burns. He was a great coach. Pat was what I would call an old-school coach. He just wanted us to go out and play hard. We had a system in place, but it was a pretty loose one. He just wanted us to focus on the fundamentals and work hard. If you did that, then he would reward you with ice time."

Jamie Langenbrunner
Dallas 1999 and New Jersey 2003

"Scotty [Bowman] was a genius. He made sure everybody had a role, and he made them feel valuable to the team. He knew how to prepare each individual too. He knew which buttons to push on each player in order to motivate him. For instance, sometimes he would be really hard on me in practice. He knew that I would get mad at that and then respond by playing harder out on the ice. He knew that I wanted to prove him wrong. He knew that I wanted to show him that I was better than he thought I was. He just knew everything, which was why he was such a great coach. He brought the best out of his players, usually without them even really realizing it at the time. He was also really good at facilitating the team chemistry with us. We had guys from all different nationalities on those teams, and he made sure that we all got along and that we were able to work together, despite the language barriers and other obstacles. We were a very close-knit team during those two Stanley Cup runs, and I think Scotty had a lot to do with that. We were all focused on the same goal, and that was the glue that bonded us together."

Martin Lapointe
Detroit 1997 and 1998

Montreal Canadiens coach Scotty Bowman (left) and Chicago Blackhawks coach Billy Reay pose with a replica of the Stanley Cup in 1973.

"Scotty Bowman was a great coach, a true professional.
I learned a great deal from him. He knows the game
so well. He understood every little detail. Whatever the
situation or with the game on the line he was always
prepared and always ready to react. He prepared us
well and just treated us with respect. Behind the bench
he was like a general; he could lead his troops to success
in any situation."

Igor Larionov
Detroit 1997, 1998, and 2002

"As for my coaching style, I think I am the type of person
who will coach the way the players want me to coach. I
am a guy who will stick with his ideas, and I try to go with
what I know. With regard to coaching and how to handle
people, I think my players play a big part in that. I mean,
if they want me to be tougher, for instance, then I get
tougher. If they want me to ease up on them, then that is
what I do, depending on how they respond to what I am
asking of them. You know, every coach tries to find a way
to win. The goal is to win. Period. You also have to work
with the type of players that you have. You just have to find
a certain way to play that will help the individual to perform. You know, people talk about my defensive philosophy and the 'neutral zone trap' and that kind of thing, and
that is okay. But I don't know one coach who doesn't want
his players to score. Believe me, scoring is a good thing,
and it is good for your team. But you just have to consider
what is best for your team and what you can do to get the
most success possible from your players. Then, after all
that, you have to sell that to your players and get them to
buy into it. If things are not going well, then you have to

find another route. And if your second route is no good, then you need to find a third. When you run out of routes, you are done as a coach. That's it."

Jacques Lemaire
Montreal 1968, 1969, 1971, 1973, 1976, 1977, 1978, and 1979

"Bob Johnson was our coach for that 1992 season, and what made Bob so unique was the fact that he was such a positive person. Bob was very good at putting guys in roles. He was able to put people into situations where they could excel, that was his gift. He was so good at that. He was able to bring us all together and really motivate us through positive reinforcement. Scotty Bowman was the coach for the 1993 team, and he was a very different type from Badger Bob. He was a great coach but very matter-of-fact and to the point. They were two totally opposite coaching styles. Both were effective, though, and both were able to get us to play at an extremely high level. Beyond that, I would have to give credit too to Craig Patrick, our GM, who put all the pieces together for us those two years by making some great trades that really helped us out."

Troy Loney
Pittsburgh 1992 and 1993

"Glen Sather was an unbelievable coach. He was a master at getting the right mix of players on his teams, from good-character locker room guys to role players. What a great motivator too. Next to my parents I owe all of my success to him. I had no confidence whatsoever when I got there and was just spinning my wheels trying to keep up with everybody, but he believed in me and gave me an opportunity. He kept patting me on the back and telling me I was doing all right. It was just fantastic. He changed my life dramatically by bringing me on to that team, and I will forever be grateful for that. Another thing that he did that was unique was he would always make his trades early in the year. If guys didn't work out they would be gone. He wasn't one of those coaches who waited until the trade deadline; he wanted to know what he had before he was going into the playoffs. That was very unique. The guy was just a genius as a coach, he really was."

Kevin McClelland
Edmonton 1984, 1985, 1987, and 1988

"Terry Crisp brought a lot of energy, emotion, and enthusiasm to the team on a consistent basis. He was a really good coach. He also used ice time as a reward. We had three really good players sitting out every night as a healthy scratch, so you had to play well to stay in the lineup on that team. Talk about motivation. And it didn't matter who it was either. Case in point: both of our captains, Jim Peplinski and Mark Hunter, sat out the championship game. I mean, that is pretty much unheard of. So if you wanted to play you had to work hard and produce. Otherwise you were going to be on the bench, and nobody wanted to sit out. Nobody. As a result, guys were more competitive in practice. I think after a while we all could sense that we were on the verge of doing something pretty special, and everybody wanted to be a part of it."

Brian MacLellan
Calgary 1989

"Randy Carlyle was very consistent in what he said and
what he taught. He didn't waver too much. One of the
words that Randy would use a lot was 'process.' He
reminded us that it was the process that would get you
to that ultimate goal. It was being disciplined, playing
with structure, working hard—all of those things added up
to a process. So Randy's ability to get us to buy into his
vision of how we should execute our overall game plan
was certainly a big reason as to why we won the Stanley
Cup that season."

Todd Marchant
Anaheim 2007

"I learned a lot from Jacques [Lemaire]. I really liked him
as a coach. He was great for a guy like me because he
simplified the game. He just told you very matter of factly:
this is where you should be; this is who you should pass to
in this situation; and this is how we do things on this team.
Everything was in layman's terms with Jacques. It was
black and white too, never gray. You just knew where you
stood with him at all times because he made his expectations of you very clear and concise. And either you did it
his way or you didn't play. That was it. If you couldn't do
the job then he would get someone else to do it. You had
to buy into his philosophy or you were going to be out of a
job. That was okay, though, because we all bought in and
wound up having tremendous success. Jacques was a man
of conviction; when he believed in something he was going
to stick with it. I will never forget starting out that '95 Cup
season really slow. We were losing a lot of games, but I
remember him not being upset with us at all. He just kept
reminding us to hang in there and to keep doing what we

were doing, following his system. He loved the neutral zone trap, and this defensive-first system, and he was very determined to make it work. He knew that we were trying, but that things just weren't clicking yet. So he just kept encouraging us to stick with it and to hang in there. Sure enough, eventually it clicked. And once it did, we were off to the races."

Chris McAlpine
New Jersey 1995

"Toe Blake was a fine coach. He was very particular that we followed the fundamentals. You had to play both ways with Toe too; he wouldn't tolerate anybody loafing or not back-checking. It was the little things with Toe. He wanted you to finish your checks and play your position, little things that led to big things—like Stanley Cups. And he won a whole bunch of them."

Ab McDonald
Montreal 1958, 1959, and 1960;
Chicago 1961

"Glen Sather was the head coach, and his two assistants were John Muckler and Ted Green. We had a tremendous coaching staff in Edmonton. They worked very well together and were great at putting game plans together that would showcase our strengths. Glen had to deal with a lot of big egos on those teams, yet he was able to excel in that environment and get the most out of his players. On a personal note, he was very good to me, and I will always appreciate the opportunity he gave me. He was the one individual who really believed in me at this level, and he enabled me to thrive in my specific role. He put me into situations where I could succeed, and I will forever be grateful for that."

Marty McSorley
Edmonton 1987 and 1988

"Ken Hitchcock was a great coach. His preparation and game planning was second to none. He was very methodical and organized and was always well prepared. Our assistant coaches were great too, in Bob Gainey, Doug Jarvis, and Rick Wilson, who had a ton of experience and insight that really helped us."

Mike Modano
Dallas 1999

"Al Arbour was such a commanding presence on the bench. I would compare him to a stern father figure who you respected because he pushed you to be your best. He would kick you in the butt when he felt like you needed it, and he would pat you on the back when he felt like you needed it. He and GM Bill Torrey, they *were* the New York Islanders—no two ways around it. What a great tandem they were. For them to be able to keep that team together for all those years was just amazing. We had a lot of strong personalities on those teams too, which I am sure was not easy as far as keeping everybody happy and focused on winning. So hats off to them for doing what they did behind the scenes during those years."

Ken Morrow
New York Islanders 1980, 1981, 1982, and 1983

"Jacques Demers taught me a lot about the power of communication. He had a two-way street with the players, and when he said his door was always open, he actually meant it. He never came across like he had all the answers, and he truly valued the input from his players. He would always welcome new suggestions and ideas, anything that would benefit the team. Jacques would gather up all of this information directly from his players and assistants and then put together a game plan based on it. It was really effective. The players really appreciated that, and that is why they had so much respect for him."

Kirk Muller
Montreal 1993

"Al Arbour was a great coach and a tremendous motivator. His style was really different. Maybe he would tell us a story at the pregame meeting, something poignant and meaningful, and as a result it would make you want to go through the boards for him. He always told us to expect the unexpected too. Case in point: if we were in a stressful situation and everyone figured he would be ranting and raving, that's when he would be quiet and calm. He was a unique guy. He instilled in me the idea that the crest on the front of the jersey means a heck of a lot more than the name on the back. It's an old cliché, but it means so much. He was able to get everybody on the same page so that we could all work together toward a common goal. The guy was like a father figure to us, especially the younger players, he really was."

Bob Nystrom
New York Islanders 1980, 1981, 1982, and 1983

"Randy Carlyle is a pretty intense coach. He's hands on, and the guys have a lot of respect for him. He really wanted to win it that year, and that emotion and energy definitely rubbed off on us. It was his first head coaching job in the NHL so he probably felt like he had something to prove as well. There was a lot of pressure on him too. We had gone out and gotten several big-name players to ramp up for it, guys like Scott Niedermayer, Chris Pronger, and Teemu Selanne. So the expectations were running high coming into the season, for sure. Randy is just a really good guy. He did an amazing job in motivating us that season, and I am just grateful that it all worked out for us the way that it did."

George Parros
Anaheim 2007

"In my opinion Jacques Lemaire is the best coach of all time. From matching up lines to tactical issues to putting together game plans, there's just nobody better. He didn't say a lot, but he was a great communicator, whether it was hand signals from the bench or group talks in the locker room. He also emphasized what we should say to the press after games too, which was really unique. He talked about the importance of giving our opponents praise and about respecting them. He would rather we say how good they were than anything else. He reminded us that if we said the wrong thing in the newspaper during a key series in the playoffs, it could change the whole momentum. Opposing players and coaches will use that as bulletin board material, and it will come back to haunt you. Well, Jacques made sure we were prepared for any ambush questions that the media may have had for us, and it was very helpful. It was a little thing, but an important thing.

Jacques simply did not want us to add any fuel to the fire. The guy had won a boatload of Stanley Cups and been through the wars—so when he told us to do something, we did it. That's why we won that year; his leadership and direction. It was awesome."

Mike Peluso
New Jersey 1995

"Bob Hartley was a very good tactician. He studied the game and was really a student of the game in every sense. The main thing I learned from him was the importance of paying attention to detail. He continually stressed the importance of paying attention to all the little things and about how collectively those things all added up to one big thing at the end of the season."

Shjon Podein
Colorado 2001

"Fred Shero was a great coach. He was a very low-key guy, but when he spoke we listened. We had a lot of respect for him, and he really knew how to motivate us. He relied on his leaders, his dressing-room guys, to make sure everybody was on the same page. That was very important to him. He understood how it worked. His approach was very unique, though; he didn't say a whole lot. He was somewhat aloof too. He would say certain things at certain times that would make you think a little bit, but there was definitely a method to his madness. Look, he embraced fear and intimidation as a tactic, and it worked. It was revolutionary; it completely changed the game. The league ultimately changed the rules because of our tactics. The 'Philly flu' was the real deal; teams did not want to face us. The fans loved those rivalries, though. We sold out buildings wherever we went. Nobody else could do that in those days, nobody. Freddy was the guy who made all of that possible."

Dave Schultz
Philadelphia 1974 and 1975

"Scotty Bowman had a great knowledge of the game. He really understood our competition too. He did his homework and prepared us well. We all knew that he was a Hall of Famer, so that kept us honest because nobody was bigger than he was in our eyes. He expected a hundred percent accountability on each and every shift, and he held us to it. You had to play defense too; that was really important to him. He was very specific about what we should do and where we should go. We all knew that if we messed up, regardless of our stature, that somebody else was going to come in and play for us. That was his way of motivating us, and it was very effective. We had to be accountable for our actions, no matter what."

Brendan Shanahan
Detroit 1997, 1998, and 2002

"Jean Perron was a very good coach. He had taken over for Jacques Lemaire, who had a defensive-first philosophy. Jean took the reins off of us a little bit and let us be a bit more offensive minded, yet he still wanted us to focus on our defensive responsibilities. So it was sort of a hybrid style of both philosophies, which worked out great for us in the end."

Bobby Smith
Montreal 1986

"Glen Sather was my coach in 1987 and 1988. His biggest strength was that he had such a strong understanding of people. He could just read people. He could sense who was playing well at any given time and get guys into situations where they could have success. He was a great motivator too. I mean, he's the type of person who, within a 10-minute conversation, makes you think you're the worst player in the league—and by the time you're done you think you're the MVP. I think he had a real psychological edge over most coaches. John Muckler coached us to the Cup in 1990. As a coach, John was more of a tactician. He was on Glen's staff for a very specific reason, and that was because the guy understood the game as well as anybody out there. He was an Xs and Os type of coach and was very detail oriented. For him to lead us to the Cup without Wayne Gretzky in the lineup was a huge accomplishment too; a lot of people forget that. Wayne had gone to L.A. at that point and everybody had sort of written us off. Well, we had something to prove, and it felt pretty good proving it. It just said a lot about the character and leadership in our locker room. Wayne is the greatest to ever play this game, but hockey players don't win championships—teams do."

Steve Smith
Edmonton 1987, 1988, and 1990

"The transition from Bob Johnson to Scotty Bowman was pretty drastic. Bob led us to the Cup in 1992 against Minnesota and then Scotty led us back in 1994 after we swept Chicago. Their personalities were polar opposites, but they were both great coaches and both great guys.

Bob was more of a teacher while Scotty was more of a bench coach. It just goes to show that you can win with different styles of play. I feel lucky to have been able to play for each of them. That was tough, to see Bob pass away so quickly that next season. He inspired us, though, and I think that was a big part of us going back to back the way we did. We had some great players on those two teams too, from Mario Lemieux up front to Tom Barrasso back in goal, and we just found ways to win. Everybody just found a way to contribute, whatever their role was, and raise their game to a higher level. We had a hot goalie, we got a few lucky breaks along the way, and beyond that we just worked hard. It was a pretty amazing time, it really was."

Kevin Stevens
Pittsburgh 1992 and 1993

"Crispy [Terry Crisp] was a good delegator. He was good at handing off responsibilities to his assistants, Pierre Page and Doug Risebrough, and letting them take ownership of certain things. He was also a very emotional guy. He was real loud and vocal and could get the guys charged up. He was a good coach, and he was able to bring us all together that year, so I give him a lot of credit."

Gary Suter
Calgary 1989

"Terry Crisp was a hard-driven, loud, enthusiastic coach. He inherited a very good team in Calgary a few years earlier from Bob Johnson, and his job was to lead them across the finish line, which he did in '89. He tolerated no excuses, and he worked the team hard. As a result he was able to take that team to the next level. Overall he was a very good coach; the players respected him."

Tom Thompson
Calgary 1989 (Scout)

"When we won our first Cup in '75 we got beat in Boston in the last minute of play in Game 1. We were tied at 2–2, and then Bobby Orr got the game winner, which really took the wind out of our sails. So after the game Freddy [Shero] told us that it was our choice as to what we wanted to do the next day, which was an off-day. He said we could either go golfing together, or we could go back to the Garden and practice for an hour. The stipulation was that if we played golf we had to each turn in our scorecards to him. That was Freddy, always throwing in odd little things like that which made no sense whatsoever. I mean, what difference would it have made whether we turned in our scorecards or not? Well, we all chose to go golfing and clear our heads. Sure enough, we took Game 2 in dramatic fashion. Moose [Dupont] tied it up, and then Bobby [Clarke] got the game winner in overtime to even up the series and send it back to Philly. Anyway, I always wondered about why Freddy let us go golfing that day and not had us practice like most every other coach would have done. I mean, had we lost that night everybody would have criticized his decision. It would have seriously damaged his reputation. So I asked him about it just before he died. He just looked at me and told me about courage. He let us make that decision, and then he had the courage to live with the ramifications. He knew we were in good enough shape, and he knew we needed to let our hair down a little bit to come together as a team. He wanted us to forget about the pressure of the moment and have some fun. Sure enough, it worked brilliantly. Freddy was so unique that way. He just was always thinking way outside the box. The guy was truly an innovator."

Bill Clement
Philadelphia 1974 and 1975

"Big Al [Al Arbour]...what a great guy and what a great motivator. He still motivates me today. His calmness, his ability to lead, the way he set the example—he just had all the right tools. Even today, whenever things get shook up or I get riled over something, I stop and think about what Al would do. I can still picture him all nice and calm behind the bench, just thinking and not reacting in a negative way. That is something that I really took away from my time with him, to stop and think when things go wrong. He was a great coach and was a huge part of our success, no question. He was dealing with 24 very different personalities, yet he had the ability to make all of those players work together and concentrate on their own contributions to the team. That is a tough thing for a coach to do too, believe me. He did it, though, and that was why the guys really respected him."

John Tonelli
New York Islanders 1980, 1981,
1982, and 1983

"Ken Hitchcock was very good at studying the opposition and figuring out ways to pull them out of their element. He was very good at finding favorable matchups for us as players. That was his specialty, game planning. Hitch used

to always ask us, 'What would make them crack?' He
wanted to find ways to make them uncomfortable when
they played us. He was very good at figuring out that
aspect of the game. We were a veteran team, and we
believed in his message, which is why I believe we had so
much success that season. He also let us older veteran guys
handle situations in the locker room, which was important.
I think that there was a learning curve for him on that ini-
tially, but eventually he realized that it was better for us
players to handle certain situations among ourselves. As
players we appreciated and respected that."

Pat Verbeek
Dallas 1999

"Peter Laviolette is a great coach and a great person. He
got everybody involved and really motivated us to be our
best. I have never seen a guy more prepared; he didn't
miss a thing. He knew our opponents' strengths and weaknesses and was really able to get us to capitalize on that
stuff. He really did his homework, and that gave us a lot of
confidence as players. His philosophy was just unique. For
instance, he wanted us to have our families around. He felt
that if we had our wives and kids around, then we would
be more relaxed and better focused on doing our jobs.
That was important to him. That whole year was just amazing. When I see that team picture of all of us out on the ice
with the Cup after we won it, I think about how it was such
a total team effort. Everybody was involved, and that was
all because of Peter. Then to watch guys like Rod
Brind'Amour, Glen Wesley, and Bret Hedican, all 15-to-20-
year veterans who had never won a Cup before, it was
pretty incredible. That was a moment I will never forget. I
can still picture Roddy, our captain, waiting so anxiously

for Commissioner Bettman to hand him the Cup. He was so excited; he just wanted to grab it so badly. As soon as the commissioner started to pick it up to present it to him, Roddy practically tore it out of his hands. It was great."

Niclas Wallin
Carolina 2006

"Scotty Bowman is an awesome coach, probably the best of all time. For starters, he has so much experience, which gives him so much credibility with the players. He is so innovative too, just very creative in his ideas about strategy and game planning. He was a great motivator too. He was the guy who kept us calm when we got too excited, and he was the guy who prodded us when we needed a kick in the butt. He was our leader. We couldn't have done it without him."

Steve Yzerman
Detroit 1997, 1998, and 2002

CHAPTER
7

Hands on the Prize

There is a protocol for what a player is supposed to do immediately after he wins the Stanley Cup. It goes something like this: first, he cries as the clock ticks to zero, and then he tosses his equipment a la "yard sale" all over the ice. From there he leaps on top of his goalie in utter bedlam, hugs his teammates, and then celebrates like a rock star. After a few minutes of that he will get in line, single file, to do the customary handshake at center ice with his teammates. He will be respectful of his devastated opponent and try not to act too excited. Next, he will stand around laughing and smiling with his teammates as he waits for the commissioner to come out with the Cup. In the meantime, he will compare playoff beards, see who has the most stitches and/or missing teeth, and even maybe sing a few verses of "We Are the Champions" along with the fans—assuming the Cup was clinched at home. If not, he hums it to himself. Either way, he's singin'.

Then, after the Cup Keeper rolls out Stanley and the commissioner congratulates the other guys for coming in second, he waits patiently for his turn to touch the Cup. The commissioner will first hand it to the team captain and then awkwardly pause for a photo of the two while trying to prevent the captain from ripping it out of his hands in excitement. Once the captain frees the Cup from the commissioner's clutches, he hoists it proudly for all to see. He will then have the choice of doing a victory lap around the rink, all the while cautiously watching for TV cords and confetti, or he will pass it off to the teammate of his choice.

Whom he decides to hand it to is always the million-dollar question. It's one of the most exciting moments for die-hard hockey fans. Will he go seniority and give it to the oldest guy on the team? Or will he give it to his buddy, who he has been to war with and feels is most deserving? Who will he honor? Nobody knows. One thing is for sure, though, nobody can talk about the said pecking order. No way. That would jinx it. It can be thought of ahead of time but never discussed openly. Ever. Once the handoff is made to the second player, it becomes that guy's choice as to who he will hand it to. He will then choose, and so on and so on, until everybody has had their turn raising Stanley. Eventually the management gets involved. You know...the suits, and the best part about that is watching to see who will fall flat on his back after raising the heavier-than-expected 35-pound Cup on slippery ice while sporting leather wingtips.

Later they will all pose for an on-ice photo at the faceoff circle. All the players will smoosh together on top of each other with the Cup in the middle. Stars up front, role players in the back. Everybody holds up his index finger to let the world know "We're No. 1!" This tradition, by the way, was started in 1988 with Edmonton and then continued when Calgary repeated it in 1989. Now it's the moment everybody waits for. Players don't want to be doing a random TV interview when this is going on because this is the photo that will hang in their office or bathroom until they are 90. It's the "money shot" of the best memory of their life.

The tradition of the on-ice passing of the Cup is wonderful for the fans, but it certainly hasn't always been that way. Looking back, it's widely believed that the first time that the Cup was awarded out on the ice as opposed to in the locker room was in 1932 with the Toronto Maple Leafs, but the practice did not become a tradition until years later. Over the ensuing years it was common for the commissioner to place the Cup on a table that was brought out onto the ice after the game. He would hand it to the captain, and then the players would come by and pose for pictures standing next to the Cup on the table. Nobody hoisted it until they got back to the locker room.

In 1950, however, Detroit's Ted Lindsay became the first captain to hoist the Cup over his head, and then he added a twist—he skated around the rink. According to Lindsay, he did so as a courtesy to the fans who wanted to have a better view of the Cup. It wasn't a victory lap per se; that tradition wouldn't come until 1971, when Montreal Canadiens captain Jean Beliveau skated around the ice at the Chicago stadium with the Cup held high and his teammates following behind. The reason he did it wasn't to draw attention to himself; it was to say good-bye to the fans, as the 40-year-old promptly retired following the game.

There are many poignant stories about who the captain has chosen to hand the Cup to over the years. In 1997, after the Red Wings won the Cup they gathered for a golf outing that summer. Afterward, defenseman Vladimir Konstantinov and team masseur Sergei Mnatsakanov were going home in a limousine. Sadly, the driver fell asleep at the wheel and got into a terrible accident. Both men suffered brain injuries, and just like that Konstantinov's career was over. The next year the team beat Washington to repeat as champions, and when team captain Steve Yzerman got the Cup from Commissioner Bettman he skipped the traditional victory lap and instead skated straight over and handed it to Konstantinov, who was sitting proudly in his wheelchair. The team had dedicated the season to him, and there weren't too many dry eyes in the house that night.

In 2007, after the Anaheim Ducks won the Cup, it was all about the Niedermayer brothers, Rob and Scott. Scott had played the good younger brother on a couple of prior occasions by going home to Cranbrook, British Columbia, to celebrate with his older brother when he had won the Cup. Happy and proud of his sibling, yet tormented that he could not touch the Cup himself, he eventually signed on with Anaheim in 2007 in hopes of finally getting to hoist it for himself. He had been to a pair of finals over his career but had lost both times. They had even faced off against each other in 2003 when Scott's Devils beat Rob's Ducks. Their mom openly admitted that she was rooting for Scott that time too, because she so desperately wanted him to share the experience that Rob had. So when they finally won it together in '07, Scott, the team captain, chose to hand it to Rob first—in what he would later call the "highlight of his career." To celebrate, the two brothers chartered a helicopter on their day with the Cup and partied on top of a nearby glacier in the Canadian Rockies—standing literally and figuratively on top of the world.

And when the Pittsburgh Penguins beat the Red Wings to win the championship in 2009, Sidney Crosby handed the trophy to Billy Guerin. Eventually, after all the players had their turns, the Cup reached team owner Mario Lemieux, who then returned it to Sid, symbolizing a passing of the championship torch from one generation to the next, from one captain to another. The fans went crazy. Afterward, Sid was asked about his thoughts at that moment. The 21-year-old superhero smiled and quipped, "It's heavier than I thought!" He then got serious, though, and said, "It's everything I dreamed it would be. I feel lucky to be a part of this group."

"This kid, that's all he thinks about, winning championships," Lemieux said. "His whole life is about training and playing hockey and practicing. He's the perfect hockey player. He prepares himself every day. It's amazing. I wish I would have had that discipline back then."

Here are some more stories…

Stanley visits the top of Fisher Peak in the Canadian Rockies with New Jersey Devils defenseman Scott Niedermayer, celebrating his team's 1999–2000 Cup victory.

WHO HANDED YOU THE CUP
ON THE ICE AFTER YOU WON IT?

"I got it from Eric Desjardins, and then I handed it to Mike Keane. It was all a blur, but I knew where my family was sitting so I skated over and held it up in front of them. That was pretty neat; a moment I will definitely never forget."

Brian Bellows
Montreal 1993

"There is definitely a pecking order based on seniority. Nobody ever talks about it, though, that would be taboo— you would jinx it for sure. Call it superstitious or whatever, but you just don't talk about it. It's just understood, I suppose. Guys just figure it out as they go, and each guy hands it down to the next. It all works out somehow. When I won it the first time in 1992 I got it from Ulf Samuelsson, and from there I handed it to Bryan Trottier. I have a wonderful picture of it in my office; it's such an amazing memory."

Phil Bourque
Pittsburgh 1992 and 1993

"In 1995 in New Jersey, Kevin Stevens got it first because he was the captain, and from there it went to the two assistants, Ken Daneyko and Bruce Driver. There really isn't a set order, but one thing is for sure, you don't ever talk about it or discuss it beforehand. That will jinx it for sure. And for that matter, you never talk about winning the Cup either, you just win it. Period."

Shawn Chambers
New Jersey 1995 and Dallas 1999

"When I won the Cup for the second time in my career in 2009 with Pittsburgh I could tell I was now an old guy. When I won it in New Jersey back in '95 I was one of the last guys to get handed the Cup out on the ice based on seniority, whereas this time in Pittsburgh I got it directly from our team captain, Sidney Crosby, which was quite an honor. I mean, for him to give it to me ahead of the two

The Penguins' Bill Guerin celebrates his second Stanley Cup, one earned in 2009 after Pittsburgh's seven-game series win over the Detroit Red Wings.

assistant captains was just an incredible gesture on his part and something I will always remember. I then gave it to Sergei Gonchar, which was pretty emotional too. He was the second-oldest guy on the team and was next in line. It's weird how it all shapes up, the handing of the Cup afterward, because it is never discussed. Never. Absolutely not. That would be completely taboo and way out of line."

Bill Guerin
New Jersey 1995 and Pittsburgh 2009

"Our captain, Rod Brind'Amour, got it first, and after he raised it he handed it to Glen Wesley, who had been with the organization since they were the Hartford Whalers. Then, and I will never forget it, he yelled out, 'Where's Heddy? Where's Heddy?' It totally caught me off guard because I didn't think I was going to get it at that point, but what a thrill. What an honor. You never know how that pecking order is going to pan out because it's never discussed. When I grabbed it I just about passed out I was so excited. I thought back to the two previous Stanley Cup Finals I had been in and lost, including the one in 2002 when Detroit—which had a $90 million payroll compared to ours, which was $24—beat us. What a moment, though, to raise that Cup for those amazing fans down there in Raleigh. Wow. I thought about my family and about the journey; it's like your whole life sort of flashes before your eyes in those few incredible moments. Then when it was my turn to hand it off, I called out for Ray Whitney. Ray and I had been teammates together down in Florida several years prior, and he had called me that summer, just nine months earlier, to ask me what I thought about him possibly playing for the Hurricanes. I said, 'Ray, we could really use a guy like you because I think we can win the Stanley Cup. I think we're two players short, and you would be one of them.' He said, 'What? Are you kidding? You guys didn't even make the playoffs last year.' I replied, 'Ray, you can believe me or not, but I think we have the right ingredients down here to get it done, and we would love to have you.' Well, my sales job obviously worked, and what a cool feeling it was to hand him the Stanley Cup out at center ice. As I gave it to him I just smiled and said, 'Ray, I told you so!' What a wonderful memory; I will never forget it."

Bret Hedican
Carolina 2006

"When we won the Cup back in '86 our captain, Bob Gainey, hoisted it out on the ice, and we pretty much followed him around. We didn't each take a turn holding it like they do today. Well, I remember skating up behind him, and for whatever reason, he turned and tried to hand me the Cup. It was so completely unexpected—I mean, I still had my gloves on, for goodness' sake. I was a rookie fresh out of the University of Wisconsin who got called up for the postseason just a few months earlier, and here is this Hall of Famer about to hand me the Cup. I was like, 'Are you kidding me?' I panicked. It caught me completely off guard. I am looking around at guys like Larry Robinson, Guy Carbonneau, and Bobby Smith, and feeling completely unworthy. So I sort of held it there for a second and then shoved it right back into his hands. There wasn't a pecking order, per se, like we see today, but I knew my place on the team, and it certainly wasn't ahead of those guys. It was such an awkward moment; I just didn't feel right about it. I guess it's a respect thing. Just to be around a guy like Bob Gainey at that stage of my career was pretty exciting. I remember afterward he said that winning it that year was the most meaningful to him of all his other Cups because he said at that stage of his career it was the one time where he needed the team much more than they needed him. It was pretty humbling."

Dave Maley
Montreal 1986

"One of my best memories came back in 1981, our second Stanley Cup victory, when I got to be the first guy to hoist the Cup. It was payback for my teammates completely ignoring me the year before, when I was off doing TV interviews out on the ice. By the time I was done, the festivities were over. I was crushed. So luckily I got to make up for it in a big way that next season. It was actually a motivating factor for me that next season, believe it or not, to make sure we won it so that I wouldn't miss out on something that I had always dreamed about as a kid. Then when it finally happened, it was just an incredible feeling. I held that thing up there for a while too, absolutely. What a thrill."

Bob Nystrom
New York Islanders 1980, 1981,
1982, and 1983

"The year before we won the Cup, Edmonton took a team picture out on the ice immediately after winning the game with the Cup. Some of our guys thought that was pretty neat and thought it would be a good new tradition to continue, so they did it after our game in the Forum in Montreal as well, where we clinched it. Well, I didn't know about that tradition, so sadly I am not in the greatest

What was your role on that Stanley Cup team?

"My role was to contribute in a lot of different ways; whether it was to shut down the other team's top line or just hitting, fighting, or scoring goals. I tried to do whatever I could to help my team win, that was the bottom line for me. I tried to be aggressive, and I worked as hard as I could, that was it."

Bob Nystrom
New York Islanders 1980, 1981, 1982, and 1983

picture ever. I had gone to the locker room after we had paraded the Cup around the ice, figuring everybody was right behind me, and wasn't aware of it. It's probably my biggest regret in hockey. I see that picture today, and it just kills me that I'm not in it. I'm tempted to make a comeback just so I can win it again and get in that darn picture!"

Joel Otto
Calgary 1989

"Sure, there is a pecking order and whatnot, as far as who goes first, but in '89 it was all about Lanny McDonald. I will never forget watching him raise the Cup. What a moment. He was the captain and the veteran who we were all playing for that year. He was in and out of the lineup during the playoffs and Crispy [Coach Terry Crisp] put him in for Game 6, where we clinched it, and sure enough he scored a big goal. It was unbelievable. So when he hoisted the Cup there were not a lot of dry eyes in the house. Everybody was pulling for him to finally get his moment with Stanley. Everybody. This was going to be his last season, and everybody was rooting for him. What a wonderful person, a true professional; he was so deserving. To see him out there smiling with that big old red beard—classic. Just classic."

Rob Ramage
Calgary 1989 and Montreal 1993

"Back in my day we would all kind of stand around the Cup and congratulate each other. We would sort of hoist it together for a moment, en masse, not really individually too much. So it has definitely evolved since then, the late '70s, into much more of a structured event, with the oldest players getting to touch it first and then each player sort of parading around the ice with it. Another unique tradition that came about in 1989 when I was an assistant coach with Calgary was that they were the first ones to do a team picture all sprawled out on the ice with the Cup. Nowadays it's just expected, but back in the day that kind of celebration was more reserved for the locker room. I think that is a really neat thing too because it captures the raw emotion of the moment, with everyone smiling and with those big scruffy beards, versus a staged team picture later on."

Doug Risebrough
Montreal 1976, 1977, 1978, and 1979;
Calgary 1989 (Assistant Coach)

"I will never forget winning it the first time. Scotty Bowman handed it to me, which was pretty neat. Then in 2002, after winning my third Cup, we let all of the guys who had never won it raise it first. We had so many veterans on that team who had won it before that we just thought this would be the right thing to do. We veterans just took a backseat and watched the other guys get their moment. It was pretty neat to see their expressions and to see how they reacted. Seeing guys like Steve Duchesne and Luc Robitaille and Dominik Hasek getting to finally raise it was pretty special."

Brendan Shanahan
Detroit 1997, 1998, and 2002

"I will never forget how honored I felt when our captain, Wayne Gretzky, accepted the Cup from then-commissioner John Ziegler and immediately turned and handed it to me. There's a pecking order for who gets the Cup, and I was blown away at that moment; it was pretty special. I had accidentally shot the puck into our own net the year before in the playoffs against Calgary in '86, which ultimately cost us the series and ended our season. I was absolutely devastated. Well, Wayne knew how badly I felt, and he wanted to let me know that it was okay. It was one of the great gestures in hockey, truly. I was just as in awe of Wayne as the fans were, so that was a moment I will always remember."

Steve Smith
Edmonton 1987, 1988, and 1990

"When we won it for the first time in 1997 I handed it to our owner, Mike Ilitch. As the team captain I skated a lap with it first to let the fans see it, and then I handed it to Mike, who was sitting in the first row of the stands at the time. We had been through a lot together over the past 14 years leading up to that point, and I thought it would be a fitting gesture. I think he really appreciated it. It was a neat moment for sure."

Steve Yzerman
Detroit 1997, 1998, and 2002

Barry Melrose on *not* winning the Cup

"Hockey is the only sport where the players play for a trophy, the Stanley Cup. In baseball they play for a World Series; in football they play for a Super Bowl; in basketball they play for the NBA Championship. In the NHL, it's the Stanley Cup Finals, and the players all play for the Cup. It's all about the Cup. That's why it's so special. The other sports bring out their trophies when it's time to crown a new champion, but in my opinion they mean nothing. The coach or the MVP might lift it up for some photos, but it's meaningless. In hockey, meanwhile, when a player gets to raise that beautiful silver Cup above his head it means everything. You can tell that it is something that they have genuinely dreamed about their whole life. It's literally a dream come true. I mean, how many people in life get to live out a childhood fantasy that they have thought about since they were five years old?

"As for me, I have never touched the Cup, and that is something I will just have to live with. You can't touch the Cup unless you've earned that right. If you don't win it then you don't deserve the right to pick it up and carry it. No way. I am a firm believer in that and think it's a great tradition. I came so close to winning it as the coach of the Kings in '93, but we lost to Montreal in the finals, and that's something I have to live with. I never got the job done, and as a result I didn't get to raise Stanley. I didn't earn it. It's just so hard and so tough to win it, and that's what makes it so special in my opinion. That's why it's the greatest trophy in sports. To be honest, I don't even like to be near the Cup. I just feel as though I don't deserve to be that close to it. Again, I haven't earned it. It's as though I'm not worthy, and I will always regret that. Like most kids from Canada, I too grew up dreaming of one day hoisting it. I wanted so badly to drink champagne out of it with my teammates. That motivated me and drove me to push harder. I've now come to the realization that I've had my chances and that I probably won't get another one. I've come to grips with that. Look, there are many more guys like me who never got the chance to drink out of it than there are guys who have, so I just have to accept it and learn to live with it. That's tough, it really is."

CHAPTER
8

Celebrating with Stanley

Ever since Lord Stanley donated his Cup to the hockey world back in 1893 the players have been trying to spend as much time with it as they possibly can. In 1896 the Winnipeg Victorias became the first team to drink champagne from the shiny silver chalice, and the tradition has only grown from there. Everybody wants to be around the Cup because of what it symbolizes—championship success—and seemingly everybody wants to drink from hockey's holy grail in the hopes of finding eternal youth. Back in the 1930s and '40s after the teams were awarded the Cup, they would usually have a congratulatory party to celebrate. Typically it wasn't too much of a big deal because in those days the players could hardly even earn a living from playing hockey full time, with many having summer jobs that they had to get back to after the season ended. The owners and management would spend some time enjoying the Cup, and then it would be put in a trophy case or out in the front office for the rest of the year, until they had to pass it on to the next champion. The public would only get to see a glimpse of the Cup at the victory parade, which only added to its mystique.

Eventually, as the popularity of the game grew because of radio and TV, the Cup increasingly gained a celebrity status. The images of teammates all celebrating and drinking champagne out of the Cup served as big motivating factors, ultimately inspiring players to win in hopes of getting a chance to do the same. As time went on teams loosened up and started to allow some of their players to take the Cup around town to celebrate with their teammates at local bars or taverns.

By the 1970s some of the star players were being rewarded by getting to take the Cup home overnight, to enjoy it with their families. In 1979 Montreal Canadiens star forward Guy Lafleur grabbed the Cup and drove it to his parents' house in Thurso, Quebec, where he had a backyard party with friends and family. Not having told anybody about his intentions, officials thought that the Cup had been stolen and began searching frantically for it. When Guy showed up the next day with the Cup they were relieved yet perturbed over his stunt, and they begged him not to do it again.

When the New York Islanders were in the midst of their dynasty in the early '80s the rules surrounding the Cup were relaxed big time, and this is where most of the great stories with it begin to take shape. There was no set plan with the Cup in those days either, the players just worked it out among themselves who would get it each day during those summers. Guys would have parties with it and then throw it in the back of their cars to drop it off at the next guy's house. Typically there was one guy who kind of coordinated the whole thing via phone calls, but that was about it. The Edmonton Oilers, who had the next dynasty in the mid- to late '80s, continued the tradition, and it just grew from there.

Before long the parties were getting bigger and bigger, and the stories more outlandish and shocking—starting with the Cup winding up battered and bruised at the bottom of Mario Lemieux's swimming pool in the early '90s. Perhaps the final straw came in 1994, when the New York Rangers won it and then proceeded to party like it was 1999 in the Gotham City. Many thought that some of the players simply went too far. Brian Noonan and Nick Kypreos appeared with the Cup on

MTV's *Beach House*, where they had Stanley dressed in a T-shirt, baseball cap, and fake mustache, and then allowed it to be stuffed with raw oysters. Strike one. Ed Olczyk apparently took Stanley to the Belmont racetrack and let Kentucky Derby winner "Go for Gin" eat oats from it. Strike two. Then, and this was the clincher, Mark Messier hauled it to Scores, a notorious NYC strip club, where it reportedly became a part of the on-stage show. Strike three…you're out! Shortly thereafter the NHL and the Hockey Hall of Fame got together and decided that hijinks like this were not only bad for PR at a time when the league was trying to grow and expand to nontraditional hockey markets throughout the southern states, it was just downright disrespectful to the history and tradition of the Stanley Cup.

So they concluded from that point on that each player on the championship-winning roster would be allowed to have the Cup for a day. The catch, however, was that it was going to include bodyguards of sorts, chaperones known as "Cup Keepers" who would provide constant 24-hour supervision to make sure the Cup was not damaged or disrespected. First and foremost, no longer would fans be allowed to raise the Cup and drink from it. That would be reserved only for the player who had *earned* it. If said player so chose to let a friend or family member drink from it, he could assist, but no hoisting. It was now up to the Cup Keepers to enforce the rules. Their job would entail delivering the Cup to each player, regardless of where he lives in the world, and remain by his side for the entire 24-hour period. Yes, that means sleeping there too. It would be his job to make sure the Cup didn't wind up in any more strip clubs, casinos, or swimming pools—because let's face it, chlorine wreaks havoc on the silver and nickel alloy. If players disobeyed, then they would lose the privilege of having the Cup. No Kodak moment with Mom and Dad, no charity golf tournament, no partying like a rock star.

One thing you don't want to do is to disrespect the Cup, otherwise the hockey gods may punish you. Such was the case back in 1940, when several players from the New York Rangers apparently burned the deed to the old Madison Square Garden in the Cup and then pissed on it to put out the fire. Needless to say, it took the Rangers another 54 years before they won it again, in 1994, and we all know what happened in the aftermath there. It may be another 54 years, New York…who knows?

No question, the Stanley Cup has been around the block over the past century or so, starting in 1905 when, after a night of celebrating their Stanley Cup victory, members of the Ottawa Silver 7s drop-kicked the Cup onto the (fortunately) frozen Rideau Canal. The Cup remained in the canal until the next day when more sober heads prevailed, and Stanley was rescued. Two years later members of the Montreal Wanderers left the Cup at the home of a photographer they had hired to document their victory. They forgot it there, though, and the photographer's mother, upon finding it, decided to use it as a flower pot in the backyard. It remained there for several months, growing lilies, before anybody realized it was missing.

During the 1962 playoffs between Chicago and Toronto the Cup was nearly kidnapped by a die-hard Montreal fan who snatched it out of a trophy case in the lobby of the Chicago stadium. As he was making his getaway a police officer busted him just as he was about to exit the building. When asked why he was removing the Cup, the guy replied, "I want to take it back where it belongs, to Montreal." After that season the Cup's original bowl and collar were retired and put on display at the Hockey Hall of Fame in Toronto. A few months later they were stolen in what some felt was the ultimate hockey caper. They remained missing for seven years before an anonymous tip led authorities to them in the back room of a Toronto cleaning store. Fifteen years later the Cup was nearly stolen again from the Hall, this time by a group of suspicious men lurking around it with a large hockey bag, but thankfully an alert employee thwarted their attempted heist and scared them off. Police later found detailed photos of the Hall's floor plan in the suspects' getaway car.

In the 15 years since the players have had their official "day with the Cup," the stories, as you will read in the ensuing pages, are hilarious as well as heartwarming. Whenever a player walks into a bar or a restaurant or wherever with Stanley in tow, it's like a major celebrity entering the building. He is the star attraction, without a doubt. People just love seeing him out in public. As for the players, they just love putting stuff in that big beautiful bowl—the more exotic, the better. Here are some of my favorites: in 1996, Colorado's Sylvain Lefebvre christened his newborn child in the Cup. Detroit's Joey Kocur used it as his live well for the trout he had just caught while fishing up at his lake home in Michigan. Edmonton's Doug Weight made an ice-cream sundae in it for his kids to eat, Carolina goalie Cam Ward ate Froot Loops out of it, and several members of the New Jersey Devils made a gigantic margarita in it at a nightclub, even salting the Cup's rim for good measure.

They also love to take it to memorable locales for that "money shot" photo. Luc Robitaille got permission to take it up to the Hollywood sign in Los Angeles, while Stars defenseman Craig Ludwig strapped it to the back of his Harley and took it for a spin around Dallas. Red Wings players Igor Larionov, Slava Fetisov, and Slava Kozlov took the Cup to Red Square in Moscow, while Anaheim's Teemu Selanne took Stanley for a traditional sauna back in his native Finland. And in 2004 Lightning winger Andre Roy proposed to his girlfriend in a helicopter, placing the ring in the Cup as a surprise.

The Stanley Cup travels more than 320 days a year for various charitable and official NHL functions and has logged more than a million miles on trips around the world. Stanley has visited the Parliament in Canada, the White House in Washington, and the Kremlin in Russia. It even came under attack from an incoming missile in Afghanistan but emerged unscathed. Phil Pritchard's official title is vice president and curator at the Hockey Hall of Fame, but his unofficial title is "Cup Keeper-in-Chief." It's his responsibility to coordinate Stanley's travel itinerary with each team, as well as with the other couple of Cup Keepers. Phil was the star of those award-winning MasterCard "Priceless" commercials and probably has the greatest job on earth. He gets to bring the Cup out onto the ice, white gloves and all, where it is then presented by the NHL commissioner to the winning team's captain, who then raises it over his head and does a victory lap before sharing it with his teammates. What a front-row view that must be.

As you can see, not only has Stanley been beat up, dented, stolen, and lost, it's served as a flower pot, baptismal font, and yes, even a urinal. Like all hockey players, though, he's tough, and that's what makes him the coolest trophy on earth. In what has become one of the greatest traditions in all of sports, here are some more stories from the players themselves about what they chose to do with hockey's most revered trophy on their "Day with Stanley."

WHAT DID YOU DO ON YOUR DAY WITH THE CUP?

"We held a big party at my parents' house afterward and put on a big fundraiser for the YMCA in St. Catharine's. I will never forget walking out to my backyard and seeing the Stanley Cup. How surreal was that? I mean, as a kid I had played for it a million times out there and in the driveway, and now to actually see it right there—amazing. Beyond that, I remember going to a party at Patrick Roy's house. At one point, every player, trainer, wife, and girlfriend was in that pool, passing the Cup around. What a great memory.

And what is so great about that day was the fact that Patrick made it all happen in a way only he could do. You see, after winning the MVP he was asked to do the postgame Disney commercial. You know, where the voice says, 'Patrick Roy, you just won the Stanley Cup, now what are you going to do?' To which Patrick says, 'I'm going to Disney World!' We all made fun of him because he couldn't say the words very well with his thick French Canadian accent, but what happened afterward totally blew us away. You see, he wound up making a hundred grand for doing it, and when it was all said and done he gave half of the money to the trainers, and the other half he spent on that pool party. What a great gesture. To him, it wasn't *his* commercial, it was all of ours. What a great leader."

Brian Bellows
Montreal 1993

"On my day with the Cup I took it back to my family farm where I'd grown up—in Simcoe, Ontario—where I spent the morning with my family. I will never forget the moment when the Cup Keeper showed up and took the Cup out of its case and set it down in the living room. What a surreal moment. I just sat there staring at it, thinking about all the early morning practices and about all the things that my mom and dad sacrificed over the years so that I could pursue my passion. So to be able to share that moment with my family was extremely important and meaningful to me. After that we put the Cup on display in town and let everybody enjoy it."

Rob Blake
Colorado 2001

The playoff beard

The playoff beard is simply synonymous with playoff hockey. One of the greatest traditions in sports, its purpose is pretty basic: once the postseason starts, you don't shave until your team is either eliminated or wins the Stanley Cup. Fans can even track their team's progress during the playoffs by monitoring their favorite player's facial hair growth. The bigger the beard, the longer the playoff run. Its origins can be traced back to the early '80s and the New York Islander dynasty. Players such as Butch Goring, Ken Morrow, Clark Gillies, Gord Lane, and John Tonelli all grew out their beards in an act of camaraderie while in the midst of winning 19 straight playoff series.

The playoff beard went into a brief hiatus after that but made a comeback with the '93 Montreal Canadiens as well as the '95 New Jersey Devils, who both embraced it as a sort of Cup-like superstition. Since then it has become a rite of passage for players, regardless of whether they are follicularly challenged or not. Some guys wind up looking like Grizzly Adams with huge bushy beards: Jean Sebastien Giguere, Bret Hedican, and of course the Niedermayer brothers, to name a few. Other guys can only muster up a little bit of peach fuzz, including Pittsburgh's Sidney Crosby, who sprouted just enough to lead his Pens to the Cup in 2009, or Chicago's Patrick Kane, who grows a playoff mullet instead.

Other players put their own twist on it, including Carolina's Mike Commodore, who sports a bright red afro/beard combo that truly sets him apart from the pack. Others sport "staches," "fu-man-chus," "pork chops," and goatees—all in the quest for hockey's ultimate prize. If a team suffers a tough loss, then modifications may be made, too, such as trimming, primping, and grooming in an effort to change the team's luck. Beard-a-thon contests often-times emerge during the postseason as a way for the players to help raise money for charity. You can't jinx it by publicly talking about it, though, which may have been the case in 2009 when the Red Wings used the slogan "The Beard Is Back" for their Stanley

Cup Finals run. Needless to say, the Penguins beat them to win the Cup. You just can't mess with the hockey gods; karma is a you-know-what.

"My beard totally rocked," said Carolina winger Matt Cullen, who won the Cup in 2006. "The local TV station in Raleigh even had a 'beard watch,' and I was the guy who they would take before and after pictures of every week, to track my growth. It was pretty funny. After we won it I shaved off the entire beard but kept this huge, thick Tom Selleck—Magnum P.I. mustache for a while, which was hilarious. In reality I looked more like Jason Lee, the guy from the TV show *My Name is Earl,* just a total tool. I actually got more recognition around town from the mustache than for winning the actual Cup. Go figure!"

"After we won the Cup we all got together at Mario's house. He has this huge place with a gorgeous pool out back, complete with a tiered waterfall that had colored lights in it. It was amazing. Well, Tom Barrasso decided to hike up this waterfall with the Cup and was posing for pictures up there. It was a great shot, with the lights and the water cascading by, just beautiful. Anyway, I am watching this photo op take place from afar as I am sitting in the hot tub drinking a few adult beverages. Feeling that the party needed to get kicked up a notch or two, I decided to take matters into my own hands. I mean, this was *the* Stanley Cup, and we needed to start partying as such. So I climbed up the waterfall like King Kong going up the Empire State Building and grabbed the Cup. I then hoisted it up over my head. Everyone started chanting, 'Throw it in the pool! Throw it in the pool!' Then, in a moment of insanity, I succumbed to peer pressure and threw it in. Everybody just started cheering and going crazy. Well, I threw the thing in the deep end of the pool and sure enough, the base of it filled with water and it sunk straight to the bottom like the *Titanic*. Everybody dove in the pool at that point to rescue Stanley. Guys started diving down to get it, but they were struggling. It was full of water and it weighed a ton. It finally took about four guys to haul the thing up; it was crazy. Once we resuscitated him, we decided that he had better stay on dry land from there on out. Luckily I didn't destroy it, or I don't know what I would have done. In retrospect, I felt bad because I didn't want to disrespect the Cup or anything like that, I just lost myself in the moment. Hey, it was a helluva moment, one I will never forget—that's for sure.

"Later, I wound up getting to have the Cup for like five days; it was totally different back then. Nowadays the guys get it for 24 hours, and they have a chaperone with them; well obviously it wasn't like that in the early '90s. In fact, it was probably because of me that the players have to have the chaperone nowadays. Sorry, guys! Anyway, when I had the Cup for five days, I took it everywhere. It was just a nonstop party, just insane. Eventually, when I had to bring it back for the next guy, I heard something rattling inside of it. Something was loose. I figured maybe something broke off when I threw it into the pool, so I decided to fix it. Now, I am not the handiest guy on the block, but I did have a little toolbox. So I took a screwdriver and pried the bottom off of the Cup. I then put a pen light in my mouth and crawled into the base as far as I could go. I soon realized that a nut had come loose, so I tightened it up. While I was in there, however, I noticed that three French Canadian guys from Montreal had engraved their names on the inside and dated it from back in the mid-1960s. They too had popped it open to repair it, and once they did so, they signed their handi-work and dated it. I thought that was pretty damn cool, so I decided to do the same. Three long hours later, I too had engraved my name inside the Cup with a screwdriver. I etched: 'Enjoy it: Phil Bourque, Pittsburgh Penguins, 1992 Champs.' I figured it would be in there forever, but I later found out that it was removed years later when one of the bands was replaced. You see, the Cup never gets any taller, so they retire the bands of metal every so many years so they can get more names on it. I was pretty bummed out when I found that out, but it's still a great memory. Looking back, had I been smarter I would have engraved it way up at the top so that it would be there forever. Those pieces way at the top, right by the actual cup, are permanent. Oh well, I guess I can always tell my grandkids about how their grandpa was one of just a few players ever to have his name on the inside of the Stanley Cup."

Phil Bourque
Pittsburgh 1992 and 1993

"The best memory I have from my time with the Cup actu-ally came the night we won. Being the captain, they let me bring it home after the game. I will never forget getting home about five in the morning and putting it in my kids' bedroom. To see their reaction when they woke up next to the Stanley Cup was just priceless."

Rod Brind'Amour
Carolina 2006

"My wife trains horses, so we thought it would be pretty neat to feed one of her favorite horses some oats out of the Cup at our ranch here in River Falls, Wisconsin. We just made sure to do it *after* we had drunk out of it though!"

Neal Broten
New Jersey 1995

"I grew up four doors down from Kevin and Derian Hatcher in Detroit, and when I had the Stanley Cup at my house for a big party they stayed away from it. They were both playing in the NHL at the time, and they both understood the unwritten rules regarding it; you don't touch it unless you've won it. I really wasn't aware of it because I guess it had never come up, but it was pretty neat to see that firsthand. It made it even more special when Derian and I won it together four years later in Dallas too. We had played many a hockey game in the neighborhood for the Stanley Cup, so to win it now together for real was pretty amazing."

Shawn Chambers
New Jersey 1995 and Dallas 1999

"We had a big day planned, but my first stop with the Cup might have been my favorite. As soon as I got it I took it to the Bloomington Ice Garden, one of the many arenas where I spent my childhood in Minnesota honing my skills. I wanted to say thanks to Denny May. Denny had been the rink manager there forever, and he used to let me and his son, Chris, who was my line mate in high school, have the keys to the place so we could go there late at night and practice. I thought it would be pretty neat to let him know how much I appreciated that all those years later, and he was really moved by my gesture, which made me feel awesome. Word got out pretty quickly from there, and people started coming out of the woodwork to come see the Cup. It was amazing. People are just drawn to it; it has a sort of magical quality to it. Having the Cup is like being the grand marshal of a big parade in your honor; it's just really a trip."

Tom Chorske
New Jersey 1995

"My day with the Cup was pretty neat. I had it for two nights, which was a fluke, but that was just how it worked out. On the first night I took it to Uptown in Minneapolis, to this swanky place called Chino Latino. I never called ahead either; I just showed up with it and wanted to be spontaneous. This 16-year-old hostess had no clue what I was holding, and she then proceeded to seat us in a private area in back. Well, I wanted to be out in the open and share the Cup, so I requested a big table for my friends right in the middle of the joint. It was in the summer and the doors were all open, so people could see in and see the Cup. It was amazing. What made it even more amazing was when a good buddy of mine, who was a fireman, showed up with his crew in two giant fire trucks outside, with the sirens blazing and all. We all got up and went outside to take pictures and stuff; it was such a great moment. Before I knew it I was up on top of a fire truck on the corner of Lake and Hennepin, hoisting the Cup. Traffic came to a stop, and everybody just went nuts; it was insane. I will never forget it—what a night.

"Then the next day I decided to do what I would normally do on a typical day—as a sort of social experiment: 'My day with Stanley.' It was awesome. I got up at seven in the morning and like every other day, I went to work out at the Calhoun Beach Club. I showed up by myself, with Stanley, and did my thing. I got a lot of strange looks, but it was great. From there I went and had coffee with Mike Bolt, my Cup Keeper, and he proceeded to tell me about the history of the Cup and about all the unique things on it—from typos to interesting facts; it was really neat. I then went back to my old stomping grounds in Bloomington, the Twin Cities suburb where I grew up. First stop was Westwood Sports, where I got my skates sharpened as a kid and continue to get them sharpened to this day. After that I took it to the Bloomington Ice Garden, where I spent probably thousands of hours as a kid learning to play this great game. We had it there for a few hours, and it was wonderful to be able to share it with the community. I saw a lot of excited kids that day— mites, peewees, bantams, and high schoolers—all wide-eyed as they looked at the Cup, and it made me wonder just how many of them might be raising it one day as well. That was pretty profound, it really was. You hope in some small way you can inspire them to think, 'Hey, if he can work hard and do it, maybe I can too.' You hope to be able to pay it forward a little bit, and hopefully I was able to do that. Who knows? I had some good family time after that, and it just capped one of the greatest days of my life. What a great memory."

Ben Clymer
Tampa 2004

"I took it back to my hometown of Moorhead, Minnesota, right on the Minnesota–North Dakota border. My wife and I have a children's foundation for pediatric cancer research, Cully's Kids, and we had our annual charity event the day I brought it back, which was pretty special. We had a golf outing and had all the kids there with us, and we even filled up the Cup with fruit punch so they could all drink out of it with straws. It was just awesome. We had a huge barbeque at our house too for friends and family, complete with a celebrity Wiffle ball game for the Stanley Cup. It was amazing. My wife Bridget and I then went to bed with Stanley, for our first "threesome," I suppose! How great is that? The next day the Keeper of the Cup had to leave to take Stanley to Aaron Ward, who lived in Michigan. I was sad about having to say good-bye to Stanley so I decided to call Aaron and mess with him a little bit. I called him, and I was like, "Hey man, sorry, but one of my buddies got out of hand and actually broke the Cup, and they have to send it back to Toronto to get it fixed. So is there any way you can reschedule your events?" He was so pissed, it was hilarious. He had this huge day planned with all of this stuff going on, and he was just beside himself. I finally came clean, and he about had a heart attack. It was pretty funny. He vowed to kill me, and I am still waiting for him to get back at me, which is kinda scary. Anyway, I remember a few days later the cleaning lady came over, and I wouldn't let her vacuum the big circular ring on the carpet where we had kept the Cup; I just didn't want the memory to fade. So we had the Stanley Cup carpet ring for a good month after that, just as a reminder of our incredible day and our even more incredible season."

Matt Cullen
Carolina 2006

"I slept with Stanley the first night I had it. I also had my kids eat cereal out of it, which was pretty neat too. From there I took it everywhere I could throughout the state of New Jersey. I just wanted to share it with as many people as I could. The fans love Stanley. My favorite thing to do was to surprise friends and family with it and just show up to their offices or wherever, unannounced. That was the best. Their reaction was priceless."

Ken Daneyko
New Jersey 1995, 2000, and 2003

"What a day. It started with breakfast with my family, and from there I took it to the Monmouth racetrack, where I got to spend the day with everybody—from my friends to all my ex-coaches that I had invited. Then, after spending a few hours at my sister's bar, we took it back to my house where we all watched the Tyson versus McNeely fight on TV and then proceeded to party until about 6:45 the next morning. All I can say is that we drank a lot of beer and champagne out of that thing. Wow, what a blur."

Jim Dowd
New Jersey 1995

"Sadly, I never got the opportunity to have the Cup for a day, like the players today get to do. What a wonderful tradition, absolutely the best in sports. Whoever thought of that deserves a huge thank you. There are very few traditions in all of sports that are as good as that one. It's fantastic, just magic. Truth be told, as a politician up here in Canada I have made several inquiries to the Hall of Fame about the possibility of letting the veterans who never had that opportunity have it for a day. I really hope that they do because I already have my day all planned out. I have thought about it many times, as a matter of fact. I'm keeping my fingers crossed. I never got to raise Stanley out on the ice either, and that's something that I regret. In our day the captain raised it, and that was about it. We didn't get to do a victory lap and pass it around from player to player. Seeing the players do that today is wonderful, and it's something that I certainly wish I could have done. I just think the Stanley Cup is by far the most beautiful trophy in all of sports. Bar none. Whether it's the World Cup in soccer or the World Series or the NBA Finals or the Super Bowl, none of those trophies compare to the sheer beauty of the Stanley Cup. What makes it so perfect is that it's big enough for both hands. All the other sports, it's really only one hand in triumph. The World Series trophy is too fragile to handle while celebrating, but not the Stanley Cup—it's made for two hands and two arms way up in the air. It's the timeless and universal symbol of triumph."

Ken Dryden
Montreal 1971, 1973, 1976,
1977, 1978, and 1979

"On my day with the Cup we had a combination ninth birthday party for my son and celebration out in the backyard. We even served cake out of the Cup, which was pretty neat. You don't realize at the time how many people take pictures with the Cup until you get all the holiday cards a few months later with everybody posing with Stanley."

Chuck Fletcher
Pittsburgh 2009 (Assistant GM)

"Bringing the Cup back to Sweden was wonderful. To share it with so many people who came out to see it for a day was very special. The fans over there follow the NHL much more so today than we did when I was a kid growing up, which is great to see."

Peter Forsberg
Colorado 1996 and 2001

"We had a big party at my house one year the night after we won the championship. It was about four o'clock in the morning, and we were all feeling pretty good so I decided to fill up the Cup with dog food, and I let my big German shepherd, Hombre, eat out of it. He looked like he was feeling left out, so I decided to let him enjoy the moment too. It was classic."

Clark Gillies
New York Islanders 1980, 1981,
1982, and 1983

"When I won it the first time in 2000 I was the first player ever to bring it to Alaska, which was really neat. The funny thing about it was that I wasn't even allowed into the bars because I was too young at the time. Finally some cops saw what was going on, and they gave me a police escort to get me in. It was pretty hilarious. I even got to bring it to my dad's bar in Anchorage, the Crossroads Lounge, which was pretty special too. The next day we took it to some nursing homes and hospitals and then had a big party for my whole town at a park, where people could come out and see it and touch it. I just wanted everybody to come out and enjoy it; I wanted to share it with as many people as I could. Later that night I had a

Clark Gillies (center) greets Dennis Potvin while Bobby Nystrom (left) and Bryan Trottier laugh it up during a 2008 reunion of the 1979–1982 Islanders, who won four straight Stanley Cups.

big party, and the best advice I got was from my team-mate, Randy McKay, who told me to set the Cup up on one end of the room and then make sure I stood at the other. It was brilliant. Everyone wants their picture taken with it, and if you are standing there you wind up doing that all night, versus spending time with your friends and family—which is way more important. You want to use that time to thank them for all their sacrifices so you could pursue your dream. It was an incredible time, very mean-ingful and very fun."

Scott Gomez
New Jersey 2000 and 2003

The New Jersey Devils' Scott Gomez raises the Stanley Cup during a parade in his hometown of Anchorage, Alaska, on July 15, 2003.

"I have a great picture of my youngest daughter sitting in the Cup, smiling at Daddy. That's what it's all about right there. That's it."

Butch Goring

New York Islanders 1980, 1981, 1982, and 1983

"The first time with the Cup it was all about sharing it with the fans back in my hometown and using it to raise money for charity. The second time, however, we did some of that, but mostly it was about my family. My wife and four kids have sacrificed so much for me over the years, and I wanted it to be for them. So my kids hosted a party for their friends in the afternoon, and then my wife and I hosted a party that night. What a great day."

Bill Guerin
New Jersey 1995 and Pittsburgh 2009

"My day with the Cup was spent near my home near Brainerd, Minnesota. I have spent a lifetime in hockey, and at 70 years old, to finally hoist the Stanley Cup was quite a thrill. What a dream come true, it really was. The highlight for me was being able to bring in all my kids and grand-kids, and we even got to baptize my new granddaughter in the Cup—holy water and all. What a wonderful experi-ence that was. Beyond that, I have always felt that when something good happens to you that you should give back. So of the 11 hours we had the Cup, only one was for me and my family. The other 10 hours, meanwhile, were used to take it around and raise money for charity. We wound up raising about $7,000 for some local cancer patients that day, which I felt very good about. I saw a lot of joy in people's eyes that day. Having the Cup and being able to do something good with it was one of the high points of my life, it really was. What a day. I will never forget it. It shows the class of the Pittsburgh organization too, to let an old scout like me have it for a day. Most teams don't do that. Usually it is just the coaches and players who get to have it, but they felt strongly that each scout should be rewarded for our hard work as well. We even got rings, which just meant the world to me. They let me know that I was important to the team's success and that I made a difference. Mario Lemieux even doubled our bonuses the day after we won it. What a classy thing to do. There is a reason they are the Stanley Cup champions, they 'get it.'"

Chuck Grillo
Pittsburgh 2009 (Scout)

"I took the Cup to Belarus after we won it, and it was really neat. We even had a celebrity hockey game in which the president of the country played, which was very special."

Nikolai Khabibulin
Tampa Bay 2004

"We never got to have the Cup for a day like they do nowadays. We just all sort of hung out with the Cup in Montreal with it instead. One of my best memories with it, though, was going to Henri Richard's restaurant in downtown Montreal for a celebration luncheon exclusively for winners of the Cup. It was like being initiated into a secret society or something, just really neat. It was as if I was now officially a member of the club. To have a connection to all of those great people, wow, what an honor. Talk about a who's who of the hockey world in there too, holy cow. I was in awe. The thing I remember the most was when Toe Blake entered the room—everybody stood up and clapped. He was sort of No. 1 in the pecking order, and it was as if the president walked in or something. It was just surreal. It was a moment for me as I was sitting there thinking, 'If only my buddies back in Minnesota could see this.' What a neat day."

Tom Kurvers
Montreal 1986

"In 1999, when I won it with Dallas, I took it back to my hometown of Cloquet, Minnesota. One of my teammates with the Stars was Derek Plante, who was also from Cloquet, so we had a joint party at the rink and just shared it with the town. It was pretty neat. The second time, in 2003, after winning it with New Jersey, I actually took Stanley tubing with me behind the boat at our summer home on Island Lake. The Cup Keeper was a bit nervous about it, so I put a life jacket around Stanley, and off we went. Everybody was out in their boats and on their docks cheering us on; it was awesome. From there we had a big party back out at our house for all our friends and family. What a day; I will never forget it."

Jamie Langenbrunner
Dallas 1999 and New Jersey 2003

"On my day with the Cup I took Stanley home with me to Montreal. We took it to some hospitals and all over town to let as many people as possible enjoy it. Then, after we had a big party, I took Stanley to bed with me and had my wife sleep on the couch. I was so drunk at the time she was more than happy to accommodate me!"

Martin Lapointe
Detroit 1997 and 1998

"I was very fortunate to have been able to bring the Cup to Moscow on two separate occasions. In fact, in 1997 it was the first time the Cup had been outside of North America. It was a very special moment for me, to share it with so many people. We brought it to Red Square and let the fans see it and touch it. It was wonderful."

Igor Larionov
Detroit 1997, 1998, and 2002

"I am from a small prairie town in Alberta of about 1,000 souls, Bow Island, and to bring the Cup back to my hometown was something I will never forget. We had a big fundraising event and parade; it was pretty special. We even auctioned off a bottle of champagne that the high bidder could drink out of the Cup at my golf tournament, which was pretty fun. It just meant a lot to the people there that I brought it home, and that made me feel great that I was able to share it with them. I will never forget walking home late that night from the party with a few of my old buddies, back to my parents' house. We had to cross over Highway 3, and as we were walking along, a big semi-truck came zooming past us. So I held up the Cup above my head to let him know what we were doing. Well, he saw that and just went crazy. He flashed his lights and blasted his air horn to celebrate with us; it was amazing. He probably woke up the whole town—it was nuts. Beyond that, I didn't do anything too crazy—other than eat a big bowl of Wheaties out of it. Best bowl of cereal I ever had."

Troy Loney
Pittsburgh 1992 and 1993

"My neatest memory from the day that I got to spend with the Cup would have to be when my two sons slept with the Cup. My son Ryan, who now plays in the NHL, really thought that was neat. They had all their friends over, and we filled the Cup up to the top with ice cream for them, and they all just gorged themselves. It was a pretty special moment; I will never forget that day."

Greg Malone
Pittsburgh 1992 and 1993 (Scout)

"My day was pretty cool. I got it on the Fourth of July and was able to have a huge backyard party in my hometown of Buffalo, New York. Buffalo has never won a championship in anything, so to bring home a championship felt pretty amazing. To see the looks in people's eyes when they got to see it and touch it and have their pictures taken with it felt great. What a day."

Todd Marchant
Anaheim 2007

"My day with the Cup was insane. I drank things out of that Cup that I am not even sure are fit for human consumption, but oh well—when in Rome, I suppose. For my day I wound up bringing it to the Minnesota State Fair, which is like the biggest state fair in the country. Just huge, over a million people come to this thing. It's nuts. I kind of got talked into it and figured sure, why not. I wanted to share it with as many people as possible, and I certainly accomplished my objective, I think. In retrospect, I regret not doing more with my immediate friends and family. There were a lot of people who I should have thanked and shared it with that I never got to see, which still bums me even today. The whole day at the fair was just a blur. I was young and dumb, though, and just went with the flow. As a cocky rookie I figured I would have many more days with the Cup to do those things. Well, we all know how that turned out. I remember being with St. Louis a few years later and getting into the conference finals against Detroit. We had such a great team that year, and I thought we were going to win the Cup for sure. I mean, I already had plans all mapped out for my next "day with the Cup." I had my invitations all ready to go, from old coaches to old teachers to old childhood neighbors; I was going to totally do it up with a big party—the whole nine yards. Well, the Red Wings kicked our asses, and sadly that was the end of my big party. Bummer."

Chris McAlpine
New Jersey 1995

"My greatest memory with the Cup came in 1961 when I was with the Chicago Blackhawks, and we had just beaten the Detroit Red Wings to win the championship. We got stuck in Detroit because of a snowstorm that night so we started celebrating in our hotel. We were all drinking champagne out of it and just making a helluva mess. It's not the easiest thing to drink out of, as you can imagine, because when you tip that big thing over ever so slightly to take a swig out of it everything inside winds up spilling all over you. Well, eventually somebody figured out that you could actually screw the top Cup piece off of it. So we did just that, and we wound up having a ball drinking out of that thing all night!"

Ab McDonald
Montreal 1958, 1959, and 1960;
Chicago 1961

"My best story with the Cup came after our fourth victory. I had just picked up the Cup from Stefan Persson's house and had put it in the backseat of my compact car. I was driving back home and got pulled over by a policeman while I was driving through this small town. I wasn't speeding so I didn't know what was up. Well, the cop came over to my window and says, 'Aha! I thought I saw the Stanley Cup in your backseat!' It was pretty funny. So I am sitting there, pulled over on the side of the road, while this cop and his partner are reading all the names on the Cup. Their sirens were going off and everything—it was crazy. All I could do was laugh."

Ken Morrow
New York Islanders 1980, 1981,
1982, and 1983

"I brought the Cup to my lake place in Kingston, Ontario, between Montreal and Toronto, and spent the day with friends and family. Dan Akroyd also has a place on that lake too, so he came over and joined our party—which was pretty cool. We later brought it over to his house so he could take some pictures, and he later told me that it was the most memorable day he had ever had at the lake, which means a lot, considering he's had the Rolling Stones over as house guests before."

Kirk Muller
Montreal 1993

"My best memory with the Cup came in 1982, when we won it on the road up in Vancouver. Afterward, on the flight home, we filled up the Cup with every single tiny bottle of booze that they had on board and then all took turns drinking out of it. It was about a four-hour flight, and I think we sang and drank and partied the whole way home. It was pretty amazing; I will never forget it."

Bob Nystrom
New York Islanders 1980, 1981,
1982, and 1983

Greatest 24 hours with the Cup—ever

"I will never forget when my teammate and good buddy, Poads [Shjon Podein], showed up at an after-bar party a bunch of us players had the night we won the Cup in Denver. It was about three in the morning, and all of a sudden we hear this super loud *clomp-clomp-clomp* sound coming up these wooden steps in the bar we were at. We didn't know what was going on and figured maybe it was a bunch of cops coming to shut us down or something. So we all look over at the steps anxious to see who was coming up so loudly, and who do we see? Poads, still in his full gear! And I mean full gear: helmet, jersey, pants, socks, gloves, and even his skates. He didn't want to take anything off and just wanted that day to go on forever; it was the greatest moment ever! It was classic Poads, just classic."

Dan Hinote
Colorado 2001

"I had a great day with the Cup. I started the day off by taking it back to my high school in Morristown, New Jersey. From there, I took it down to Princeton University, where I went to college. I was the first-ever player to win it from there, which was pretty cool. I then was able to fly up to Pittsburgh, courtesy of my then-girlfriend's (now wife's) dad, who was a pilot. A lot of my extended family lives there, and I really wanted to share it with them as well. My uncle has a dairy farm just outside of town, and he had a big pig roast for us. The food was amazing. In fact, my Cup Keeper, Walter, said it was the best meal he had ever had at a Cup party—so I take great pride in that too. Three stops in 24 hours, a real whirlwind, but it turned out to be just a fantastic day. For sure one my most memorable ever."

George Parros
Anaheim 2007

"I grew up in Cloquet, Minnesota, with a population of about 10,000 people, and we had two guys on that '99 Dallas team from there: myself and Jamie Langenbrunner. Plus Brett Hull lives nearby in the summer, so when the Cup came to town it stayed for a while. It was pretty awesome. Jamie and I shared it for some of the time and just tried to share it with as many people as possible. We brought it to the rink in town, and about 5,000 people showed up to have their pictures taken with it, which just blew us away. From there I took it to a local hospital and then out to the lake, where I had a big party with my family. I will never forget driving around the lake in my boat with Stanley. We got some pretty odd looks from people as we went by; it was pretty funny. It was just such a memorable day."

Derek Plante
Dallas 1999

"When I brought the Cup to my hometown of Rochester, Minnesota, it was the first time that a professional champi-onship trophy had ever been there. So it was a big deal. I felt so privileged to have been able to share something that meant so much to me with all of the people who had helped me and encouraged me along the way. To let the community be a part of it was so cool; I will never forget that day. I took it everywhere; it was just a blur—people's houses, businesses, you name it. I just wanted everyone to be a part of it."

Shjon Podein
Colorado 2001

"To see the impact that the Stanley Cup has on the world at large is so profound to me. You know, I never got to have Stanley for a day back in the early '70s, but they did let me have it in 2008 for a fundraiser I was a part of that ultimately raised over $65,000 for two charities that are near and dear to me. You know, one of the rules for drinking out of the Cup is that it has to be held up and poured by somebody whose name is on it. Well, I actually got tendonitis from pouring so much champagne into people's mouths out of that thing that day. What a fantastically amazing experience that was, though, to witness firsthand the power that the Stanley Cup has. To see the response in those people's eyes was something I will never forget. Everybody was so excited and happy and friendly and positive and thankful. I was blown away. We had over 4,000 fans show up that day to see Stanley and to just be around it. It almost never happened either, because the Cup was supposed to be flown in the night before to Philly from Toronto, but a storm shut down the airport. I thought we were going to have to cancel the entire thing, but then two guys up there volunteered to drive all night through a blizzard with the Cup to make sure it would be there. Amazing. It was on that day that I developed a true feeling and understanding for just what the value of the Cup really is. It has such a unique unifying ability. It has the power to evoke an incredible charitable response in people from all walks of life. The lore of the Cup brings it out of people. It has a magical quality. I dare to think that if you were somehow able to plunk it down in the middle of a war zone, so long as both sides knew what it was and what it stood for, that everybody would stop fighting out of respect for it. It's just unlike any other trophy in sports. It's just so totally unique and awesome. It truly stands for love."

Bill Clement
Philadelphia 1974 and 1975

"We never got to have it individually, but they did give it to us as a team. So we would take it around town to various places, particularly bars, to let the fans enjoy it. It would sit on the table, and everybody would come over and celebrate with it and tell stories. It was great. Sometimes I would find myself just staring at it, looking in awe at all the great names. To think that mine was alongside so many of those of my childhood heroes was so humbling. In those days the names were hand engraved, literally, by a craftsman with some primitive tools. The letters are all oddly shaped and totally unique. And I've got a long name too, so it really stands out!

"Another really neat thing that Montreal would do was they would have a huge party for the entire organization after the season, a celebration with the Cup. And when I say the entire organization, I mean the *entire* organization—from the players to the janitors to the Zamboni drivers, as well as their wives. Everybody. It was the organization's way of saying thanks. It was really special. We would take pictures and tell stories and just let our hair down. Everybody appreciated it so much. What a classy, respectful thing to do. That was Montreal, though, they just got it."

Doug Risebrough
Montreal 1976, 1977, 1978, and 1979;
Calgary 1989 (Assistant Coach)

"The first time I won it I took the Cup and drove up to the cemetery where my father is buried. I brought it out and sat there with my dad; it was pretty emotional. The cemetery was empty too, just me and Stanley, talking to my dad. I wanted to pay respect to the man who had tied my skates for me as a little kid and had just made so many sacrifices. Sadly, he wasn't there to watch me win it, so this was my way of saying thanks. It was a completely private moment and just very peaceful. It was a moment I will never forget, ever."

Brendan Shanahan
Detroit 1997, 1998, and 2002

"Back when we won it each player didn't get it for a day, we all just sort of shared it for a few weeks instead. There was no Keeper of the Cup in those days either; guys just took it and pretty much did whatever they wanted to with it. Stanley made his way around Pittsburgh those two summers, let me tell ya. I will never forget the party at Mario [Lemieux's] house either, when Stanley wound up at the bottom of his pool. What a day that was!"

Kevin Stevens
Pittsburgh 1992 and 1993

"If winning the Cup is the best day of your life, then your day with the Cup is a close second. I brought it back to Quebec and shared it with as many people as I could. That night we had a huge celebration on a private island for my friends and family; it was pretty amazing. In addition to that, I also got to spend an afternoon with the Cup at Mario Lemieux's house with my two brothers and my mom and dad. We just hung out and chilled in his backyard with it, lying in the grass visiting and telling stories. I mean, here I was sitting with the Stanley Cup in Mario Lemieux's backyard—never in my wildest dreams did I ever think I would be doing something like that. It was such a great afternoon, very memorable and special, just something I will never forget."

Max Talbot
Pittsburgh 2009

"The first year we won it I got to touch it out on the ice, and then I basically never saw it again. I had heard about a bunch of the guys taking it all over town and whatnot, so the next year when we won it again I made sure to get my day with Stanley. I did it up right, too. I rented a big stretch limo and took it to 18 different places—from the police station to the fire hall to my golf club—I went everywhere with that thing. It was a nonstop party, all day. I just wanted to share it with as many people as I could. What a great day, just unbelievable. I will never forget it."

John Tonelli
New York Islanders 1980, 1981,
1982, and 1983

"When the Stanley Cup sunk to the bottom of Mario Lemieux's swimming pool, I was the one who dove in and rescued it. I saved Stanley. It was a fun moment, but I was actually a bit taken aback by it all. Things had gotten out of hand, and when I saw it at the bottom of the pool I just thought that we had crossed a line. The Cup is all about respect, and I didn't want to disrespect it. So I told everybody there that the Cup was not going to go back in the pool again, and that was that. I didn't hear any arguments. How it got in there in the first place is another story altogether. I will never forget seeing Phil Bourque climb way the hell up to the top of Mario's waterfall, maybe 30 feet up there on this rock outcropping, ready to jump into the pool with the Cup. I just yelled up to him, 'Bourquey, the Cup will survive, but you might not!' That was when he tossed it in and decided to climb back down. I then went into lifeguard mode and dove in after Stanley. What a day that was."

Bryan Trottier
New York Islanders 1980, 1981, 1982, and 1983;
Pittsburgh 1991 and 1992;
and Colorado 2001 (Assistant Coach)

"I took the Cup back to Sweden, which was pretty neat. I am not too crazy, so I just spent some time with my family and had a nice party for my friends. It was great, though. I invited all of my old coaches over too, which was a lot of fun, especially for my old soccer coaches who had told me that I was making a mistake by choosing hockey over soccer. That was fun. It was a great day and certainly a moment I will never forget. Lots of great memories."

Niclas Wallin
Carolina 2006

Mike Bolt, keeper of the Cup, traveling with Stanley

"Even though it's an inanimate object, the Stanley Cup leads a far more interesting life than most people do. Stanley is without a doubt the biggest celebrity in hockey—he really is. I started working at the Hockey Hall of Fame back in 1995, and a few years later I got asked if I wanted to be a Keeper of the Cup. I said absolutely, and since then it has been a dream job. Like most kids in Canada, I had dreamed of raising the Cup all my life. The problem was I just wasn't a very good hockey player. Now, luckily, I get to watch the greatest players in the world raise it on an annual basis. What a great gig. I have been to the White House several times and gotten to meet the president. I got to go inside the Space Shuttle on an unbelievable off-the-books tour at the Kennedy Space Center. I have been all over the world—from every province in Canada to every state except Hawaii, as well as Japan, Russia, Sweden, Finland, Czech Republic, Switzerland, Slovakia, Ukraine, Belarus, and Afghanistan. It has been an amazing adventure.

"As a part of my job, I get to take the Cup to each player from the Stanley Cup–winning team every season. As a reward, each player gets one day with the Cup, and it is my responsibility to personally escort the Cup to him in his hometown or wherever, regardless of where he lives in the world. I can be in Boston one week and Moscow the next, you just never know. The guys get so excited when I show up too; they are like little kids at Christmas. And I get to be Santa, bringing them the greatest gift of all—how awesome is that? As soon as the schedule is released after their team has won it, guys start planning their parties, golf tournaments, family outings, and charity events. Sometimes guys will call me every single day, to ask questions or to just let me know that they can't sleep because they are so pumped up about getting their day with Stanley.

"When the big day arrives I show up with white gloves on and proudly present the Cup to that particular player. From then on, I am a part-time bodyguard/passive observer. I usually just wind up sleeping at the player's house so I can keep an eye on the Cup. I am there to make sure it is treated with respect and that nobody gets too out of hand with it. I mostly stay behind the scenes, but there have been a few times where I have had to step in and make sure the Cup was being treated properly. Most of the time when that happens, it is not the players doing something wrong, it is someone else who has probably had too much to drink or is trying to show off. The players have so much respect for the Cup; they treat it like it is sacred. Whenever I hand over the Cup to a player I always tell him to have a great, safe, but respectful time with it. We want the guys to have a wild and fun time with it, but we want them to respect the history and the tradition. Yes, it has been in swimming pools, and yes, it has been in lakes and oceans, but we try to keep it out of the water because chlorine and salt water are really bad for it. Sometimes we have to tell guys no, which sucks, but it's just the reality of our job. I mean, one player wanted to parachute with it, and I had to draw the line right there, no way. The tradition of getting the Cup has been around for decades, but in the mid-'90s they really tightened up the rules to keep it respectful, so no casinos and no strip joints anymore.

"Accidents do happen, though. Once in a while the Cup will get dinged up. This is a trophy that doesn't hide behind glass; it is meant to be enjoyed. So occasionally it will get dropped or something, but we can fix it. I have banged out a few dents over the years, but just like hockey players—it's tough. It only adds to Stanley's character. One of the questions we're asked most often is if the Cup we carry around is the real one or a replica. The answer is the Cup that we carry around is the real deal. The one the players get to have for a day is the same one that they hoist over their heads after winning it out on the ice after the Stanley Cup Finals. They play for the real thing, and they get to have the real thing. The replica sits permanently on display at the Hockey Hall of Fame in Toronto.

"To watch a player bring it to his parents' house up in Canada or wherever, and to see them break down and cry—it is pretty incredible. What a thank you for all those early morning practices, or for working that extra job so that they could buy new skates, or whatever. The amount of emotion that pours out every single time I bring it somewhere is almost overwhelming. I get to see this on a daily basis, and I just have to pinch myself sometimes. The best part of my job for sure, though, is the reaction that I get from all of Stanley's fans around the world. To see how excited and giddy people get when I take it out and let them enjoy it, what a feeling. That never gets old. I have seen grown men cry when they have gotten close to it, and that is pretty powerful stuff. Again, what a job—I get to bring smiles to people's faces for a living.

"I am also a true believer that you have to earn the right to raise it too. I don't believe a player's cousin or buddy has the right to lift it up above his head. That is sacred and should only be done by those who have won it and earned it. So when guys want to take a drink out of it, I have the player lift it up for them. Again, you have to earn that right. It's a respect thing, and I am there to make sure the tradition is upheld. It's important, it really is. Sometimes it's hard for the players who have never won it to be around it. I feel awful for them. They know the tradition; they'll never touch it unless they have won it. Sometimes after their careers are over, however, some of them decide that they just can't wait any longer to touch it.

"Such was the case with Ron Tugnutt, who I spent some time with over in Kandahar, Afghanistan, on a trip to visit the troops. We had just flown in, and the guys were telling us that the Taliban wasn't that far away and that we had to be ready to take cover in case of a missile attack. We even wore flak jackets; it was pretty intense. Ron had unfortunately never won it over his 17-year NHL career and had always been superstitious about not touching it unless he had earned it. Well, he was so moved by seeing what was going on over there with the soldiers that he just broke down and gave Stanley a huge hug. He said that he had finally come to terms with the fact that his career was over, and he just couldn't take it any longer. It was pretty neat.

"I will never forget that trip. When we landed I was hot and tired, so I went back to my barracks to take a shower. Suddenly, I heard an air raid siren go off, and I didn't quite know what to do. I was all by myself, standing there in nothing more than a towel. I came out, and everybody was gone, so I just sat down on the Stanley Cup case and waited for someone to tell me what to do. I sat there for 15 minutes, reading a magazine, and eventually the siren stopped. Pretty soon all the soldiers started rolling back in, and they saw me standing there. A couple of officers came over, and one of them said, 'Hey Mike, where were you during the missile attack?' I was like, 'What do you mean, missile attack?' They then proceeded to tell me that the base had been under attack by enemy missiles and that everyone else had taken cover in bunkers. I was like, 'Holy crap!' I told them that I was sitting there with Stanley the whole time. They all just looked at me in awe and were like, 'Wow, you are so dedicated to your job and so brave; we really admire your courage.' In retrospect, it was pretty hilarious because here I was sitting around with absolutely no idea what the hell was going on in the middle of a war zone, and these hardened soldiers think I am this tough guy willing to put my life on the line in order to protect this trophy. Little did they know that I was just too damn stupid to know any better! Truth be told, if I had known what was actually going on I would have ditched the Cup and been like George Costanza [from *Seinfeld*] pushing women and children out of the way. Luckily I survived, but what an experience that was.

"The Cup is on tour 320 days a year, which is pretty amazing. Throughout the year, while the season is going on, we travel to minor league games, corporate sponsor outings, and charity events. I personally am on the road with it about 250 days a year, and there are four of us Cup Keepers that do this full time. Needless to say, I am single. What sane woman would marry a guy with a schedule like that? I have been to so many airports and hotels, sometimes I wake up and simply have no idea where I am. I can't even count all the frequent flier miles that I have earned, no way. Although that isn't always bad, though, because sometimes the only time I get to sleep is on planes. Oftentimes as soon as you hit the ground, guys will pick you up in a limo and you are off to parties and appearances for the next 24 hours straight, literally. The players are so jacked up to see me that they go crazy; they can't wait for the party to get started. It can get pretty wild, trust me.

"Hanging with Stanley is like being the bodyguard of a world-famous rock star. The stories are endless. One of my favorite experiences with the Cup was when Chris Chelios had it back in 2002 after winning it with Detroit. Some of the marquis players get the Cup for two days and such was the case for Chris. His first day with it he had this huge party in Malibu down on the beach. It was insane. Everybody from Kid Rock to Ray Liotta to David Spade to Cuba Gooding Jr. to John C. McGinley to D.B. Sweeney to Pamela Anderson to Sylvester Stallone to Wayne Gretzky was there. We even had a party crasher show up by the name of Tom Hanks, who had heard the Cup was in the neighborhood and decided to jog a couple of miles down the beach to come see it. He was so excited; it was really cool.

"The next day we flew to Chicago to do it all over again. This time we started out in a limo bus that took us first to Wrigley Field, where Chris and Stanley got to throw out the first pitch at a Cubs game. His catcher was his buddy, Eddie Vedder, from Pearl Jam—who was along for the ride. Also hanging with us for the day was actor John Cusack, who lives in Chicago and is really well known around town. From there, we headed over to the White Sox game. Well, as we were driving down to the South Side of Chicago, the guys, after many beverages that afternoon, had to go to the bathroom. We didn't have one on our limo bus, so we had to improvise. We were driving through this residential neighborhood, and Chris yelled for the driver to pull over at this house where a bunch of kids were playing baseball in their front lawn. Chris jumps out, at which point he is immediately recognized, and tells the kids that they can take their pictures with the Cup if we can use their bathroom. They were all like, 'Heck yeah!'

"So we all go inside, and once we are in there we realize that it is a neighborhood party going on, with about 40 people in there—all hanging out and watching the baseball game that we had just come from. Once they realize what was happening, they all start going nuts. They couldn't believe it. Now, the funniest part of the story is that after about 20 minutes of hanging out, this woman suddenly blurts out, 'Oh my God, you're John Cusack!' It was hilarious. He and Eddie loved having the Cup around because it was like they were invisible. They were walking 10 feet behind it all day, and nobody recognized them; everybody was just glued to Stanley. It just goes to show you how big of a rock star Stanley actually is. That night we all went to the Pearl Jam concert. There I was sitting next to John Cusack, Chris Chelios, and Sean Penn—who had decided to join us—and Stanley. What a day.

"Another of my favorite stories was when I got to go to Martin Brodeur's childhood home after he had won it in 1995. His dream was to recreate the street hockey game that he and his buddies had always played as kids, only this time they got to play for the actual Stanley Cup. As kids they had played for the Cup every day, only this time it was for the real deal. Sure enough, he got them all together, and they played out there in the front of his house, just like they had done after school so many times before. Well, Brodeur's team lost that day, and he was so upset about having to watch his buddies drink out of the Cup that when he won it again in 2000, he demanded a rematch. Sure enough, he got the same guys together and formed the same teams. He even pulled out the same old battered net, which was held together with duct tape. This time, Brodeur's team won. Martin smiled and told me the irony of what that game meant to him. He said that when he was a kid the neighbors used to yell at him to get off the street. Sometimes they would even call the cops on him. And his mother had tried and tried to get him to throw that old ugly net out. Now, here he was, 20 years later, using that same old net, out in the same street playing hockey—only this time the neighbors were all out there cheering him on as this famous celebrity. And so were the cops, who even blocked off the street for him so he and his pals could play uninterrupted. How amazing is that? Later that night Martin took Stanley to the movies and let his kids eat popcorn out of it. He had asked them what they wanted to do with it, and that was what they asked for—so off they went. It was great.

"The stories go on and on, from Evgeni Malkin holding it out of the sunroof of his limo in Moscow's Red Square to Cam Ward taking it with him bowling in Saskatoon to Mike Babcock taking it waterskiing in Regina. I will never forget being in the middle of Siberia with Pavel Datsyuk on the Asia-Europe border, two continents at the same time, with these Russian dancers all dancing around us. It was pretty cool. And I will never forget Shjon Podein's day with the Cup. He set a record for the most appearances ever with the Cup: 28 different stops throughout Minnesota back in 2001. Just nuts.

"Sometimes guys will go to great lengths to put Stanley on display for their big day. Scott Parker and Darren McCarty even had custom harnesses designed for the back of their bikes. I got to do something like that as well, which was pretty neat. It was back in 2004, at the NHL All-Star Game up in St. Paul. We had a big snowmobile rally from Eveleth, home of the U.S. Hockey Hall of Fame, to Xcel Energy Center in the Twin Cities. They customized my snowmobile with a Plexiglas case for the Cup, like the pope mobile, and off we went—about 200 miles. When I showed up with Stanley it was like a mob scene.

"Another time I was in a bus with [Ducks forward] Corey Perry on the 401 to London, Ontario. There was a major accident, and traffic was not moving for like two hours. These kids outside were sitting on top of their parents' car waiting patiently and could see the Cup in the bus, so they started motioning us to hoist the Cup. Well, Corey went a step further by grabbing the Cup and heading outside. The next thing you know, we're having a tailgate party in the middle of Canada's biggest highway. It was awesome.

"Not all the memories are great ones, though. Case in point, back in 2003 I flew to Slovakia to spend the day with Jiri Bicek, who had just won it with New Jersey. He was so excited because this was the first time the Cup had ever been to Slovakia. Well, I got there all right, but Stanley got lost. We used to be able to bring him with us on flights, but after September 11, he now has to ride in the cargo hold along with all the other luggage. Poor guy. Anyway, I felt horrible when I showed up at Jiri's big party where over 10,000 fans were waiting anxiously to see the Cup. Needless to say, I got booed pretty badly. Luckily we were able to track down Stanley and get him rerouted, and Jiri was able to spend about six hours with him. What a nightmare, but luckily it had a happy ending.

"Yes, the stories are endless, and they just keep coming year after year. Some are heartwarming and others are pretty crazy—no, *really* crazy—you can use your imagination. As a Cup Keeper, however, I am sworn to secrecy. No matter how many drinks people try to give me, I won't crack under pressure. So don't even try…you're not getting it out of me!"

All-Time Stanley Cup Champions

2010—Chicago Blackhawks

2009—Pittsburgh Penguins

2008—Detroit Red Wings

2007—Anaheim Ducks

2006—Carolina Hurricanes

2005—Lockout

2004—Tampa Bay Lightning

2003—New Jersey Devils

2002—Detroit Red Wings

2001—Colorado Avalanche

2000—New Jersey Devils

1999—Dallas Stars

1998—Detroit Red Wings

1997—Detroit Red Wings

1996—Colorado Avalanche

1995—New Jersey Devils

1994—New York Rangers

1993—Montreal Canadiens

1992—Pittsburgh Penguins

1991—Pittsburgh Penguins

1990—Edmonton Oilers

1989—Calgary Flames

1988—Edmonton Oilers

1987—Edmonton Oilers

1986—Montreal Canadiens

1985—Edmonton Oilers

1984—Edmonton Oilers

1983—New York Islanders

1982—New York Islanders

1981—New York Islanders

1980—New York Islanders

1979—Montreal Canadiens

1978—Montreal Canadiens

1977—Montreal Canadiens

1976—Montreal Canadiens

1975—Philadelphia Flyers

1974—Philadelphia Flyers

1973—Montreal Canadiens

1972—Boston Bruins

1971—Montreal Canadiens

1970—Boston Bruins

1969—Montreal Canadiens

1968—Montreal Canadiens

1967—Toronto Maple Leafs

1966—Montreal Canadiens

1965—Montreal Canadiens

1964—Toronto Maple Leafs

1963—Toronto Maple Leafs

1962—Toronto Maple Leafs

1961—Chicago Blackhawks

1960—Montreal Canadiens

1959—Montreal Canadiens

1958—Montreal Canadiens

1957—Montreal Canadiens

1956—Montreal Canadiens

1955—Detroit Red Wings

1954—Detroit Red Wings

1953—Montreal Canadiens

1952—Detroit Red Wings

1951—Toronto Maple Leafs

1950—Detroit Red Wings

1949—Toronto Maple Leafs

1948—Toronto Maple Leafs

1947—Toronto Maple Leafs

1946—Montreal Canadiens

1945—Toronto Maple Leafs

1944—Montreal Canadiens

1943—Detroit Red Wings

1942—Toronto Maple Leafs

1941—Boston Bruins

1940—New York Rangers

1939—Boston Bruins

1938—Chicago Black Hawks

1937—Detroit Red Wings

1936—Detroit Red Wings

1935—Montreal Maroons

1934—Chicago Black Hawks

1933—New York Rangers

1932—Toronto Maple Leafs

1931—Montreal Canadiens

1930—Montreal Canadiens

1929—Boston Bruins

1928—New York Rangers

1927—Ottawa Senators

1926—Montreal Maroons

1925—Victoria Cougars

1924—Montreal Canadiens

1923—Ottawa Senators

1922—Toronto St. Pats

1921—Ottawa Senators

1920—Ottawa Senators

1919—No decision

1918—Toronto Arenas

1917—Seattle Metropolitans

1916—Montreal Canadiens

1915—Vancouver Millionaires

1914—Toronto Blueshirts

1913—Quebec Bulldogs

1912—Quebec Bulldogs

1911—Ottawa Senators

1910—Montreal Wanderers

1909—Ottawa Senators

1908—Montreal Wanderers

1907—Montreal Wanderers

1907—Kenora Thistles

1906—Montreal Wanderers

1906—Ottawa Senators

1905—Ottawa Senators

1904—Ottawa Senators

1903—Ottawa Senators

1903—Montreal AAA

1902—Montreal AAA

1902—Winnipeg Victoria

1901—Winnipeg Victoria

1900—Montreal Shamrocks

1899—Montreal Shamrocks

1898—Montreal Victorias

1897—Montreal Victorias

1896—Montreal Victorias

1895—Montreal Victorias

1894—Montreal AAA

1893—Montreal AAA